THE LEVEL AND COMPOSITION OF HOUSEHOLD SAVING

THE LEVEL AND COMPOSITION OF HOUSEHOLD SAVING

Edited by
PATRIC H. HENDERSHOTT

BALLINGER PUBLISHING COMPANY
Cambridge, Massachusetts
A Subsidiary of Harper & Row, Publishers, Inc.

International Standard Book Number: 0-88410-987-9

Library of Congress Catalog Card Number: 84-20497

Printed in the United States of America

Library of Congress Cataloging in Publication Data
Main entry under title:

The Level and composition of household saving.

Includes bibliographies and index.
1. Saving and investment—United States—Addresses, essays, lectures.
I. Hendershott, Patric H.
HC110.S3L47 1985 339.4′3 84-20497
ISBN 0-88410-987-9

CONTENTS

List of Figures vii

List of Tables ix

Preface xv

Part I
Introduction 1

Chapter 1
An Overview
Patric H. Hendershott 3

Chapter 2
Saving in the U.S.: Some Conceptual Issues
Alan J. Auerbach 15

Part II
Household Saving and Wealth Accumulation 39

Chapter 3
Real Household Capital Gains and Wealth Accumulation
Patric H. Hendershott and Joe Peek 41

Chapter 4
Household Saving: An Econometric Investigation
Patric H. Hendershott and Joe Peek 63

Chapter 5
Microeconomic Evidence on the Composition of Household Savings in Recent Years
Edward J. Kane 101

Chapter 6
Inflation and the Accumulation of Wealth by Older Households, 1966 to 1976
Nancy Jianakoplos 151

Part III
Household Saving in Specific Vehicles 181

Chapter 7
Household Formations
Patric H. Hendershott and Marc Smith 183

Chapter 8
Investment in Consumer Durables
Richard C. Lemmon 205

Chapter 9
The Growth in Pension Saving
Sheng-Cheng Hu 235

Chapter 10
Investment in and Returns from Education
George Johnson 267

Index 297

About the Contributors 303

About the Editor 305

LIST OF FIGURES

7–1 Endogenous Household Formations and Some Key Determinants, 1960–82. 193

8–1 Gross Investment in Consumer Durables as a Percentage of Disposable Personal Income. 207

8–2 Ratio of Deflator for Consumer Durables to Deflator for Total Personal Consumption. 208

8–3 Net Stock of Consumer Durables Per Househould (1972 dollars). 209

8–4 Net Investment in Autos and Parts Per Household (1972 dollars). 218

8–5 Net Investment in Furniture and Household Equipment Per Household (1972 dollars). 220

8–6 Net Investment in Other Consumer Durables Per Household . 223

8–7 Index of Attitudes about Current Personal Finances. 226

9–1 Net and Gross Pension Saving. 251

9–2 Inflation and the Rates of Return on Pension and Nonpension Saving. 252

LIST OF TABLES

2–1 Saving Rates Based on National Income Accounts (percentage). 16

2–2 Saving Rates Based on Flow-of-Funds Balance Sheets (percentage). 20

3–1 Real Household Wealth Accumulation (billions of 1972 dollars). 42

3–2 Adjusted Real Household Wealth Accumulation (billions of 1972 dollars). 43

3–3 Changes in Real Household Balance Sheet Components, 1950–82 (billions of 1972 dollars). 49

3–4 Changes in Household Balance Sheets, 1949–82 (billions of 1972 dollars). 50

3–5 Expected Percentage Capital Gains Equations, 1951–82. 54

4–1 Alternative Measures of the Saving Rate (percentage). 69

4–2 Various Saving Adjustments (millions of 1972 dollars). 71

4–3 Various Saving Rate Adjustments (percentage). 73

4–4 Data Summary. 83

4–5 Estimated Saving Equations, 1952–82. 84

4–6 Explanation of Broad Swings in the Saving Ratio. 92

5–1 Comparison of Survey and Time-Series Estimates of

	Cumulative Growth Rates between Survey Dates in the Mean Value of Components of Net Transactable Wealth (percentage).	105
5-2	Comparison of Homeownership Rates for Married Households and One-Person Households in the Edited 1977 SRC Sample with Census Estimates for the Same Year (percentage).	107
5-3	Estimates of Cumulative Price Appreciation and Cumulative Inflation-Adjusted Total Returns on Selected Assests between Survey Dates (percentage).	109
5-4	Incremental Mean Saving and Per-Year Real Savings Rates between Survey Dates, for Households in Specific Age Classes.	115
5-5	Cumulative Percentage Change in the Real and Nominal Value of Accumulated Mean Savings between Survey Dates, by Age of Household Head (percentage).	117
5-6	Dollar Increments between Survey Dates in the Mean Value of Real-Estate Assets and Three Components of Net Transactable Wealth, by Age of Household head (dollars).	118
5-7	Distribution of Cumulative Changes in the Nominal Value of Mean Transactable Wealth between Survey Dates by Age of Household Head (percentage).	119
5-8	Distribution of Selected Assets and Respondent Population across Age Classes at 1962, 1970, and 1977 Survey Dates (percentage).	120
5-9	Homeownership Rate, Mortgage Status, and Mean Dollar Value of Net Transactable Wealth in 1962, 1970, and 1977, by Age of Household Head.	123
5-10	Changes in the Real and Nominal Value of Accumulated Mean Savings between Survey Dates, by Age Cohorts Determined by the Age of Household Head in 1962 and 1970 (percentage).	128
5-11	Dollar Increments between Survey Dates in the Mean Value of Real-Estate Assets and Three Components of Net Transactable Wealth, by Age Cohorts Determined by the Age of a Household Head in 1962 and 1970 (dollars).	130
5-12	Distribution of Cumulative Percentage Change in the Nominal Value of Mean Transactable Wealth between	

Survey Dates, by Age of Cohorts Determined by the Age of Household Head in 1962 and 1970 (percentage). 131
5–13 Percentage Distribution of Selected Assets and Respondent Population across Age Cohorts of the 1962 and 1970 Age Classes, at the 1970 and 1977 Survey Dates. 132
5–14 Homeownership Rate and Mortgage Status in 1962, 1970, and 1977, by Age Cohorts Reflecting the Age of a Household Head in 1962 and 1970 (percentage). 135
5–15 Age of Heads of Households of Different Sizes in 1962, 1970 and 1977 (years). 136
5–16 Accumulated Mean Savings in Dollars and Savings Per Year as a Percentage of Mean Survey-Date Incomes, for Households in Different Size Classes. 137
5–17 Cumulative Percentage Change in the Real and Nominal Value of Accumulated Savings between Survey Dates, for Households in Different Size Classes (percentage). 138
5–18 Distribution of Selected Assets and Respondent Population across Household Size Classes at 1962, 1970, and 1977 Survey Dates (percentage). 139
5–19 Dollar Increment in Mean Wealth and Ratio of Accumulated Mean Saving Per Year to Average Survey-Date Incomes, by Type of Household. 141
5–20 Cumulative Percentage Change in the Real and Nominal Value of Accumulated Mean Savings between Survey Dates by Type of Household Head (percentage). 142
5–21 Age of Heads of Different Types of Households in 1962, 1970, and 1977 (years). 143
5–22 Homeownership Rate and Mortgage Status in 1962, 1970, and 1977, by Household Type (percentage). 145
6–1 Rates of Price Change (percentage). 161
6–2 Means of Selected Household Variables. 165
6–3 Observed Changes in Household Portfolio Composition, 1966–76 (percentage of household net worth). 167
6–4 Observed versus Simulated Changes in Portfolio Composition, 1971 and 1976 (percentage of household net worth). 167
6–5 OLS and WLS Regression Results (dependent variable: average annual change in net worth). 169
6–6 OLS Regression Results Employing First Differences of Variables (dependent variable:DSAVE). 175

6–7	Regression Results Using Fuller–Battese Pooled Time-Series and Cross-Section Model (dependent variable: average annual change in net worth).	176
7–1	Headship Rates.	185
7–2	Data Summary.	192
7–3	Household Formations, 1961–82.	194
7–4	Elasticities of Headship Rates.	196
7–5	Increase in Households, 1961–82 (millions).	196
7–6	Changes in Headship Rates.	198
8–1	Data Summary for Consumer Durables.	214
8–2	Net Investment in Autos and Parts Per Household, 1954–82.	215
8–3	Net Investment in Furniture and Household Equipment Per Household, 1962–82.	219
8–4	Net Investment in Other Durables Per Household.	221
8–5	Long-Run Elasticities Evaluated at Mean.	222
8–6	Impact of a 9 Percent Increase in the Real Interest. Rate and a 40 Percent Decline in Consumer Confidence.	225
8–7	Impact of a 9 Percentage Point Increase in the Real Interest. Rate and a 40 Percent Decline in Consumer Confidence.	227
8–8	Impact of Tax Increases on Net Durable Stocks Per Household (in 1972 dollars).	228
8–9	Estimates of Net Investment in Consumer Durables for 1983 (in 1972 dollars).	229
8–10	Forecast Evaluation: Net Investment in Durables Per Household (1972 dollars).	230
9–1	Pension Saving and Wealth (per capita, in 1972 dollars).	247
9–2	Pension Saving Function, Labor Income.	254
9–3	Pension Saving Function, Disposable Income.	256
10–1	GNP, Direct Schooling Costs, and Gross Private Nonresidential Investment, 1929–79.	268
10–2	Distribution of Labor Force by Educational Attainment, Selected Years 1952–79.	269
10–3	Estimates of Determinants of Logarithm of Earnings Level from Aggregate Data 1949.	282
10–4	Selected Estimates of The Impact of Schooling on the Logarithm of Hourly Earnings.	283
10–5	Estimated Impact of Schooling on Monthly Earnings with Adjustments for Cognitive and Affective Ability Traits.	

10–6 Ashenfelter–Ham Estimates of the Effect of Schooling on Earnings and Wages for White Males. 286
10–7 Estimated Coefficients on Logarithm of Annual Labor Earnings from the Current Population Survey (CPS) and from the Panel Study on Income Dynamics (PSID), 1968 and 1981. 287
10–8 Estimated Coefficients on Schooling for White and Black Males Age 21–35, 1972 and 1978. 287
10–9 Estimates of Intensive and Extensive Rates of Return to Education. 291

PREFACE

This study of The Level and Composition of Household Saving was funded by a grant from the American Council of Life Insurance (ACLI), arising from its continuing interest in the savings process. Since the inception of the project in early 1982, specific studies were commissioned, written, revised, and completed. I am grateful to the ACLI and the authors for making this volume possible. Special thanks are extended to Joe Peek, my collaborator, and Ed Kane, my colleague.

Many others have played important roles in bringing this volume to fruition: Kenneth M. Wright, Vice President and Chief Economist of the ACLI and his Economic Research Committee (especially Francis Schott) for their advice and input throughout the project; my wife, Carole, for her editorial assistance on the entire volume; my secretary, Sharon Ford, for her patient and tireless revision of large parts of the manuscript; and the Ohio State University and the sponsors of the Galbreath Chair for aiding and abetting my participation in projects like this one.

Patric H. Hendershott
June 1984

I INTRODUCTION

1 AN OVERVIEW

A nation's net capital formation is ultimately determined by its total net saving (plus that supplied by foreigners), and the composition of its capital formation is influenced by the form that the saving takes. Concern exists over both the low level of total saving in the United States and the small share channeled to industrial capital, largely because of their negative implications for economic growth (Feldstein 1977, 1983; Boskin 1983). Household saving is of special interest for two reasons. First, households have provided well over 90 percent of aggregate net saving, as officially measured, in the United States since 1951. Second, the composition of household saving crucially affects the allocation of the U.S. capital stock among human capital, household capital, and industrial capital because household saving in the form of outlays on higher education, housing, and consumer durables largely determines the economy's investment in these forms of capital. Given these outlays and total saving, investment in industrial capital can be derived residually.

This book focuses on the quantity and quality (form) of household saving. The main body of the text is divided into two broad parts. The first contains analyses of wealth and portfolio changes of all households in the aggregate, national samples of relatively wealthy households taken at intervals of seven and eight years, and a longitudinal sample of older households observed at five-year intervals. Econometric estimates are reported for the aggregate household sector and the older households. The chapters in the second part of the book focus on specific economic decisions: formation of households, purchases of consumer durable goods, the demand for pension savings, and investment in human capital (education).

Auerbach's (Chapter 2) analysis of personal (household), private and national saving places the study of household saving in perspective. A fundamental question he addresses is the importance of corporate and government saving in the determination of household saving: Do households see through the veils of corporate and governmental accounts to offset or undo the saving of these sectors or does household saving evolve independently of corporate and governmental saving activity? The veils, Auerbach argues, may be impenetrable to many, and numerous other households may not even be looking. Older households offset tax-cut induced government deficits only when they have a remarkably strong bequest motive. Younger households do so only in the absence of a liquidity constraint, a constraint that low-wealth households in the early stages of their life cycle generally find binding (Dolde 1978). Even if households wish to see through the veils, their perception of government saving must be highly uncertain given the difficulties economists experience measuring it (Eisner and Pieper 1984). The differential taxation of corporate source income and, again, difficulties in measuring a corporation's "permanent" retained earnings suggest that households face parallel difficulties in systematically undoing corporate saving. Moreover, the relationship between equity values and measures of retained earnings is highly uncertain. Households likely respond to observed stock price changes (the well-established inverse saving-wealth relation), rather than to perceived movements in retained earnings.

THE MEASUREMENT AND EXPLANATION OF HOUSEHOLD SAVING

A number of authors (Auerbach, Jianakoplos, and Kane) define saving synonymously with the change in real wealth. This makes saving a (real) balance sheet concept: net worth at the end of the period less net worth (times one plus the inflation rate during the period) at the beginning of the period. The increase in real wealth is the increase in real resources available for future consumption. As straightforward as this definition might seem, both Auerbach (Chapter 2) and Hendershott and Peek (Chapter 3) emphasize the conceptual and practical difficulties that make it hard to determine just what constitutes an increase in real resources.

While the change in real wealth is clearly an important concept, perhaps "saving" could be employed to describe some other useful concept, with the expression "change-in-real-wealth" being reserved for that concept. Historically, saving has been defined in flow terms as income less taxes and consumption. Given expectations regarding after-tax income, saving and consumption are simultaneously determined behavioral variables. In contrast, if saving is defined residually as the *ex post* change in real wealth, movements in saving can be largely the result of exogenous wealth changes (stock market gains or losses, housing and land booms, etc.), and one must be careful not to attribute such movements to active household behavior.[1]

For saving to be a useful variable, it must be measured correctly; that is, income, consumption and taxes must be measured accurately. Hendershott and Peek (Chapter 4) emphasize a number of measurement errors in the official government data: the treatment of net purchases of consumer durables as consumption instead of saving, the treatment of net contributions to government life insurance and retirement funds as taxes instead of saving, and the inflation-induced conversion of some fixed-income wealth into interest income (some of the inflation premium in new-issue interest rates is built into recorded after-tax interest income). Correction of the saving and income variables results in a household saving rate nearly 5 percentage points greater than the officially measured rate in the 1965–75 period, but the corrected rate exhibits a sharp 7 percentage point decline between 1975 and the early 1980s.

Auerbach's discussion of adjustments to the official saving measure varies somewhat. While he agrees with the Hendershott-Peek adjustments in principle, the magnitude of his adjustments differs owing to his definition of saving as the change in real net worth. His upward adjustment for consumer durables is far less in recent years because capital gains on durables have been negative, and the inflation premium adjustment (downward) is far larger because he subtracts the entire capital loss on fixed-valued assets due to inflation, not just that part of the loss actually converted into after-tax interest income. Auerbach also notes that some other "consumption" outlays are at least partially investment in human capital and thus should be treated as saving (outlays less "depreciation," he emphasizes), and he argues for including real changes in implicit claims, such as social security and unfunded pensions, in the definition of changes in real wealth.

The adjusted saving rate (adjusted saving divided by disposable labor income) of Hendershott and Peek (Chapter 4) exhibits major movements during the 1951–82 period. The rate declines from over 15 percent in the early 1950s to around 11 percent in the early 1960s, rebounds to over 14 percent in the middle 1960s and then plummets in the late 1970s. The most important variables explaining these movements are real wealth and income. Large real gains on equities and on housing and land in the second halves of the 1950s and 1970s, respectively, accounted for most of the sharp declines in the saving ratio in those periods. While wealth also grew rapidly during most of the 1960s, again owing largely to stock-market gains, the saving ratio actually increased because of unparalleled real income growth. This growth raised the saving ratio both directly, because the marginal propensity to save out of income exceeds the average propensity, and indirectly, because the wealth-income ratio is lowered. Jianakoplos (Chapter 6), too, reports large and significant income and wealth effects in her study of older households.

Two forces acted almost continuously to depress the saving ratio throughout the 1951–80 period: A marked increase in the retired portion of the population and rapid growth in unfunded pension wealth (both social security and pensions for government employees). The former resulted from both a 3 percentage point increase in the share of the population over age 65 (from 8 percent to 11) and a doubling of the proportion of males below age 65 choosing early retirement. The precise role of these two forces is uncertain, but together they would have reduced the saving rate to near zero in the absence of real income growth.

HOUSEHOLD PORTFOLIO ALLOCATION

Three studies consider household portfolio allocation, albeit from perspectives established by substantially different data sets. Hendershott and Peek use balance sheet data from aggregate flow of funds accounts covering the 1950–82 period to analyze the distribution of household net worth among owner-occupied housing, consumer durables, corporate equity, noncorporate equity, and other net financial assets (pension and life insurance reserves are allocated to equities and other financial assets). Kane (Chapter 5) analyzes data from three samples of roughly 2,000 households collected in 1962, 1970, and 1977. Because the distribution of wealth is highly skewed and wealthy households are deliberately oversampled, average behavior tends to be dominated by the richest respondents in any class. Kane investigates the allocation of what he calls "net transactable wealth" among its components: retail financial assets (deposits and savings bonds), wholesale financial assets (corporate equities and bonds other than savings) and equity in real estate (real estate assets less mortgage debt). Jianakoplos follows a panel of 5,000 older households (aged 45 to 59 in 1966) over the decade 1966–76 and analyzes the allocation of net worth among retail financial assets (plus personal loans), wholesale financial assets, owner-occupied housing, noncorporate equity, and (negative) debt.

All authors recognize the possible importance of relative asset-price movements on observed household portfolios. And relative asset-price changes in the past quarter century have been large indeed: real equity prices rose sharply prior to the late 1960s, real equity and bond values then declined markedly during the late 1960s and all of the 1970s, and real house prices and social security wealth increased greatly in the 1970s. A (possibly temporary) major reversal of these trends has occurred in the early 1980s, with real equity and bond values rising and real house and social security values declining (the latter owing to the taxation of future benefits). A question of substantial interest is to what extent households passively accept changes in portfolio shares induced by relative asset-price changes and to what extent they actively manage their portfolios, shifting part of real gains in a specific form to other asset forms and offsetting part of real losses in a particular asset by reallocating other assets to the category in which a loss occurs.

Jianakoplos provides specific evidence against active portfolio management by her older households. She projects portfolio shares from 1966 to 1971 and from 1971 to 1976, assuming no active portfolio shifts. Observed and projected portfolio shares for the five asset categories she investigates do not differ significantly in any instance. However, although the differences are not statistically significant, the raw data show that sample households did convert housing capital gains into liquid assets by increasing mortgage debt throughout the

1966–76 period. Also, Jianakoplos projects a substantial increase in noncorporate equity for households in her panel between 1966 and 1971 when none occurred, suggesting active liquidation of these assets.

With the entire 1950–82 period and aggregate household data as a base for inference, Hendershott and Peek (Chapter 3) find both passive and active responses to varied rates of real capital-gain accruals on various asset categories. Households seemed to accept passively the portfolio consequences of the incredible stock-market boom of the 1950s and 1960s and bust of the 1970s and the housing and land boom of the 1970s. For equities, and possible housing too, this likely reflected changes in expected risks and returns in response to prolonged periods of extraordinary large *ex post* gains (or losses). In contrast, households did not accept continuing real gains on noncorporate equity (owing largely to rising real land prices) and real losses on consumer durables and net financial assets (the latter caused by general inflation) throughout the 1950–82 period. Active household actions have, in fact, reduced the share of portfolios in noncorporate equity (this is consistent with Jianakoplos' result for 1966–71) and raised (slightly) the shares in consumer durables and net financial assets.

Looking at the 1962–77 period and analyzing samples that overrepresent wealthier households, Kane finds definite evidence of active portfolio management in response to changing after-tax returns and risks. Most importantly, his data show household deposit holdings shrinking relative to other assets during the 1962–70 period in response to binding rate ceilings and then expanding between 1970 and 1977 as rate ceilings were circumvented by depository institutions broadening their product lines to less regulated liabilities and expanding their payment of implicit interest on regulated accounts. Kane also documents marked changes in real wealth accumulation by age of household between the 1960s and the 1970s.[2] In the 1960s, households over age 55 were large accumulators, while in the 1970s younger households were. This corresponds with the acceptance by Jianakoplos' older households of the increase in equity values in the 1960s and with the probable demographic effects of the decrease in equity values and rise in housing values in the 1970s. Equities are held in disproportionately large amounts by older households (this proves particularly true for Kane's 1970 data where the one-third of the households over age 55 held three-quarters of the equities). Thus, increases in share prices in the 1960s gave older households enormous gains, while increases in house values and decreases in the real value of their outstanding mortgage debt gave younger households large gains in the 1970s when the housing gains of older households were only mildly reinforced by implicit capital gains on their fixed-rate mortgage debt and were offset by stock market losses.

THE COMPOSITION OF HOUSEHOLD SAVING AND ECONOMIC EFFICIENCY

In allocating their accumulated savings, individual households equalize risk-adjusted net (of taxes and subsidies) private rates of return earned on alternative forms of saving. In the absence of externalities, differences between private and social risk, and differential government taxation and subsidization of alternative economic activities, household responsiveness to net private returns would also equate risk-adjusted social returns on all assets, as required to maximize economic efficiency for a given level of societal wealth. When externalities and risk differences exist, government policy would promote efficiency by subsidizing activities with positive externalities or whose social risk is less than their private risk and by taxing activities with negative externalities or whose social risk exceeds their private risk.

Efficiency losses occur when risk-adjusted social returns are not equalized. The magnitude of these losses varies with the product of the differences in adjusted social returns on the various forms of saving and the amount of savings (capital) that is prevented from earning its maximal adjusted social return. Optimal tax and subsidy policies would minimize differences in adjusted social return. The sensitivity of household portfolio allocation to differences in net private rates of return on alternative forms of saving, in conjunction with the differences, determines the amount of capital that is misallocated. Measuring sensitivity and studying how government policies could significantly improve the allocation of household saving/investment are critical topics.

Various forms of household saving are taxed and subsidized differentially in the United States. For example, dividends paid on corporate equity and most income from debt instruments and human capital is taxed, while income in kind from owner-occupied housing and durables is not and income from pension assets and capital gains on financial assets is tax-deferred. At the same time, substantial subsidies are available to investors in human capital (purchasers of higher education), although depreciation deductions are not allowed. The chapters in the third part of this book consider household demands for and returns from these supposedly tax-favored household "investments."

Considerable research on housing demand supports a general consensus that the price elasticity for housing is roughly −0.5 (Hanushek and Quigley 1980), while its income elasticity is slightly less than unity. Much less research has been devoted to study of the determinants of household formations, even though over 25 million households were formed in the 1960s and 1970s (an increase of 50 percent). Because there are obvious economies to individuals living together, this surge in households likely absorbed significant resources.

Hendershott and Smith (Chapter 7) attribute a third of the increase in households to population growth, another third to changes in the age-structure of the population (the aging of the postwar baby boom) and a final third to an increased demand for privacy (an increase in age-specific headship rates). Of this last eight million additional households, the doubling of real per capita income accountsfor three million and the decline in the real price of owner-occupied housing (generated by a falling real after-tax mortgage rate) explains nearly another million. The remaining four million is attributed in roughly equal proportions to the expansion of the aid to families with dependent children (AFDC) program in the late 1960s (increase in real benefits and expanded eligibility) and a greater taste for privacy. The latter was evidenced predominantly among the elderly (who experienced a continuing increase in health and longevity) and young adults (those born after the late 1930s).

In the early 1980s, a sharp divergence in headship rates has occurred; those for population under age 35 have fallen, while those for the population over age 44 have continued to rise. Hendershott and Smith attribute the reduced headship rates for the young to both the marked increase in the real price of owner-occupied housing (again dominated by movements in the real after-tax mortgage rate) and the cutback in real benefits and increased eligibility standards for the AFDC program. Each of these tends to fall more heavily on younger households who are more mobile (and thus are more likely to have to pay the market mortgage rate) and are more likely to have dependent children.

Like housing demand, demand for consumer durables undergoes substantial cyclical variation. Disagreement exists as to the source of this variation because economists have less confidence in estimates of the income and price elasticities for durables than for housing. Lemmon (Chapter 8) attempts to shed light on this issue in his analysis of three separate components of durable goods: autos and parts, furniture and household appliances, and "other." He partitions the service prices (user costs) for these categories into their real asset price and real interest rate components and estimates demand elasticities with respect to each component and income. His estimates of income elasticities are just under unity for furniture and appliances (consistent with the elasticity of the demand for housing) and about 1.5 for the other components. Real asset price elasticities are also high, ranging from (minus) 1.5 to 2, but the estimated interest rate response, while statistically significant, implies a low -0.05 elasticity.[3]

What do these estimates suggest regarding stabilization policy and economic efficiency? First, high real interest rates cannot greatly curtail durable demand (as they obviously have not in 1983 and 1984). However, a high real asset price, as could be induced by an excise or value-added tax, can. Second, efficiency losses from the nontaxation of implicit income on durable goods is small. These losses can only be great if a significant misallocation of capital occurs, and the small size of the estimated interest-rate response belies such a misallocation.

Hu's analysis (Chapter 9) suggests that the demand for pension wealth is positively related to real income and the real pension rate of return and negatively related to social security wealth and the real after-tax nonpension rate of return. The long-run income elasticity of demand is quite high (3 to 6), but the interest rate elasticities are low (0.5). The elasticity with respect to social security is 0.5 to 1.0. Short-run elasticities are only about one-twentieth of long-run elasticities.

A number of sharp changes occurred in the determinants of the demand for pension wealth in the 1970s. First, expected returns on pension wealth (which is largely invested in equities) fell significantly relative to the returns on nonpension wealth, owing to the poor performance of the stock market. Second, the 1972 social security amendment raised social security wealth by nearly 40 percent. Third, passage of the Employee Retirement Income Security Act (ERISA) in 1974 significantly reduced the risk of pension saving. The first two of these changes are estimated to reduce pension demand by 20 and 30 percent (with large standard errors), respectively. (Even when the elasticity is near unity, pension wealth is reduced by only 5 percent of the increase in social security wealth because the former has been well over 10 times the latter.) ERISA, in contrast, is estimated to be increasing pension wealth by 50 to 100 percent. Thus ERISA seemingly does little more than offset the negative impacts of declining returns and increasing social security wealth. Much of the growth in pension wealth in the 1970s was simply a lagged response to the enormous real income gains of the 1960s.

The United States invests an enormous quantity of resources in education. By Johnson's (Chapter 10) calculations, gross outlays (including the opportunity cost of forgone earnings) in 1979 roughly equaled gross investment in private nonresidential plant and equipment. As a proportion of GNP, investment in education about doubled between 1950 and 1980 and the educational attainment of our population reflects this. In 1979, three-quarters of the labor force were high-school graduates and nearly one-fifth were also college graduates. These proportions are nearly double the ratios observed in 1950. The growth in education outlays reflects increased absolute and relative government support of education; the governments' share of direct outlays for higher education rose from less than half in 1955 to over two-thirds in 1978. However, Johnson argues that even today education should not be viewed as a subsidized good. While government pays a large share of the direct costs, neither private direct outlays nor indirect opportunity costs (after-tax income forgone) are depreciable.

After reviewing a large number of studies, Johnson concludes that the real social rate of return to investment in years of schooling is 6 to 8 percent and that returns to the *quality* of education (smaller class size, better equipment, etc.) are even greater. Moreover, in spite of the enormous increase in the supply of educated labor he can find no clear evidence of a decline in these rates of return. Apparently, the demand for educated labor has increased *pari passu* with the supply.

NOTES

1. Jianakoplos avoids this problem by including unexpected real wealth changes as a regressor in her equations explaining the change in real wealth.
2. Kane examines household wealth accumulation by size and type of household, as well as by age of head.
3. It is possible that estimates from micro data would yield significantly larger elasticities. This is the case with studies of housing demand.

REFERENCES

Boskin, Michael J. 1983. "Saving Incentives: The Role of Tax Policy." In *New Directions for Federal Tax Policies for the 1980s,* edited by Charls E. Walker and Mark A. Bloomfield, pp. 93–111. Cambridge, Mass.: Ballinger Publishing Company.

Dolde, Walter. 1978. "Capital Markets and the Short Run Behavior of Life Cycle Savers." *Journal of Finance* 33 (May):413–428.

Eisner, Robert and Paul J. Pieper. 1984. "A New View of the Federal Debt and Budget Deficits." *American Economic Review,* 74 (March):11–29.

Feldstein, Martin S. 1977. "National Saving in the United States." In *Capital for Productivity and Jobs,* pp. 124–154. The American Assembly. Englewood Cliffs, N.J.: Prentice-Hall, Inc.

———. 1983. "Fiscal Policy for the 1980s." In *New Directions for Federal Tax Policies for the 1980s,* edited by Charls E. Walker and Mark A. Bloomfield, pp. 23–34. Cambridge, Mass.: Ballinger Publishing Company.

Hanushek, Eric A. and John M. Quigley. 1980. "What is the Price Elasticity of Housing Demand?" *Review of Economics and Statistics* 62 (August):449–454.

2 SAVING IN THE U.S. Some Conceptual Issues

Alan J. Auerbach

WHAT IS SAVING?

In 1982 personal saving in the United States constituted 6.5 percent of disposable personal income, a slight rise in the saving rate over the previous year (see Table 2–1). If one looks at a broader measure of saving, though, the trend is different. By adding undistributed after-tax corporate profits both to saving and to measured after-tax income, we obtain a rate of private saving that declined from 8.4 percent to 7.9 percent over the same interval. An even bleaker picture materializes if we consider a still broader measure of the saving rate that encompasses the government sector as well. Subtracting the total government deficit from private saving and dividing this number by the net national product (total output less depreciation) yields a national saving rate of 2.1 percent in 1982, compared with 5.6 percent in 1981.

Do we face the prospect of a higher standard of living because personal saving out of income increased, or should we be alarmed that national saving declined so much? While simple answers cannot be provided for such questions, much can be said about the relative usefulness of various saving measures that differ not only with respect to the level of aggregation, as with the three measures just cited, but also in their comprehensiveness and the adjustments made to raw figures. For example, all of the measures in Table 2-1 utilize a *net* saving approach, whereby depreciation is subtracted both from gross income and gross saving. The logic of this and other corrections will be explored below. In some cases, desirable corrections are not made in practice because of the lack of available data, while in others it is not clear which of many approaches is most suitable. However, it is important that these issues be understood, for such corrections can be the source of markedly varying results about both levels and trends in measured saving.

This chapter discusses these issues of scope and aggregation, exploring both the relevant arguments and measurement problems and considering their impact on the measurement of saving. We begin with a brief review of what common saving measures indicate about trends in postwar U.S. saving behavior.

Table 2-1 presents time series for the three saving ratios mentioned above: personal saving, private saving, and national saving. The measures differ primarily in the degree to which they extend beyond the

Table 2-1. Saving Rates Based on National Income Accounts (percentage).

Year	*Personal Saving*		*Private Saving*[a]		*National Saving*[b]	
1946	8.6		9.7		10.7	
1947	3.1		5.7		11.3	
1948	5.9		10.7		12.3	
1949	4.0		8.7		5.8	
1950	5.8	6.0	8.9	9.8	10.3	9.0
1951	7.1		10.1		9.8	
1952	7.3		10.4		6.8	
1953	7.3		9.9		5.6	
1954	6.6		9.6		5.5	
1955	6.0	6.9	10.2	10.1	8.9	7.0
1956	7.3		10.5		9.7	
1957	7.2		10.2		8.3	
1958	7.4		9.7		4.7	
1959	6.2		9.9		7.5	
1960	5.6	6.3	8.7	9.6	7.6	6.7
1961	6.3		9.4		6.5	
1962	6.0		10.2		7.3	

Table 2-1. Continued.

Year	Personal Saving		Private Saving[a]		National Saving[b]	
1963	5.4		9.9		7.9	
1964	6.7		11.5		8.8	
1965	7.1	6.9	12.6	11.9	10.1	8.9
1966	7.0		12.5		9.6	
1967	8.1		12.8		8.2	
1968	7.1		11.2		8.0	
1969	6.4		9.6		8.5	
1970	8.0	7.2	9.9	10.3	6.6	7.4
1971	8.1		10.8		6.5	
1972	6.5		9.9		7.4	
1973	8.6		11.8		9.8	
1974	8.5		9.7		7.2	
1975	8.6	7.7	11.0	10.4	4.3	6.7
1976	6.9		9.7		5.4	
1977	5.9		9.6		6.6	
1978	6.1		9.9		7.9	
1979	5.9		8.9		7.7	
1980	5.8	6.1	7.8	8.6	4.8	5.6
1981	6.4		8.4		5.6	
1982	6.5		7.9		2.1	

Source: *Economic Report of the President* (1983).

a. The private saving rate equals personal saving plus undistributed corporate profits (with inventory valuation and capital consumption adjustments) divided by disposable personal income plus undistributed corporate profits.

b. The national saving rate equals private saving plus total government surplus divided by net national product.

household sector. By all measures, the saving rate has declined in the past five years, although the severity of this decline varies. In addition, the trends in the saving rates vary. While personal saving peaked in the mid-1970s and is now at levels comparable to those in earlier years, private saving and especially national saving have been declining since the mid-1960s and are now at levels below those typical of earlier years.

The relative stability of private saving has been the subject of much discussion in the literature, starting with the work of Denison (1958). However, Denison's law about the constancy of private savings does not necessarily apply once various corrections are made to the figures presented in Table 2-1.

ADJUSTMENTS TO MEASURED SAVING

This section discusses the construction of existing saving measures, particularly that of personal saving, and the adjustments that might be made in order to make the series a more meaningful measure of household saving. Questions of aggregation are deferred until the next section.

Changes in Wealth

How should changes in asset values be treated in the measurement of saving? Generally, saving is viewed as an accumulation of resources that will enable an increase in future consumption. Using a simple model of the economy, one can apply this definition to decide how asset value changes should be treated.

Consider a stationary economy in which generations overlap and each generation lives for two periods, working a fixed amount in the first period and then purchasing a fixed stock of wealth from the previous generation as a store of value to permit consumption during retirement in the second period of life. The wealth may be thought of as land, possessing a certain marginal product. As long as the productivity of land and labor remains constant, so does aggregate consumption. The price of land (and hence the market interest rate) is determined by the demand for land, which is determined in turn by the younger generation's preferences; in equilibrium, the price will be such that the implicit price of second-period consumption relative to that of first-period consumption causes the younger generation to desire to purchase just the amount of land available. The higher the price of land, the greater the fraction of aggregate consumption done by the elderly. Saving in this economy is zero in the aggregate, though the model could easily be extended to allow for positive output and population growth rates that would yield a positive aggregate savings rate.

Suppose that we observe in this economy a one-time increase in the price of land. Should this revaluation be considered a contribution to savings? On a flow basis, it obviously is not. But this may not be relevant. If we are interested in the extent to which future consumption prospects have been enhanced, the answer depends on the *cause* of the price rise. If land has become more productive, future consumption will be higher. If, however, land has become more expensive because of an increase in the desire of the young to defer consumption until retirement, aggregate consumption will remain unaffected. Intuitively, then, we should include increases in wealth in savings (and income) to the extent that they reflect increased productivity. Put another way, increases in wealth, adjusted for nominal price changes, should be included in measured savings. This has certain direct implications for actual savings measures. Stocks of nominal assets, such as long-term bonds, decrease in purchasing power in the presence of general price inflation. This decline should be subtracted from both income and savings. The same argument holds for physical assets that decline in value because of reduced productivity. On the other hand, if the price of an asset declines or rises at a rate below that of prices in general because other more productive assets have appeared, this does not constitute dissaving. Rather, adjusting for quality, the nominal price of the asset has declined.

While one can imagine these corrections theoretically, empirical implementation is much more difficult. First, there is no single measure of purchasing power. There are as many "market baskets" as consumers, each with its own price. To measure "the " change in the price of consumption goods, we must be satisfied with a representative index. Second, even to the extent that used capital goods' prices can be observed, separating changes in such prices into components associated with declining productivity and cheaper competing new assets remains a difficult task.

The personal saving rate reported in Table 2–1 makes only some of the corrections just discussed. Income from physical assets included in personal income (primarily propriety income and imputed rent from owner-occupied housing) is measured net of estimated capital consumption or depreciation. To the extent that this adjustment is intended to correct for reduced productivity (as opposed to embodied technical progress), it is appropriate. However, no adjustment at all is made for changes in the value of corporate securities, not even to the extent of realized capital gains. Moreover, there are no corrections made for the loss in real value of financial assets caused by inflation. This may have a major impact on estimated saving rates. For example, in 1982 personal interest income was $371.8 billion.[1] Using an estimate of 10 percent for the average interest rate on the underlying bonds, this implies $3.718 trillion in financial assets. Given the 6.1 percent year-to-year change in the consumer price index from 1981 to 1982, this implies a loss of $226.8 billion in the purchasing power of these assets. By comparison, measured personal saving itself was only $141.1 billion in 1982. Thus, this single correction would make measured personal saving negative!

The impact of making wealth corrections can be seen by constructing alternative series for saving based on year-to-year changes in wealth. The Board of Governors of the Federal Reserve System (1983) provides estimated end-of-year balance sheets for sectors in the U.S. economy from 1945 through 1982, based on Flow-of-Funds (FOF) data. These balance sheets provide current cost estimates for each sector's tangible and financial wealth, although bonds are valued at par. More precise wealth estimates are not available. Using these balance sheets, one can estimate saving as the real increase in a sector's wealth over a given period. For example, one would subtract deflated end-of-year wealth in 1981 from the comparable value for 1982 to obtain a constant-dollar figure for 1982 saving, and then reflate by a 1982 price index to obtain a real current-dollar saving estimate. This method would naturally incorporate the price-level adjustments outlined above.

There is a sufficient level of detail provided by these accounts to perform calculations of this type for the three levels of aggregation used in Table 2-1 for series based on data from the national income accounts. The three comparable series based on the flow-of-funds wealth data are reported in Table 2-2. For the sake of simplicity, we divide by the same income measures used in Table 2-1 (personal in-

Table 2-2. Saving Rates Based on Flow-of-Funds Balance Sheets (percentage).

Year	*Personal Saving*[a]		*Private Saving*[b]		*National Saving*[c]	
1946						
1947						
1948	9.2		18.4		21.2	
1949	19.8		19.6		13.6	
1950	24.0	17.1	19.6	17.3	23.4	16.5
1951	14.6		11.5		12.6	
1952	18.0		17.3		11.7	

Table 2-2. Continued.

Year	*Personal Saving*[a]		*Private Saving*[b]		*National Saving*[c]	
1953	7.9		15.2		10.0	
1954	45.3		21.2		13.9	
1955	37.6	20.0	26.1	18.6	21.6	14.5
1956	18.0		21.6		19.0	
1957	-8.6		8.8		8.1	
1958	45.2		14.8		8.7	
1959	19.2		15.1		11.1	
1960	3.2	20.1	6.4	12.7	5.2	8.8
1961	40.2		13.1		9.0	
1962	-7.1		14.2		10.0	
1963	26.2		8.2		6.6	
1964	26.5		18.1		14.0	
1965	26.9	22.6	16.9	14.9	14.0	11.7
1966	-4.3		15.8		13.4	
1967	37.5		15.5		10.7	
1968	32.5		14.6		11.6	
1969	-23.5		6.3		7.4	
1970	-3.5	12.2	6.7	13.5	4.8	10.5
1971	24.6		14.3		9.2	
1972	30.8		25.7		19.6	
1973	-19.1		21.5		19.4	
1974	-30.7		17.7		13.8	
1975	21.9	2.1	10.4	19.5	5.1	14.8
1976	30.6		26.6		19.1	
1977	7.8		21.4		16.4	
1978	19.1		26.5		22.4	
1979	-0.7		-2.0		0.8	
1980	11.9	4.4	-0.1	2.7	-1.3	1.7
1981	-11.4		-2.8		-2.5	
1982	3.1		-8.3		-10.9	

Source: Board of Governors of the Federal Reserve System, (1983).

a. The personal saving rate equals end of year household wealth (measured on a sector basis) less previous year's wealth multiplied by rate of current December's Consumer Price Index to previous December's divided by personal disposable income.

b. The private saving rate equals real change in wealth of private sector, consolidated, calculated in the same manner as personal saving, divided by disposal personal income plus undistributed corporate profits.

c. The National Saving Rate equals the real change in total domestic net worth divided by net national product.

come, personal income plus undistributed profits, and net national product), although a strictly consistent procedure would be to add wealth changes not included in the national income accounts to the income measures used. To the extent that saving is small relative to income, this should not introduce serious errors.

Although general trends in the three savings series reported in Table 2-2 are similar to those in Table 2-1, the absolute levels are quite different, as is the volatility of each series. The series that incorporate changes in wealth are much more volatile and show higher average savings rates for the postwar period. Whereas personal saving, based on national income accounts, has varied between 3.1 percent and 8.6 percent of disposable income, the wealth-based version has varied between -23.5 percent and 45.3 percent of disposable income. For the period 1948-82, the average personal saving rates were 6.7 percent and 14.1 percent, based on the NIA (Table 2-1) and FOF (Table 2-2) measures, respectively. Thus, the differences in the series are not cancelled out by aggregation of temporary fluctuations in the less stable wealth-based series.

Though private saving, based on the flow-of-funds data, is more stable than personal saving, it still fluctuates more than the very smooth private sector series reported in Table 2-1, varying between -8.3 percent and 26.6 percent, as opposed to a range of between 5.7 percent and 12.8 percent. Again, the FOF measure has a higher average for the period 1948-82, 14.2 percent versus 10.1 percent. National saving also is more volatile (a range of -10.9 percent to 23.4 percent versus one of 2.1 percent to 12.3 percent) and higher on average (11.2 percent versus 7.4 percent).

The relationships *among* saving rates are much less stable in Table 2-2 also. Whereas the years 1973-74 look bad from a personal saving perspective, this was a period of very high private and national saving. The explanation is quite clear, and instructive as well. This was a period of high inflation and a decline in equity values *relative* to the measured replacement cost of assets. The inflation eroded the real value of financial assets, which households hold in positive supply, and coupled with the decline in equity values led to low measured personal saving. However, to the extent that these household financial assets were debts of corporations (and the government), they are not *net* assets to the private sector (or the economy) as a whole. Hence, there is an offsetting debtors' gain to the creditors' loss on the value of bonds. Moreover, once the private sector is consolidated, corporate assets are measured at their replacement cost, rather than at the market value of corporate securities. Over the period, the ratio of market value to replacement cost plunged. Which of the measures gives a true picture of saving depends on how accurately replacement cost is measured.

A final important difference between these two types of saving measures is what they imply about the severity of the decline in savings over the past few years. By the wealth-based measures, personal, private, and national savings have averaged -7 percent, -3.3 percent, and -3.5 percent over the period 1979–82. According to these calculations, national wealth declined by nearly 11 percent in 1982 alone!

The implications of these alternative ways of measuring saving and the level of aggregation most helpful for policy analysis will be discussed in the final section. What a comparison of the two tables clearly indicates, however, is that wealth adjustment is an important issue and that the most commonly used measure of household saving, the personal saving rate, may be a very poor indicator of actual wealth accumulation.

Consumer Durables

An important additional reason for the two household savings series to differ is the treatment of consumer durables. The personal saving rate based on the national income accounts treats expenditures on household durables as consumption. Theoretically, this makes little sense. Like household purchases of owner-occupied houses, which are treated as investment with subsequent consumption service flows, durables provide future consumption services; their purchase represents a form of saving. The importance of this difference is easily isolated by looking at net household saving each year in consumer durables. Using the FOF data, we find that durables saving by households averaged 1.9 percent of personal disposable income over the period 1948–82; this accounts for approximately one-quarter of the difference between the two measures. (At the end of 1982, durables represented 11.5 percent of household net worth and were 40.9 percent as large as the stock of owner-occupied housing.[2]) The successive five-year averages for durable goods saving as a percentage of disposable income are 4.9, 2.4, 0.8, 2.2, 1.9, 1.4, and -0.1, respectively, for the periods presented in Table 2–2. Thus, while saving through durables was extremely important in the early postwar years, it recently has been negligible.

Human Capital

Less easy to calculate, and conceptually somewhat harder to justify for inclusion in a savings measure, is human capital, the value of future earnings embodied in individual workers. To the extent that expenditures on education, job training, and so forth increase this value, they ought to be considered saving. This argument is familiar, and such an adjustment would lead to an increase in the measured saving rate. To be consistent, however, with the treatment of labor earnings streams as capital assets, such an adjustment should be accompanied by a depreciation deduction in each year for the decline in value of existing human capital, absent any new investment. Because all workers eventually die, their human capital must fully depreciate. Thus, calculations such as those in Blades and Sturm (1982), which find that adding direct education expenditures to savings increases the U.S. household saving rate by 1.8 percent over the period 1970–80, are not informative about changes in the value of human capital.

In addition to direct expenditures on education and training, one can argue that earnings foregone while a worker is being trained and educated ought to be included in savings (and added to measured income as well). At a somewhat more abstract level, a component of nearly every "consumption" expenditure represents saving. Expenditures on food, health care, and shelter (the most basic such expenditures) also influence future earnings potential. One could separate, conceptually at least, expenditures on food required for adequate nutrition from those going to provide current pleasure from food consumption.[3] Similarly, traditional "human capital" expenditures (as on education, for example) contain what may in some cases be a substantial consumption component. Whether people make such careful calculations consciously is doubtful, but the very notion of a "necessary good" with a low income elasticity of expenditure is associated with the role of nutrition in providing for the maintenance of future earnings capacity.

This expanded way of viewing saving has important implications for conclusions about the effects of changes in the income distribution on savings. It is often suggested that an equalization of the income distribution would lower the household saving rate because the wealthy have a higher propensity to save than do the poor. While this result has been disputed empirically,[4] it also ignores the additional forms of saving in human capital. To the extent that such expenditures have an income elasticity below one, they would raise the saving rate of the poor relative to the rich.

Government Assets

Neither of the savings concepts implemented in Tables 2–1 and 2–2 includes government capital goods as assets. Government expenditures are treated as consumption in the measure of national saving. But the same logic that argues, for example, for treating privately owned buildings as assets argues that government buildings should be treated the same way. While this is straightforward for buildings, valuing the Grand Canyon might prove somewhat more difficult. Nevertheless, some heroic calculations have been done recently,[5] and they indicate that government saving in this form has been positive in recent years. For example, the increase in the real value of tangible government assets is estimated to have been $21 billion in 1980.[6] This compares to a measured deficit in 1980 of $33.2 billion, according to the national income accounts, and a measured surplus of $9.9 billion, according to the FOF data. From 1950 to 1980, government assets (in 1980 dollars) grew by $355 billion, representing about 6 percent of total wealth accumulation over the same period, as reported in the Flow-of-Funds data.

Implicit Claims as Assets

Not all claims against the government are marketable. Yet in many cases they are nearly indistinguishable from the government bonds that are included in private wealth. The most frequently cited of these is the "social security wealth" that members of the household sector have in the form of social security benefits they expect to receive in excess of social security taxes they expect to pay. At the end of 1977 the excess of this social security wealth over assets in the government social security trust fund was (in 1980 dollars) over $4 billion, or roughly half as much as the measured household sector wealth used for the calculations in Table 2–2.[7] There has been a vigorous debate over the last decade about whether such "wealth" influences household decisions, beginning with the conflicting views of Barro (1974) and Feldstein (1974). However, this controversy relates to *all* government liabilities (or at least those in excess of offsetting government assets) and is a question about whether a government debt that must be repaid by the household sector in the future can be considered a net household sector asset. This is an issue we will discuss in the final section. In the current context, what is relevant is that marketable government debt obligations are included in household wealth and indirectly, therefore, in the measures of personal saving presented above. Consistency would seem to argue for the inclusion of social security wealth as well. This is particularly important because the excluded social security wealth dwarfs marketable government debt in importance. In 1977, for example, the $4 trillion of estimated social security wealth was over ten times the direct holdings of $252 billion of government debt ($182 billion in U.S. obligations and $70 billion in state and local obligations). Even the total market value of the federal government's financial liabilities is less than one-quarter the size of unfunded social security wealth. Thus, there is a serious inconsistency in the treatment of claims against the government.

Similar problems are present in the area of household claims against corporations. Promised pension benefits constitute an increasing fraction of household wealth. Yet the national income account measure of personal saving excludes accrued benefits entirely. Because the Flow-of-Funds balance sheets include pension fund reserves in household wealth, *funded* pension accruals are included in that measure of personal saving, contributing to the observed higher average level of the FOF measure. (In 1982 pension fund reserves amounted to 8.7 percent of measured household wealth, about the same magnitude as consumer durables.) Still, unfunded accruals are not counted, just as unfunded increases in social security wealth are not.

Finally, there are implicit claims (possibly negative) by households against the government in the form of future tax liabilities and benefits. We consider these in the next subsection, along with other issues related to taxation.

The Effects of Taxation

There are at least two separate problems introduced to the measurement of saving by the presence of capital income taxes. One relates to differing *levels* of taxation and the other to differences in the *timing* of tax collections. The first of these problems is a familiar one in the area of project evaluation and shadow pricing in cost/benefit analysis, while the second relates to the discussion of implicit claims just completed.

Suppose there are two types of assets available for investment, *A* and *B*, each of which costs $100. Asset *A*'s return is not taxed, while asset *B*'s return is taxed at 40 percent. One may think of asset *A* as being government capital or owner-occupied housing. If both must earn for the investor an after-tax return of 6 percent, then asset *B* must deliver 10 percent before tax, while asset *A* must earn only the 6 percent return. What is the amount of saving done when each of the assets is purchased? Any available saving measure would suggest an answer of $100. However, the value to *society* of the purchase of asset *B* is greater than that coming from the purchase of asset *A* because of the tax revenues asset *B* will generate. Evaluated at the after-tax discount rate, the total social returns to asset *B* are worth $167, rather than $100, the difference being the present value of taxes generated. The distortionary tax creates a positive externality associated with investment in the taxed asset. Indeed, it is this divergence between social and private rates of return that underlies much of the current argument in favor of increasing saving in the United States, particularly in the form of business capital.

A related issue is that different assets may be taxed in ways such that the present value of taxes paid is the same but the timing of such payments is different. While such a difference should have few real effects, it does introduce changes in measured saving. Now consider an asset *C* that receives a deduction of its entire purchase price immediately at the same rate that its future income is taxed, 40 percent. As has long been recognized,[8] immediate expensing of assets is neutral in the sense that such assets face a zero effective tax rate: The present value of taxes on such assets is zero. In the current context, expensing is in all respects equivalent to a government loan being made for 40 percent of the asset's cost, being repaid by the return over time of 40 percent of the asset's proceeds. Presumably, then, the nontaxed asset *A* and asset *C* would earn the same pretax return, which we assume to be 10 percent for the sake of this example. How will these differences in taxation affect behavior? Assuming the investor wants to save $100 and consume $10 in each succeeding year, for example, he will have to save an additional amount if he purchases asset *C*: It has a net cost of only $60 but returns only $6 a year, after tax. At the same time, the government will have to come up with $40 more revenue if asset *C* is purchased because its cost can be expensed but will receive an additional $4 a year forever in taxes from the asset. Fortuitously (but not coincidentally), the amount the government must raise by floating debt equals the amount the investor wishes to save. Hence, if the debt is issued, neither the investor nor the government will have its plans disturbed in any way. The outcome will be the same, regardless of whether asset *A* or asset *C* is purchased.

Yet this equivalence will not be reflected in measuring saving. Under the usual national income account approach to saving, personal saving would be $100 when asset *A* is purchased but $140 if asset *C* is purchased. Government saving in the latter case would decline by $40, the size of the debt issued to the private sector. It should be emphasized that this inclusion of accumulated government debt in measured personal saving is not appropriate, even if government bonds are considered to be net wealth, because there is an offsetting government *claim* against the household that is being ignored in this calculation. To see this, note what will happen to the *value* of asset *C* once it is purchased and expensed: It will drop in value to $60, reflecting the future after-tax stream of returns of $6 per year. This is because, while the *present value* of taxes on asset *C,* like those on asset *A,* are zero, the owner of asset *C* has received a tax benefit and must repay this benefit in the future. The value of this implicit government claim, $40, is capitalized into the value of the asset. Thus, the investor's wealth, *including* government bonds, is $100, not $140, and the government's net liability is zero. Unlike in the case of, say, social security, where bonds will be paid off by those alive in the future, a change in the timing of tax collections from an existing asset financed by government debt will have an offsetting wealth effect in the asset's value. This result is particularly important at present because the current state of business income taxation resembles expensing for many types of assets: very low effective tax rates, accomplished not by a low statutory tax rate but by an investment tax credit and accelerated depreciation allowances. Hence, the measured deficits associated with new investment are overstated, and private saving is overstated.[9]

When the tax law changes in a way that discriminates between old and new assets, there is an additional transfer of wealth from the household to the government associated with the decline in the value of existing assets, this time *without* any offsetting government transfer to the household. For example, suppose that the government suddenly announced, in our example above, that asset *A* would henceforth be treated like asset *C*: expensing followed by future taxes, both at 40 percent. For new assets of type *A*, there would be no *net* effect, as just discussed. But for *existing* assets of type *A* that do not receive the expensing deduction, this represents a 40 percent decrease in value: The government has taken its implicit claim without paying for it.[10] If government bonds are net private wealth, then such wealth has been decreased by this amount, essentially by a lump-sum tax, if the change was unanticipated. The outcome is equivalent to the government's simply taxing away 40 percent of the value of all existing assets of type *A*. The importance of this result is that it bears on most recent changes in capital income taxation in the United States: Only new assets have qualified. Thus, along with whatever lowering in effective tax rates occurred, there was a wealth levy on the existing capital stock.

These results about the capitalization of future taxes are relevant not only to the discussion in the next section but also to the way we measure saving; for if we used a wealth-based measure, such as the Flow-of-Funds balance sheet approach taken in Table 2–2, corporate equity values, which are carried at market, ought to respond to changes in implicit tax liabilities. Even is this were the case, however, there is no automatic correction in the corresponding national saving measure to account for the implicit *asset* this represents for the government. This would lead to an understatement of national saving.

Summary

Saving in the United States appears to have declined in recent years, regardless of the measure used, but the extent of the decline differs according to the method of measuring saving. The measure of personal saving based on the Flow-of-Funds wealth statistics suggests a higher average level of postwar saving (but a lower one in the last decade) than that taken from the national income accounts (NIA). The generally higher level of the former is due probably to three major differences. The FOF measure includes accumulations of wealth through consumer durables and funded pensions, each of which represents about a quarter of the average gap between the two measures of personal saving. The remaining discrepancy is the inclusion of capital gains and losses in the FOF measure. In principle, this effect could go either way. During periods of stable prices and rising equity values (such as the 1950s and 1960s), real capital gains are positive. However, with rising prices and bond and stock prices constant or declining in *nominal* terms (as in the 1970s), real capital gains are negative. This helps to explain the stronger downward trend in the FOF-based measure of personal saving.

Many have suggested (see, for example, Baily 1981) that much of the wealth decline in the 1970s was the result of induced obsolescence of much of the nation's capital stock as a result of the rapid rise in energy prices. By the arguments put forward above, such a decline would portend diminished future consumption possibilities and should be incorporated in measured saving. The same holds true, of course, for recent increases in wealth, to the extent that they are related to declining energy costs.

Given the lack of allowance for consumer durables, pension assets and capital gains, as well as other potential components that, while less easily measured, may be more important in magnitude, it is striking how stable the NIA-based measures of saving, particularly personal saving, are. This brings us to the second major topic of discussion: the interrelationship of different components of saving.

AGGREGATION AND IRRELEVANCE PROPOSITIONS

Three different levels of aggregation of saving, measured in two ways, have been presented above, along with ways in which these measures fail to incorporate particular aspects of behavior that, from an economic perspective, would be described as saving. One argument in favor of using a saving measure based on a higher level of aggregation is that certain corrections that would be necessary at the household level of measurement are not required at the private or the national level. For example, we discussed how the personal saving rate based on national income account (NIA) concepts does not correct for the loss in value of nominal assets that households suffer in the presence of inflation. Presumably, even if we believed that household saving is not influenced by saving behavior at the firm or government level, we would wish to make such a correction. Not doing so would amount to a rather severe assumption about money illusion on the part of households. However, this problem disappears in stages as we consider broader levels of aggregation. For private saving, one would only have to include claims against the government and debtors abroad; for national saving, only the latter. Similar arguments apply to such things as implicit claims that households may have against the corporate or government sector. Ultimately, one must weigh such benefits against other arguments for considering household saving separately. The extreme stability of the NIA-based measure of personal saving indicates that not all offsets that would be predicted by naive models actually occur. Aside from various types of "illusion" or imperfect information, this stability may also result from taxes and capital market conditions that make other forms of saving imperfect substitutes for household saving.

This section reviews first the most basic theories about how saving by different sectors should be related and then discusses why, in spite of elementary irrelevance propositions, there may exist strong reasons why the level at which saving is done does matter and why changes in the composition of national saving may have real effects.

If an individual owns a business and loans money to it, he or she has saved and the business has borrowed. If, instead, the owner increases his or her share in the business by retaining earnings from the business, the business has saved. Put this way, the distinction between business and personal saving appears arbitrary and of little use. But this distinction exists in the way household saving is measured, if the business is a corporation. Retained earnings constitute business saving that, even if they increase equity values accordingly, do not show up at the household level of saving (in the NIA measure), while issues of debt and equity are considered to be personal saving. Implicit in this approach seems to be a sense that the act of retention is different from that of floating new issues.

This rationale was attacked by Modigliani and Miller (1958, 1961), who pointed out that, holding real behavior constant, variations in a firm's pure financial policy can have no real effects under a wide variety of circumstances. As long as personal investors can undo what the firm has done, unexploited profit opportunities will exist if real effects are present. If, for example, a firm's value increases more when it sells new shares than when it retains earnings in the same amount, it can generate infinite profits for its stockholders by selling shares and distributing the proceeds as dividends, with the stock price rising without bound. In a competitive market, all that is generally necessary for the Modigliani/Miller proposition to hold is rationality on the part of investors.

At the national level, the corresponding irrelevance proposition is sometimes referred to as the Ricardian equivalence theorem. The argument here is that government can use either tax or debt finance to finance a real path of government expenditures. In the long run, however, the government's budget must be balanced. Hence, a substitution today of debt for taxes carries with it a need to raise taxes in the future. These future taxes, according to the argument, will constitute an implicit liability that offsets the "wealth" created by the issuance of government bonds, with no real effects. This argument even has been extended to claim that monetary finance is equivalent to debt finance and tax finance (Wallace 1981).

For certain types of taxes, this argument is similar to the Modigliani/Miller theorem. For example, as discussed above, debt issued to support changes in the timing of capital income taxation should be offset by implicit claims, representing postponed taxes, that are capitalized into asset values. This is analogous to a firm's equity value going down when it issues debt. However, most government debt is not repaid through such capital income taxes. In general, the view that government debt does not constitute net private wealth requires some further mechanism to connect future tax payments to current debt. As shown by Barro (1974), an operational bequest motive of a specific kind (parents bequeath based on the welfare of their heirs rather than for other potential reasons) suffices for this purpose. However, a fully functioning system of bequests is a much stricter requirement than mere household rationality.

In summary, the Modigliani/Miller theorem implies that a shift in measured corporate saving should be offset by one at the personal level. If a corporation switches from new share issues to retentions, those that would purchase the shares ought to purchase stock from existing shareholders in an amount of equal value to the forgone issue, with the existing shareholders left with stock equal to the value of all shares before the earnings were retained. The Barro/Ricardo theorem suggests that increases in government saving should have a similar offset at the private level. The latter proposition requires more than mere rationality on the part of households. In one study, David and Scadding (1974) referred to such behavior as "ultra-rational."

Once realistic features of the economy are considered, additional problems arise for the irrelevance propositions. One implication of the simple Barro/Ricardo proposition is that the government's issuing of debt in order to make lump-sum transfers should have no real effects, except for second-order effects that arise because the distribution of these transfers is different from the distribution of future taxes. However, to the extent that the transfer recipients are unemployed, they may be facing constraints against borrowing and consuming all available resources. Even if they are taxed in the future to repay the debt, their real current behavior will change: Their consumption will increase, just as if the debt were net wealth. The importance of this effect depends on how important such constraints are. In a study of consumption behavior using panel data, Hall and Mishkin (1982) estimated that 20 percent of the population was consuming out of current income rather than permanent income. Presumably, this figure would vary over the business cycle. In severe recessions, one would expect a much higher percentage to result.

There are a number of reasons why both irrelevance propositions should break down once a realistic tax system is considered. Perhaps the most obvious is that if taxes are distortionary, their timing matters because it affects the tax system's deadweight loss. A general result in public finance theory is that the welfare loss induced by a tax (or some other distortion)–that is, the social loss in excess of the revenue collected–increases in proportion to the squared value of the tax. As a result, excess burden over time, under certain assumptions, will be minimized if tax rates are kept constant, or at least vary only in unpredictable ways. Recent work by Barro (1979) offers empirical support for this proposition. Hence, issuance of debt can increase social welfare by allowing a smoothing of tax collections over time.

Taxes also influence the distribution of saving between households and corporations because of the nature of the income tax in the United States. Under our classical tax system, corporations and their owners are treated as separate entities. Since not all corporate source income is taxed in the same way, the Modigliani/Miller theorem breaks down. This was first recognized by Modigliani and Miller (1963) themselves, who pointed out that a corporate income tax with interest deductibility and without a personal income would encourage firms to use all debt finance to take advantage of the deduction. Hence, business saving through retentions would be less desirable from the viewpoint of households than direct saving through debt. Once a personal income tax is added, the situation becomes more complicated because interest payments are taxed at the personal level while equity source personal income receives preferential tax treatment of the capital gains generated by retentions.

Under one recent view of the corporate tax, equity income is essentially exempt from taxation at the personal level. This argument (discussed in Auerbach 1983a) hinges on the immediate source of equity funds. Traditionally, the vast bulk of equity finance in the United States has come through retained earnings rather than new share issues. This is particularly true once regulated utilities, with their special tax rules, are eliminated from the sample. Though the earnings generated by current retentions may, when distributed in the future, be subject to dividend taxes, such taxes on the firm's owners are avoided by the current act of retention. For example, if a firm retains $100 in earnings, an investor in a 40 percent tax bracket saves $40 in taxes. If the asset purchased generates $10 a year after corporate taxes, with all such earnings distributed, the investor will receive $6 a year after tax, for a 10 percent return on his $60 of forgone, after-tax contribution–the same return he would receive if dividends were untaxed. Hence, the dividend tax does not affect the rate of return available through retentions, just as was the case above for an income tax that provides for the expensing of investments. In fact, the two systems are analytically identical.

By this argument, business saving results in income taxation at the personal level only to the extent of capital gains taxation. Hence, business saving is less clearly discouraged relative to personal saving via debt finance. It is still the case that firms without access to a pool of retentions, or that choose to fund equity through new issues, face the "double taxation" of dividends previously thought to apply to all equity income because there is then no immediate deduction in the form of reduced dividend taxation.

Despite these many reasons for the irrelevance propositions to fail, they have prompted much investigative effort in the empirical literature and some support for them has been found. Probably the first empirical investigation about the relationship of various saving rates produced Denison's (1958) observation that gross private saving as a fraction of income was remarkably stable over time. This study was followed by that of David and Scadding (1974), who observed that this private saving rate was substantially more stable over time than either of its components–corporate saving and personal saving–suggesting the presence of an offset at the personal level to corporate saving. David and Scadding also found that such stability was not present at the level of national saving, suggesting perhaps that the Modigliani/Miller theorem has more validity than the Barro/Ricardo proposition.

Perhaps the most central criticism of these findings is the saving rates on which they are based. As emphasized in the previous section, the rates based on the national income accounts leave out many components of saving and improperly measure others. Moreover, it is not clear why one would use stability of a *gross* rather than *net* saving rate as evidence concerning behavioral trends. If the rate at which capital depreciates changes over time (as it has with the shift in business investment in the 1960s away from structures and toward equipment), this should not be ignored in a calculation of saving. Looking at the net saving rates in Table 2–1, it is not immediately evident that private saving has been more stable over time than household saving. Both measures, however, have been substantially more stable than their wealth-based counterparts in Table 2–2; in fact, national saving appears to be the most stable of the three measures. However, there are many other corrections not made to these series that would alter them substantially. Thus, the relative stability of gross private saving cannot necessarily be viewed as strong empirical confirmation for the substitutability of personal and business saving.

A potential response to this criticism might be that households and businesses do not necessarily make all the corrections we have suggested in determining how much they save. On this question, there is at least some evidence that they do make adjustments. In Auerbach (1982) I studied the aggregate dividend-retention policy of U.S. firms between 1962 and 1981. By the national income account definition of corrected, after-tax profits, it appeared that the dividend payout rate had increased over the period and had varied substantially from year to year. On the other hand, adding to profits the corporate gain on net indebtedness due to inflation reduced the trend and year-to-year fluctuations. A regression based on components of corporate profits suggested that dividend payments responded in roughly equal magnitudes to measured corporate profits and the normally excluded corporate gain from inflation. Thus, at least in this case, there is some evidence that business savings responds to real magnitudes, whether or not they are incorporated into reported statistics.

A popular way of testing various "offset" propositions concerning the effects of corporate and government saving on household behavior is through behavioral time series regressions that relate household saving decisions to those of firms and the government. However, much of this work has come under strong theoretical and empirical criticism. When all such criticism is taken into account, it becomes evident how difficult it is to use time series data to test hypotheses such as those discussed here.[11]

CONCLUSIONS

Probably the most important conclusion of this paper is that saving is very difficult to measure and that savings measures on which much of the empirical evidence on the various rationality hypotheses has been based differ quite substantially from those that would be desirable, at least theoretically. If, for example, the private saving rates based on the Flow-of-Funds data are examined, there is very little stability in recent years; such saving exceeded 21 percent for each of the three years between 1976 and 1978 and has been *negative* in every subsequent year.

In the same vein, theoretical arguments suggesting that the household level of saving is unimportant and that only private or national saving need be considered ignore very important institutional factors that make both government and corporate saving imperfect substitutes for saving at the personal level. Thus, despite the previous difficulty encountered evaluating such propositions empirically, one would not really expect them to be completely valid.

NOTES

1. This and other numbers taken from the Economic Report of the President (1983).
2. Household net worth was $9.468 trillion at the end of 1982 according to the FOF balance sheet data. The stocks of consumer durables and owner-occupied housing were, respectively, $1.09 trillion and $2.665 trillion.
3. Presumably, the expenditures on food by an obese person whose weight hinders him in his job performance would have a negative investment component.
4. See, for example, Blinder (1975).
5. See the Economic Report of the President (1982):104. Also see Eisner and Pieper (1984).

6. In 1980 dollars, the value of tangible government wealth was $727 billion at the end of 1980 and $706 billion at the end of 1979.
7. According to the 1982 Economic Report of the President (p. 104), social security wealth was $4.018 trillion or $2.895 trillion in 1977 dollars. This is 50.5 percent of the $5.733 trillion of household wealth provided by the Flow-of-Funds estimates.
8. See, for example, Brown (1948).
9. Calculations of Auerbach (1983b) suggest a correction to the 1981 deficit of $134.6 billion to allow for increased tax capitalization associated with the 1981 investment incentives. This estimate includes an adjustment for offsetting future reductions associated with the implicit repayment of the debt via deferred taxes.
10. What actually occurred is recent tax law changes more resembled treating asset *B* like asset *C*. In this case there is, in addition to the wealth effect just discussed, also a net reduction in the tax burden facing new capital.
11. Probably best known here is the work of Feldstein (1974), who looked at the impacts both of corporate saving and the social security system on household saving decisions. Feldstein's work generated substantial controversy and subsequent empirical research, but the results of this body of work must be viewed with caution. Auerbach and Kotlikoff (1983) have shown that regressions based even on the time series data *generated* by a life cycle simulation model in which social security *does* reduce saving may not give stable or sensible coefficients of the social security wealth variable because of aggregation bias and equation misspecification. A similar problem is present in the attempt to measure the response of consumption to increased retentions. Presumably, changes in retentions are correlated with other, excluded variables, such as prospects for future profitability. Hence, the increased saving that results when retentions increase may be due to changes in those other variables.

REFERENCES

Auerbach, Alan J. 1982. "Issues in the Measurement and Encouragement of Business Saving." In *Saving and Government Policy*, Conference Series No. 25, pp. 79–100. Boston: Federal Reserve Bank.

———. 1983a. "Taxation, Corporate Financial Policy and the Cost of Capital." *Journal of Economic Literature* 21 (September):905–40.

———. 1983b. "Corporate Taxation in the U.S." *Brookings Papers on Economic Activity* 2:451–505.

Auerbach, Alan J., and Laurence J. Kotlikoff. 1983. "An Evaluation of Empirical Tests of Social Security and Saving." In *Social Policy Evaluation: An Economic Perspective*, edited by E. Helpman et al., pp. 161–81. New York: Academic Press.

Baily, Martin N. 1981. "Productivity and the Services of Labor and Capital." *Brookings Papers on Economic Activity* 1:1–150.

Barro, Robert J. 1974. "Are Government Bonds Net Wealth?" *Journal of Political Economy* 82 (November/December):1045–17.

———. 1979. "On the Determination of the Public Debt." *Journal of Political Economy* 87 (October):940–71.

Blades, Derek W., and Peter H. Sturm. 1982. "The Concept and Measurement of Savings: The United States and the Industrialized Countries." In *Savings and Government Policy.* Conference Series No. 25, pp. 1–30. Boston: Federal Reserve Bank.

Blinder, Alan S. 1975. "Distribution Effects and the Aggregate Consumption Function." *Journal of Political Economy* 83 (June):447–75.

Board of Governors of the Federal Reserve System. 1983. *Balance Sheets for the U.S. Economy 1945–82.* Washington, D.C.: U.S. Government Printing Office, (May).

Brown, E. Cary. 1948. "Business Income Taxation and Investment Incentives." In Metzler et al. *Income, Employment and Public Policy.* New York: W.W. Norton.

David, Paul, and John L. Scadding. 1974. "Private Saving: Ultrarationality, Aggregation, and Denison's Law." *Journal of Political Economy* 82 (March/April):225–49.

Denison, Edward. 1958. "A Note on Private Saving." *The Review of Economics and Statistics* 40 (August):261–67.

Economic Report of the President. 1982. Washington, D.C.: U.S. Government Printing Office.

———. 1983. Washington, D.C.: U.S. Government Printing Office.

Eisner, Robert, and Paul J. Pieper. 1984. "A New View of the Federal Debt and Budget Deficits." *American Economic Review* 74 (March):11–29.

Feldstein, Martin S. 1974. "Social Security, Induced Retirement and Aggregate Capital Accumulation." *Journal of Political Economy* 82 (September/October):905–96.

Hall, Robert E., and Fredric S. Mishkin. 1982. "The Sensitivity of Consumption to Transitory Income: Estimates from Panel Data on Households." *Econometrica* 50 (March):461–83.

Miller, Merton, and Franco Modigliani. 1961. "Dividend Policy, Growth and the Valuation of Shares." *Journal of Business* 34 (October):411–33.

Modigliani, Franco, and Merton Miller, 1958. "The Cost of Capital, Corporation Finance, and the Theory of Investment." *American Economic Review* 48 (June):261–97.

———. 1963. "Corporate Income Taxes and the Cost of Capital: A Correction." *American Economic Review* 53 (June):433–43.

Wallace, Neil, 1981. "A Modigliani–Miller Theorem for Open Market Operations." *American Economic Review* 71 (June):267–74.

II HOUSEHOLD SAVING AND WEALTH ACCUMULATION

3 REAL HOUSEHOLD CAPITAL GAINS AND WEALTH ACCUMULATION

Patric H. Hendershott and Joe Peek

Real capital gains and losses contribute to or detract from the accumulation of nonhuman wealth by households. Although omitted from the National Income and Product Accounts (NIPA), these real gains and losses have been large relative to personal saving in most years.[1] Moreover, when the gains are cumulated over extended periods, they can result in a large number as the data in Table 3–1 indicate. The 1950–82 period has been partitioned into two broad spans, 1950–68 and 1969–82, which correspond roughly to surges in real corporate equity and real land and housing values in the United States. To reflect these surges, household real capital gains on corporate equities and on housing, land, and noncorporate equity (over half of the real increase in noncorporate equity can be attributed to growth in underlying real land values) are listed separately.[2] The cumulated values of these real gains, of their sum, and of real household saving as measured in the NIPA are presented in billions of 1972 dollars. As can be seen, real capital gains, largely in the form of corporate equities, dominated the cumulation of real saving as conventionally measured in the 1950–68 period. In the 1969–82 span, the collapse of the corporate equity market resulted in saving looming large relative to the sum of the two components of real capital gains, but even here

Table 3-1. Real Household Wealth Accumulation (billions of 1972 dollars).

	Real Cumulated Capital Gains			
	Housing, Land, and Noncorporate Equity	*Corporate Equity*	*Housing, Land and Total Equity*	*Cumulated Saving*
1950-68	241	825	1066	638
1969-82	643	-376	267	875

Source: Board of Governors of the Federal Reserve System (1983), *Balance Sheets For the U.S. Economy* 1945-82, calculations of the authors (see the section of this chapter on the calculations). The real gains (losses) on corporate equities held by households indirectly via their insurance and pension fund reserves are included in the corporate equity data.

real gains on housing, land, and noncorporate equity were nearly three-quarters as large as cumulated real saving.

It can reasonably be argued that these data overstate the importance of real capital gains. More specifically, the real gains on corporate equities are due, in part, to the retention of earnings, or corporate saving, rather than solely to increases in the real price of the underlying stock of physical capital. If households see through the corporate veil, then these earnings should be added to household saving and excluded from corporate equity capital gains.[3] These changes are incorporated in the data in Table 3-2 (the retained earnings data are after the inventory valuation and capital consumption adjustments), and the changes are large. Real capital gains are now slightly negative in the 1969-82 period, and the gains are only 64 percent of cumulated real saving in the 1950-68 span, about the reverse of the data in Table 3-1. But even here, the contribution of real gains is important. Moreover, in Table 3-2, the savings cumulation, instead of capital gains, is overstated, both because empirical studies suggest that households only partially see through the corporate veil and because some part of saving is simply a means of replacing the erosion of the real value of household financial assets (less liabilities) by inflation.

Rather than continuing these ad hoc adjustments, we will get on with our systematic measurement of real household capital gains. But the motivation for this measurement ought to be clear: One can hardly ignore real gains when studying either wealth accumulation or

Table 3-2. Adjusted Real Household Wealth Accumulation (billions of 1972 dollars).

	Real Cumulated Capital Gains			
	Housing, Land and Noncorporate Equity	*Adjusted Corporate Equity*	*Housing, Land, and Total Adjusted Equity*	*Cumulated Adjusted Saving*
1950–68	241	426	667	1037
1969–82	643	-724	-81	1223

Source: See Table 3-1. In the adjustment, cumulated real retained earnings are subtracted from the change in real corporate equity holdings and added to cumulated saving.

saving behavior. The next section of this chapter addresses some conceptual issues regarding the measurement of real capital gains (and income at a more general level), and the following one describes the real gains (or losses), both absolutely and relative to total real wealth accumulation in various forms, that households have experienced on various balance sheet items over the last third of a century. The final section reports estimates of expected real gains over this period. The impacts of the expected and unexpected components of real capital gains on household saving are estimated in Chapter 4.

MEASUREMENT OF REAL CAPITALS GAINS: SOME CONCEPTUAL ISSUES

The observed growth of household wealth, as customarily measured, is a result of (1) the net purchase of assets (the flow of saving) and (2) changes in asset values arising from changes in either the actual or expected income earned by real assets or the rates at which earnings are capitalized.[4] In addition, a change in the relative price of consumption goods will alter the real value of wealth in terms of consumption goods. To illustrate the sources of the change in real wealth, consider a simple world with four assets (money, bonds, corporate equity claims, and physical capital) and a single consumption good. Real household wealth (W) is defined as:

$$W \equiv \frac{p_b B}{p_c} + \frac{M}{p_c} + \frac{p_e E}{p_c} + \frac{p_k K}{p_c} = \bar{B} + \bar{M} + \bar{E} + \bar{K}, \tag{3.1}$$

where B is the number of bonds (which can be negative for households borrowing to finance purchases of physical capital or equity shares), M is the nominal stock of money, E is the number of equity shares, K is the number of units of physical capital, and p_b, p_e, p_k, and p_c are the prices of bonds, equities, physical capital, and the consumption good, respectively.

The change in wealth (dW) can be written as:

$$dW \equiv \bar{B}\left(\frac{dB}{B} + \frac{dp_b}{p_b} - \frac{dp_c}{p_c}\right) + \bar{M}\left(\frac{dM}{M} - \frac{dp_c}{p_c}\right) + \bar{E}\left(\frac{dE}{E} + \frac{dp_e}{p_e} - \frac{dp_c}{p_c}\right) + \bar{K}\left(\frac{dK}{K} + \frac{dp_k}{p_k} - \frac{dp_c}{p_c}\right), \tag{3.2}$$

if one is interested in separating the effects by asset, or alternatively:

$$dW \equiv \left[\bar{B}\frac{dB}{B} + \bar{M}\frac{dM}{M} + \bar{E}\frac{dE}{E} + \bar{K}\frac{dK}{K}\right] + \left[\bar{B}\left(\frac{dp_b}{p_b} - \frac{dp_c}{p_c}\right) - \bar{M}\frac{dp_c}{p_c} + \bar{E}\left(\frac{dp_e}{p_e} - \frac{dp_c}{p_c}\right) + \bar{K}\left(\frac{dp_k}{p_k} - \frac{dp_c}{p_c}\right)\right], \tag{3.3}$$

if one wishes to separate the change in wealth according to the flows, or net purchases, of assets (saving) and changes in the real value (in terms of the consumption good) of the assets previously held (net capital gains). The last equation is equivalent to:

$$dW \equiv S + G, \tag{3.4}$$

where S, the conventional measure of real saving, is the first bracketed term in equation (3.3), and G, total real capital gains, is the second bracketed term. Clearly the change in the real value of household wealth (dW) would be identical to the real value of saving only in the absence of real net capital gains ($G = 0$).

The above definition of changes in real wealth and real capital gains is the Haig/Simons view (Haig 1921; Simons 1938): To maintain wealth intact means maintaining its beginning of period real pecuniary value. But this is not the only possible definition of capital maintenance. The conventional measurement of income, for example, excludes all capital gains. As Seltzer (1951) notes, this measurement has been strongly affected by the agricultural origins of the income concept. Income arose from a fixed and continuing source such as land and, like the annual harvest, was separated from this permanent source at periodic intervals leaving the capital (land) intact. Because capital was regarded as a physical thing rather than a pecuniary value, the maintenance of capital was not tied to the maintenance of its pecuniary value. Under this view, capital assets were considered as quasi-permanent holdings held for the receipts they produced rather than for potential capital gains they might generate. An increase in the pecuniary value of the asset did not alter the real wealth of its holder, who still held the same asset as before. Even if the asset were sold at a profit, the entire sales price would be required to replace the asset (and the corresponding stream of income). Thus a rise in the pecuniary value of a capital asset was not an addition to either income or wealth. This position would be consistent with the view of Pigou (1941). Under this definition, $dW \equiv S$.

There is another concept of capital maintenance that lies between these extremes: Hicks's prospective-income capital maintenance. Of most appeal is his Income No. 3: "The maximum amount of money which the individual can spend this week, and still expect to be able to spend the same amount in real terms in each ensuing week" (1946: 174). The basic difference between this concept and the Haig/Simons concept adjusted for changes in the price level can be illustrated by analysis of the effect on each of a change in the discount rate. Consider a perpetuity that pays $10 a year. At an interest rate of 10 percent, its value is $100. Suppose the market interest rate falls to 5 percent, increasing the value of the perpetuity to $200. The Haig/Simons concept considers this capital gain as a part of income while the Hicks concept would not because there has been no change in the future earnings stream of the perpetuity. Even if the perpetuity were sold for $200, the entire sum would be required to purchase a comparable asset that yielded the same stream of payments, that is, maintained capital (prospective income) intact.[5]

Actually, if Hicks's concept is pushed to its limit, then the increase in the real price of an asset could even cause a *decrease* in the well-being of the holder. Consider a capital asset that will be used up and replaced periodically and for which there are limited substitution possibilities. A rise in its price could make its owner worse off because the asset will have to be replaced eventually at a higher real price (see the discussions of Shoven and Bulow 1975, 1976). While an individual who purchased the asset before a price increase would certainly be better off than if he had purchased the same asset immediately after the price increase, his position is worsened nonetheless by the need to replace the asset at the higher price in the future. The longer lived the asset, the better off (or less worse off) an individual is in that the bad aspect of replacement at the higher price is pushed further into the future. Furthermore, the intent of the asset holder, as well as the life of the asset, is an important consideration in determining the effect of a rise in the price of an asset, or good, on his economic well-being. If he trades in the asset with the intention of selling at a profit, then it would seem that he is certainly made better off by a rise in the real value of the asset. It is the value of the asset that is important. In contrast, if the intent is to use the asset until the end of its useful life (for example, many consumer durable goods), it is the physical thing that is important.

The Hicks's prospective-income view suggests expressing real gains, after allowing for i different categories of physical capital with prices p_{ki}, as:

$$G = \bar{B}\left(\frac{\lambda_b dp_b}{p_b} - \frac{dp_c}{p_c}\right) - \bar{M}\frac{dp_c}{p_c} + \bar{E}\left(\frac{dp_e}{p_e} - \frac{dp_c}{p_c}\right) + \Sigma\lambda_i\bar{K}_i\left(\frac{dp_{ki}}{p_{ki}} - \frac{dp_c}{p_c}\right), \qquad (3.5)$$

where λ's have been introduced following the above arguments. We assume that λ_b lies between zero and unity, being closer to zero the longer is the intended holding period of the bond holder. For example, if the intent is to hold the bond to maturity, nominal bond price changes in the interim are irrelevant. Such changes do not alter either the nominal par value of the bond at maturity or the stream of interest payments paid on the bond. Of course, if transactions costs are low, there may be tax advantages to selling the bond following a capital loss and then repurchasing a similar bond. In this instance, the bond price changes cause only an alteration in the timing of (Haig/Simons) income because both the stream of nominal interest payments and the nominal price of the bond at maturity are unchanged (McElroy 1976 discusses this timing of income issue).[6] As discussed previously the λ_i should vary positively with the durability of the capital, being close to unity for, say, houses and, possibly, negative for very short-lived consumer durables.

Given the unknown values of the λ's, equation (3.5) cannot be implemented directly. In the empirical work in Chapter 4, real capital gains will be measured following the Haig/Simons view (that is, with the λ's equal to unity). However, we will take care to partition the variables such that average values of the λ's can be reflected in the estimated coefficients. For this purpose, equation (3.5) is usefully rewritten as:

$$G = -(\bar{B} + \bar{M})\frac{dp_c}{p_c} + \lambda_b \bar{B}\frac{dp_b}{p_b} + \bar{E}\left(\frac{dp_e}{p_e} - \frac{dp_c}{p_c}\right) + \Sigma\lambda_i \bar{K}_i\left(\frac{dp_{ki}}{p_{ki}} - \frac{dp_c}{p_c}\right). \quad (3.5')$$

This equation suggests that the inflation-induced erosion in the values of bonds and money can be aggregated, nominal capital gains on bonds due to price changes should be isolated, and real gains on corporate equities, housing, and consumer durables should be treated separately.

MEASUREMENT OF REAL CAPITAL GAINS: THE DATA FOR 1950–82

The major data source for this study is the *Balance Sheets for the U.S. Economy 1945–82* compiled by the Flow-of-Funds Section of the Board of Governors of the Federal Reserve System. These tables provide a consistent set of annual data for stocks, flows, and revaluations of the financial assets and liabilities contained in the flow-of-funds accounts supplemented with data for tangible assets. Nominal net capital gains are calculated as the change in the value of wealth less both net investment and that portion of the change in the value of wealth required to maintain real wealth intact as suggested by McElroy (1971) and Eisner (1978, 1980) (see the appendix to this chapter for a detailed description of the actual calculation of the net capital gains series):

$$G\$_t = W\$_t\left(\frac{\bar{p}_t}{p_t}\right) - W\$_{t-1}\left(\frac{\bar{p}_t}{p_{t-1}}\right) - I\$_t, \quad (3.6)$$

where p_t is the price level at the end of period t and $\bar{p}_t$ is the average price level during period t. Because the flow of the nominal net investment in assets ($I\$_t$) occurs over the whole period, it is assumed to be in the average of the price index for the period. Both initial household nominal net worth ($W\$_{t-1}$) and end-of-year nominal net worth ($W\$_t$) are revalued to period average prices to make them comparable to the units in which the investment flow is measured. This calculation reflects the current accrual of purchasing power (with respect to the general price index) that does not arise from the net additions to the stock of assets. The net capital gains calculated with equation (3.6) are still in current dollars.

To obtain constant dollar net capital gains, one must divide nominal capital gains by $\bar{p}_t$, obtaining:

$$G_t = \frac{W\$_t}{p_t} - \frac{W\$_{t-1}}{p_{t-1}} - \frac{I\$_t}{\bar{p}_t}. \tag{3.7}$$

The cumulative real gains over n periods is simply ΣG_t from $t = 1$ to n. It would be natural to state the cumulated real gains in the prices of period 1 or period n. However, we express them in 1972 dollars following the NIPA convention of using 1972 as the base year for implicit price deflators.

The first two columns of Table 3-3 indicate the end of 1949 holdings and the percentage increases in various household balance sheet items over the 1950-82 period. Household holdings of life insurance company and pension fund reserves are divided between equities and net financial assets according to the investment policies of these institutions.[7] The table also lists the real dollar increases and the amounts due to purchases and to capital gains. Over this broad period, substantial real gains were earned on housing, land, and noncorporate equity. Nearly three-fifths of the gains on noncorporate equity were themselves attributable to increases in real land values.[8] In contrast, large losses were taken on corporate equities (when retained earnings are viewed as indirect purchases), net financial assets (owing to inflation), and consumer durables.[9] Purchases of all asset categories, except noncorporate equity, were large. In the 1970s, households pulled substantial funds out of noncorporate businesses, borrowing to cash out the substantial real gains that had been earned.

Our earlier discussion of Hicks's prospective-income view of real capital gains suggests that the consumer durables data in Table 3-3 may be quite misleading. Our conclusion was that real capital gains on durables may not be gains at all because owners need to replace the durables at higher real prices. Conversely, the decline in real durable prices during the 1950-82 period may not represent a real capital loss. The numbers in parentheses in the durables line are based upon the assumption of no real loss. Under this interpretation, the percentage increase in household real wealth held in durables was greater than the percentage increase in wealth held in any other form.

Table 3-3. Changes in Real Household Balance Sheet Components, 1950–82 (billions of 1972 dollars)

	1949 Level	*Percentage Increase*	*Real Dollar Increase*	*Real Dollar Purchases*	*Real Capital Gains*
Owner-occupied housing and land	249	410	1022	722[a]	300[a]
Noncorporate equity	446	92	410	-174[b]	584[b]
Corporate equity	200	289	578	876[c]	-298[c]
Net financial assets	422	136	573	1409	-836[d]
Consumer durables	155	235	365	708	-343
		(457)	(708)		(0)

Source: See Table 3-1.

a. Purchases do not include a likely significant volume of negative land purchases (sales of land to businesses and state and local governments), and gains are net of such sales.

b. Purchases do not include land bought from homeowners; gains do.

c. Purchases include $746 billion of real retained earnings, and real capital gains are net of those attributable to retained earnings.

d. This loss is the net of a $865 billion erosion by inflation and a $29 billion gain owing to a greater decline in the nominal value of mortgage debt than increase in the value of bond holdings in response to the increase in interest rates (mortgage debt outstanding exceeds long-term bond holdings).

Table 3-4. Changes in Household Balance Sheets, 1949-82 (billions of 1972 dollars).

	1949		*1958*		*1968*		*1978*		*1982*
Owner-occupied housing and land	17	(12)	20	(13)	21	(47)	31	(-9)	29
Noncorporate equity	30	(18)	24	(14)	18	(67)	22	(3)	19
Corporate equity	14	(112)	25	(40)	32	(-74)	15	(14)	18
Net financial assets	29	(-22)	19	(-26)	18	(-67)	20	(-28)	22
Consumer durables	10	(-21)	12	(-34)	11	(-42)	12	(-15)	12
Total	100	(13)	100	(7)	100	(-19)	100	(-7)	100

Source: See Table 3-1. Numbers in parentheses are percentage capital gains between the surrounding dates. Retained earnings are viewed as indirect purchases, not gains, in these calculations.

Table 3-4 contains the division of household wealth among the various asset categories for five different years: 1949, 1958, 1968, 1978, and 1982. The percentage real capital gains for each asset category are listed in parentheses between the years. Clearly the gains (losses) in specific assets have been substantial over significantly long periods. Continuing capital gains (or losses) on specific assets obviously alter household portfolio shares in the absence of offsetting actions by households. Households may wish to offset the portfolio shift by redistributing the gains in a specific form among other assets or by compensating for the losses by selling other assets and purchasing whatever declined in value. If households begin adaptively to expect the gains (losses), then both the expected return on the asset and the portfolio share households wish to allocate to it rise (fall). That is, there may be no need to liquidate gains (offset losses) in order to reestablish the old portfolio balance because the optimal balance has been altered toward (away from) the asset in which the gain (loss) occurred. Even if the desired portfolio balance is not altered, high transactions costs may prevent households from reestablishing that balance very rapidly, if at all.

The shifts in portfolio shares in Table 3-4 reflect a number of factors, but clearly two of the more important are the enormous changes in real corporate equity prices in most periods and the large run-up in real land and structure prices (and thus in real noncorporate equity values) between 1968 and 1978. The incredible stock market boom between 1949 and 1968 raised the share of wealth in corporate equities from 14 to 32 percent and, necessarily, lowered the other shares; the sharp decline in share values between 1968 and 1978 did the reverse. Because land and structures prices jumped in the 1969-78 decade, the offset to the fall in the equity share occurred largely in the housing and noncorporate equity categories. That is, many of the portfolio shifts are consistent with the passive acceptance, possibly owing to revisions in relative expected risks or returns, of the impact of real price changes on portfolio shares.

On the other hand, households have not accepted the portfolio implications of the continuing real gains on noncorporate equity and losses on net financial assets and consumer durables. In fact, except for the real losses on net financial assets in the 1949-58 period, households have actively liquidated enough noncorporate equity and purchased sufficient financial assets and durables to offset the impacts of these real asset price changes on their portfolio. (The acceptance of the decline in net financial assets in the 1949–58 period probably reflected a desire to liquidate part of the large holdings accumulated during World War II.)

It is again useful to consider the possibility that the decline in real durables prices between 1950 and 1982 did not, in fact, generate capital losses. If this were the case, the value of the durables stock would be two-thirds greater in 1982. As a result, the share of household wealth in durables would be 18 percent, up sharply from the 10 percent in 1949. This increase is comparable to the observed increase observed in the share of household wealth in housing (and land) and seems quite plausible.

EXPECTED CAPITAL GAINS

In our earlier discussion, we noted that individuals may not passively accept the impact of accruing capital gains on their portfolio shares or, for that matter, on the total accumulation of wealth. As capital gains accrue, wealth increases except to the extent that saving (net purchases) is reduced. This offsetting reduction in saving in response to the accrual of capital gains is referred to as deflection (see our model in Chapter 4). However, in the current period, individuals can react only to those gains that are *expected* to accrue. The unexpected gains would be passively added to wealth and would alter behavior only in future periods through a wealth effect. Consequently, it is important to distinguish between the expected and unexpected components of net capital gains.

The decomposition of total capital gains into their expected and unexpected elements is accomplished through regression analysis The predicted value from an equation with the variable in question being regressed on a set of exogenous variables is taken as the expected component; the residual series from the regression is taken as the proxy for the unexpected component. We have grouped capital gains into five categories based on equation (3.5) and the fact that structures and land account for a large proportion of noncorporate equity capital gains. The five gains categories are: (1) housing, land, and noncorporate equity (*GHLN*), (2) consumer durable goods (*GDUR*), (3) corporate equities (*GSTK*), (4) gains on net financial assets due to changes in the general price level (*GNFAP*), and (5) gains on net financial assets due to nominal bond price changes (*GNFAB*).

The dependent variable in each equation is the ratio of net capital gains to the beginning-of-period value of the corresponding assets. Thus, the capital gains are converted into a form corresponding to a rate of return. Once the expected elements are calculated, they can be reconverted to per capita constant dollar levels. Annual observations for the 1951–82 sample period are used. The set of explanatory variables in the regressions is composed of variables whose values are known at the beginning of the period when expectations are formed. Due to the limited number of available observations, we were not able to make out-of-sample, one-period-ahead forecasts. Rather, we estimate one regression for each asset category for the entire sample period.

In most instances an increase in the level of an explanatory variable will cause an increase in the price of an asset but not a continuing rise in the price. Thus we use changes rather than levels for nearly all of the explanatory variables. The set of exogenous variables considered (in addition to as many as five own lagged values) include the change in the Livingston Survey expected inflation rate (ΔPEL) and one period lagged values of *changes* in: the percentage GNP gap (ΔGAP), the $M1$ definition of the money supply (ΔM), the one-year after-tax nominal Treasury bill yield (ΔRNT), the after-tax nominal Moody's Corporate bond yield ($\Delta RNCT$), an index of marginal personal income tax rates ($\Delta TXRT$), and the corporate tax rate (ΔTXC). In addition, the corporate equities equation considered the ratio of lagged undistributed corporate profits to the beginning-of-period stock of equities ($UNDPR$) and the ratio of the change in lagged dividends to the beginning-of-period stock of equities (ΔDIV). We have also included the level of the expected inflation rate in all equations because capital gains are measured net of inflation. If an asset's price failed to keep up with (or consistently exceeded) an increase in the general price level, other things equal, there would be a role for PEL.

Our final equations are those providing the best overall fit. That is, we sequentially eliminated those potential explanatory variables whose estimated coefficients did not exceed their estimated standard errors. However, we retained all lagged values of the lagged dependent variable out to the furthest one whose coefficient exceeded its standard error. That is, if the third lag did meet our criteria but the second lag did not, we still retained the second lag for continuity.

Table 3-5 presents the regressions used to calculate the expected capital gains proxies. The equations are estimated over the full 1951–

Table 3-5. Expected Percentage Capital Gains Equations, 1951–82.[a]

Dependent VAR	*GHLN*	*GDUR*	*GSTK*	*GNFAP*	*GNFAB*
Constant	0.00727 (0.00484)	–0.0297 (0.0037)	–0.275 (0.091)	–0.00367 (0.00316)	–0.00198 (0.00173)
Dependent variable (t–1)	0.364 (0.165)	–0.165 (0.116)	–0.171 (0.177)	1.043 (0.076)	–0.806 (0.175)
Dependent variable (t–2)	0.495 (0.182)	–	0.021 (0.168)	–	–0.379 (0.194)
Dependent variable (t–3)	–	–	0.141 (0.144)	–	–
Dependent variable (t–4)	–	–	0.387 (0.145)	–	–
Dependent variable (t–5)	–	–	0.226 (0.163)	–	–
ΔRNT	–0.0325 (0.0063)	–	–0.113 (0.045)	–	0.00461 (0.00202)
ΔRNCT	–	–	–	0.0123 (0.0056)	–
ΔTXRT	–0.285 (0.160)	0.320 (0.075)	–1.82 (1.04)	0.126 (0.077)	–
ΔGAP	0.00311 (0.00185)	–	–	–	0.000821 (0.000583)

ΔM	—	-0.000428 (0.000066)	-0.00338 (0.00097)	-0.000319 (0.000075)	—
PEL	—	-0.00273 (0.00062)	—	—	0.00108 (0.00047)
ΔPEL	—	0.00497 (0.00108)	—	—	—
UNDPR	—	—	7.60 (2.24)	—	—
R^2	0.658	0.752	0.635	0.883	0.494
SEE	0.0186	0.00904	0.123	0.00959	0.00650
Durbin h	3.396	0.295	5.72	0.852	0.891

a. Standard errors in parentheses.

82 sample period using annual observations. The estimated standard errors are in parentheses below the associated estimated coefficients. Because the equations include lagged dependent variables as explanatory variables, Durbin *h*-statistics, rather than the usual Durbin-Watson statistics, are reported. Except for the corporate equities equation, only one or two lags of the dependent variable are included. The interest rate effects are as might be expected. The positive coefficients for gains on net financial assets are not surprising because households' mortgage debt outstanding exceeds their long-term bond holdings for most of the period. Thus, households earned capital gains, not losses, on their *net* financial assets when interest rates rose. The positive effect of $\Delta TXRT$ on consumer durable gains is due to the fact that the service return to durables is untaxed making durables more attractive and driving up their price. One could make the same argument for housing. However, the negative coefficient on $\Delta TRXT$ in the GHLN equation may be due to the taxability of the returns on land and noncorporate equity. The negative tax effect in the GSTK equation is due to stock market returns being taxable. The positive tax effect in the GNFAP equation may suggest that higher tax rates imply lower inflation rates (by slowing down the economy) because GNFAP can be interpreted as the negative of an inflation rate. The business cycle effect (ΔGAP) on *GHLN* is as expected. It appears that faster money growth leads to capital losses on durables and corporate equities and higher rates of inflation (makes *GNFAP* a larger negative number). The point estimate for *UNDPR* in the corporate equities equation is troublesome. It has the appropriate sign but is much too large. This may be related to collinearity problems. One might have expected to find ΔDIV included in this equation. However, its *t*-statistic was only 0.76.

SUMMARY

This chapter has presented an analysis of the measurement of real capital gains. We have been concerned with both conceptual and computational problems. Rather than considering total aggregate capital gains, our analysis indicates that one should be careful to separate the gains (and losses) into categories based on the source and nature of the particular gains. For example, we find that whether an individual trades in an asset for profit or instead plans to use up the asset and replace it is an important consideration in determining the contribution of a particular capital gain to an individual's economic well-being. Similarly, for physical assets, durability (length of useful life) is a distinguishing characteristic, while for financial assets we should distinguish between gains due to changes in nominal bond prices (interest rates) and to changes in the general price level.

We find that capital gains make an important contribution to both the total and the composition of household wealth. For example, in the 1950–68 period, corporate equity capital gains swamped cumulated personal saving, and in the 1969–78 period, enormous real capital losses on corporate equities were more than offset by extremely large real gains on housing, land, and noncorporate equity. Moreover, individuals (in the aggregate) appear to have passively accepted the portfolio composition consequences of the corporate equity and housing and land real price changes. Other changes in real asset prices have not been accepted. Even though there were large capital losses on net financial assets and consumer durables during the 1958–82 period, their portfolio shares increased slightly. Similarly, in spite of large capital gains on noncorporate equity from 1949 to 1978, its portfolio share declined from 30 to 22 percent.

Because individuals do appear to respond to portfolio changes induced by capital gains accruals, it is important to distinguish between the expected and unexpected components of total gains. In the current period, individuals can react only to the expected component of current period gains and losses. While unexpected gains are passively added to wealth in the current period, individuals can, if they choose, undo the effects of these unexpected capital gains and losses in later periods. Thus, total capital gains can affect personal saving both concurrently (through expected gains effects) and in future periods (through a wealth effect).

In the next chapter, we incorporate our theoretical analysis of capital gains into a model of personal saving behavior and find that the distinctions between the different gains categories and between their expected and unexpected components have important implications for personal saving behavior. We then use our constructed capital gains measures as regressors in personal saving equations. Even though the measures are extremely volatile, we find statistically significant effects. While the gains appear to be more important for explaining short-run movements in the personal saving rate, cumulated gains (wealth) are a major force in explaining long-run shifts in the saving rate.

APPENDIX

The household sector tables provided in *Balance Sheets for the U.S. Economy 1945–82* contain year-end outstandings for all of the assets and liabilities as well as gross revaluations for the physical assets, land, corporate equities, noncorporate equity, and life insurance and pension fund reserves. These are calculated as:

$$R\$_t = W\$_t - W\$_{t-1} - I\$_t,$$

where $R\$_t$ represents the current dollar gross revaluations and $W\$_t$ is the current dollar end-of-year stock of the asset. The purely inflationary increment to the nominal value of assets and liabilities is not eliminated as in the calculation of *net* capital gains in equation (3.6). The tables contain no gross revaluations for deposits because their nominal value is fixed, and for credit market instruments because they are measured at par, rather than market, value.

Current dollar net investment series were obtained as:

$$I\$_t = W\$_t - W\$_{t-1} - R\$_t.$$

Unfortunately, no data are available on net investment in land. Thus gross land revaluations do not necessarily equal capital gains (gross revaluations of other assets do). While gross revaluations of land are often put in the capital gains columns in the tables presented in this chapter, such "gains" are probably understatements because households likely sold land to state and local governments and businesses over the 1950–82 period.

The outstanding stocks of the credit market instruments are adjusted from par to market values with updated bond price indices from Eisner and Pieper (1984). Savings bonds were adjusted with a bond price index for federal notes. Other Treasury issues were adjusted with an index for total federal securities. An index for federal bonds and notes was used to convert federal agency issues. Indexes for state and local bonds and corporate bonds were used for state and local obligations and corporate and foreign bonds. Mortgages were converted using a federal mortgage index. The end-of-year price index was constructed as the average of the fourth quarter and following first quarter values of the personal consumption expenditures deflator.

NOTES

1. Recently, Eisner (1978, 1980) has led a revival of interest in the measurement and role of capital gains in wealth accumulation. Earlier studies include Arena (1963), Bhatia (1970), and McElroy (1971). A more recent study is Peek (1983).
2. The calculation of real gains requires two steps. First, the change in asset price is adjusted for the change in the general price index: For example, if the asset price increases by 10 percent when the general inflation rate is 6 percent, then gains are based on a 4 percent net inflation rate. Second, these gains are converted from current to constant dollars via the usual deflation by the general price index.
3. A number of other conceptual problems with the household saving data are discussed in Chapter 4.
4. Eisner (1980) discusses two additional sources of capital gains: (1) the conventional treatment of investment and (2) noncompetitive elements in the economy. These capital gains arise due to the manner in which NIPA investment is measured. A comprehensive treatment of capital investment (such as proposed by Kendrick (1976) and Eisner (1978)) would eliminate this type of capital gains. McElroy (1976) and Eisner (1980) provide more detailed discussions of the sources of capital gains.
5. The doubling in price of the perpetuity, however, does represent an increase in the purchasing power of its owner in terms of consumption goods today. Whether the asset is sold or not, its increased value provides a new opportunity for its owner. Furthermore, he might also be considered better off simply because wealth is typically measured in terms of money value rather than in terms of specific assets. Even though he still has the same right to a stream of $10 per year, its value in terms of money today has risen. Finally, to the extent that a consumer's horizon is less than infinite, he may not prefer to maintain a constant stream of income forever.
6. There are two ways to treat assets, such as long-term bonds, with fixed nominal maturity value and stream of interest payments. We can value the asset at par and treat the coupon payments as the stream of income. Alternatively, we can value the asset at market and include (in addition to coupon payments) in income the gross capital gains accruing on the asset as the market value approaches its par value at maturity. Both approaches result in the same return for an individual holding the bond until maturity. However, the second approach is more appropriate for the investor who considers the possible reinvestments of the remaining market value of the bond at the new higher market interest rate. (The market value would also be relevant if the bond holder desired to use the bond as collateral.)
7. We omit any measure of private unfunded pensions and social security

wealth. Because of the difficulties in forecasting the many economic and demographic variables required to calculate such a wealth measure, we have chosen not to include an explicit measure of such wealth and any associated capital gains. While the Employee Retirement Income Security Act of 1974 (ERISA) has reduced some types of uncertainty associated with private pensions (eligibility requirements, vesting conditions, creation of Pension Benefit Guaranty Corporation), future values of other variables (e.g., interest rates, mortality rates, labor force participation rates, social security legislation for both benefit levels and tax rates) remain very speculative in nature.

8. All of the \$154 billion real gain during the 1950–68 period is due to an increase in real land values; only two-fifths of the \$429 billion real gain in the 1969–82 span can be attributed to this source.
9. To the extent that inflation was built into interest rates (and net financial asset holdings exceeded liabilities outstanding), net interest income rose to (at least partially) compensate for the erosion of the real value of net financial assets.

REFERENCES

Arena, John. 1963. "The Wealth Effect and Consumption: A Statistical Inquiry." *Yale Economic Essays* 3 (Fall):251–303.

Bhatia, Kul B. 1970. "Accrued Capital Gains, Personal Income and Saving in the United States, 1948–64." *Review of Income and Wealth* (December):363–78.

Board of Governors of the Federal Reserve System. 1983. *Balance Sheets for the U.S. Economy 1945–82.* Washington, D.C.: U.S. Government Printing Office (May).

———. Various issues. *Federal Reserve Bulletin.*

Eisner, Robert. 1978. "Total Incomes in the United States, 1959 and 1969." *Review of Income and Wealth* 24 (March):41–70.

———. 1980. "Capital Gains and Income: Real Changes in the Value of Capital in the United States, 1946–77." In *The Measurement of Capital,* Studies in Income and Wealth, vol. 45, edited by Dan Usher, pp. 175–342. Chicago: National Bureau of Economic Research.

Eisner, Robert, and Paul J. Pieper. 1984. "A New View of the Federal Debt and Budget Deficits." *American Economic Review* 74 (March):11–29.

Haig, Robert Murray. 1921. "The Concept of Income—Economic and Legal Aspects." In *The Federal Income Tax,* edited by Robert M. Haig, pp. 1–28. New York: Columbia University Press.

Hicks, John R. 1946. *Value and Capital.* Oxford: Clarendon Press.

Kendrick, John W. 1976. *The Formation and Stocks of Total Capital.* New York: National Bureau of Economic Research.

McElroy, Michael B. 1971. "Capital Gains and the Concept and Measurement of

Purchasing Power." In *1970 Proceedings of the American Statistical Association, Business and Economics Section*, pp. 132–39. Washington, D.C.: American Statistical Association.

———. 1976. "Capital Gains and Social Income." *Economic Inquiry* (June): 221–40.

Peek, Joe. 1983. "Capital Gains and Personal Saving Behavior." *Journal of Money Credit and Banking* 15 (February):1–23.

Pigou, A.C. 1941. "Maintaining Capital Intact." *Economica* (August): 271–80.

Seltzer, Lawrence H. 1951. *The Nature and Tax Treatment of Capital Gains and Losses.* New York: National Bureau of Economic Research.

Shoven, John B., and Jeremy I. Bulow. 1975. "Inflation Accounting and Nonfinancial Corporate Profits: Physical Assets." *Brookings Papers on Economic Activity* (no. 3):557–611.

———. 1976. "Inflation Accounting and Nonfinancial Corporate Profits: Financial Assets and Liabilities." *Brookings Papers on Economic Activity* (no. 1): 15–66.

Simons, Henry C. 1938. *Personal Income Taxation.* Chicago: University of Chicago Press.

U.S. Bureau of Economic Analysis. 1981. *The National Income and Product Accounts of the United States, 1929–76.* Washington, D.C.: U.S. Government Printing Office.

———. Various issues. *Survey of Current Business.* Washington, D.C.: U.S. Government Printing Office.

U.S. Council of Economic Advisors. 1983. *Economic Report of the President.* Washington, D.C.: U.S. Government Printing Office.

U.S. Internal Revenue Service. Various years. *Statistics of Income, Individual Income Tax Returns.* Washington, D.C.: U.S. Government Printing Office.

4 HOUSEHOLD SAVING An Econometric Investigation

*Patric H. Hendershott and Joe Peek**

By official government accounts, the United States saves a substantially smaller fraction of income than do other industrialized countries. Reasons for the small fraction and the implications of it for America's future well-being are widely discussed (Feldstein 1977; Boskin 1983). Contributing to the low national rate is a low, and apparently declining (Auerbach 1985), personal, or household, saving rate. The measurement and determinants of household saving are the subject of this chapter.

Major problems in measuring saving rates (Auerbach 1985; Blades and Sturm 1982) raise questions as to just how low the U.S. household saving rate is and how much it has declined recently. We consider the sources of measurement error in the following section and compute an adjusted household saving series that includes net purchases of consumer durables, net contributions to government life insurance and pension reserves, and adjustments for income tax liabilities and for the inflation premium component in interest income. These adjustments raise the measured household saving rate by nearly 5 percentage points in the 1965–75 period but result in an extremely sharp

*We wish to thank Hu McCulloch and other participants at an Ohio State University Economics Department Seminar for useful comments.

7 percentage point decline in the rate between 1975 and the early 1980s.

We then present a model of household saving behavior and estimate it using annual data from the 1952–82 period. While saving responds to numerous influences, major swings in the saving rate—a significant decline in the 1950s and rebound in the early 1960s, as well as the decline since 1975—are largely explained by two variables: the wealth/income ratio and the growth rate of real income. A detailed interpretation of the empirical estimates is provided in the text and summarized in the concluding section.

THE MEASUREMENT OF PERSONAL SAVING

Personal saving is calculated in the National Income and Product Accounts (NIPA) as:

$$SNIA = YPERS - CEXP - TXPERS - INTPD. \tag{4.1}$$

where *SNIA, YPERS, CEXP, TXPERS,* and *INTPD* represent personal saving, income, consumption expenditures, tax payments, and interest paid to business,[1] respectively. Thus, measurement errors in any of the terms netted from personal income, as well as in personal income itself, will be embedded in *SNIA* dollar for dollar.[2] Below we discuss important measurement errors in each of these terms and describe the adjustments we make to correct the errors.

Consumption (CEXP) and Tax (TXPERS) Adjustments

Theoretical models of consumption and saving behavior (for example, the Life Cycle Hypothesis, the Permanent Income Hypothesis, and their derivatives) are stated in terms of the consumption of service flows. These flows, rather than consumption expenditures, are an argument in the utility function. To be consistent with this theory, the component of consumer expenditures representing net investment in consumer durable goods should properly be considered personal saving. The NIPA measure of personal saving, however, is constructed on an expenditures rather than a service flow basis. Consequently, we adjust *SNIA* by the difference between the value of expenditures and the value of the consumption of services (*CON*) to arrive at the theoretically appropriate personal saving measure (*SAV*):

$$SAV = SNIA + SDUR = SNIA + (CEXP - CON), \tag{4.2}$$

where *SDUR* is net investment in consumer durable goods. *SDUR* has risen, erratically, from $15 billion (in 1972 dollars) in the early 1950s to $35 billion in the late 1970s. Consumer durable goods are distinguished from nondurables and services because they need not be consumed in the same period that they are purchased. To the extent that net new purchases of consumer durable goods are carried over to the next period, current net purchases will be a poor measure of actual consumption in the period.

There are two measurement problems associated with tax liabilities. The first concerns the treatment of government life insurance and employees' retirement fund activities. In the NIPA, these transactions are treated as social insurance contributions (taxes) and payments (transfers). The flow of funds treatment of the net contributions as household claims analogous to private life insurance and pension reserves is more appropriate. Thus the net contributions, denoted by SGPEN, must be added to household saving (and subtracted from government saving).[3] This variable rose from $3 billion (in 1972 dollars) in the early 1950s to $20 billion in the early 1980s.

The second problem associated with the NIPA measurement of personal taxes occurs because personal income taxes are measured on a cash payment rather than a liability accrual basis. If individuals plan consumption and saving over a long period of time, the relevant income tax variable will be the one that represents their actual tax liabilities (see Peek 1982, 1983). The tax adjustment (STAX) is constructed as:

$$STAX = TXPERS - TXLIAB, \tag{4.3}$$

where *TXLIAB* is tax accruals taken from annual issues of the U.S. Internal Revenue Service's *Statistics of Income, Individual Income Tax Returns* (SOI). Most of the difference between tax payments and accruals (which has fluctuated between –$2 and +$10 billion in 1972 dollars) arises because the net refund for tax year t is included in the liabilities of year t and in the cash payments of year $t + 1$. The major fluctuations in the net refunds series are largely due to differences in the timing and magnitude of the changes in income tax rates and the corresponding withholding schedules.

Expected Inflation and Personal Income (YPERS)

The final proposed personal saving adjustment is due to distortions in the measurement of interest income (and payments) and capital losses (and gains) during inflationary periods. The expectation of net capital losses on fixed-dollar financial assets leads to the incorporation of an inflation premium in nominal interest rates to compensate investors for the losses. Part of the household stock of fixed-dollar assets is being converted into a flow (the inflation premium component) that is recorded inappropriately as income received and capital losses incurred. Because saving is computed as income less consumption and taxes, an extended period of anticipated inflation would result in a substantial overstatement of the personal saving rate.

Three categories of interest payments are incorporated in personal income: (1) monetary interest paid to persons, (2) imputed interest paid to persons by depository institutions, and (3) imputed interest paid to persons by life insurance companies and private noninsured pension funds. The second category is also imputed to consumption expenditures. Consequently, if it is mismeasured, the error (being added to and subtracted from the right side of equation (4.1)) is not included in measured personal saving. However, an overstatement of the other two categories will lead to a dollar-for-dollar overstatement of *SNIA*. Similarly, an overstatement of interest paid by consumers to business (*INTPD*) will result in a dollar-for-dollar understatement of *SNIA*.

Jump (1980) proposed that an inflation premium equal to the product of the anticipated inflation rate and the stock of net household fixed-income assets be subtracted from the official saving measure.[4] Because this premium implies immediate, complete adjustment of interest income to the current anticipated inflation rate, it would substantially overstate, and be more volatile than, the inflation premium component of NIPA interest income included in personal saving during a period of rising inflation for three reasons. First, binding interest rate ceilings on at least some demand and savings accounts existed in the United States for the 1965–79 period. Once these nominal interest rate ceilings were reached, the monetary interest payments on such assets could incorporate an additional inflation premium only as rapidly as ceiling interest rates were raised. Second, while additional interest from financial institutions is imputed to individuals when interest rates (inflation) rise, imputed interest generally responds sluggishly to interest rate changes. Third, a significant part of fixed-valued household assets and liabilities are long-term. For these instruments, coupon receipts/payments adjust to an increase in inflation expectations only over time as new bonds are issued to replace maturing bonds. (Yields adjust immediately via a decline in the market price of the instruments.) This analysis suggests that there will be a lagged adjustment of the inflation component of NIPA interest income and expenses to an increase in the anticipated inflation rate. (The adjustment to a decrease in inflation will occur more rapidly to the extent that high coupons are replaced by lower coupons as long-term debt is refinanced at the lower market rate.) A final problem with Jump's adjustment is that it ignores the tax liabilities incurred on monetary interest income: Only the net-of-tax inflation premium component can be used to maintain the real value of net financial assets.

We have constructed inflation adjustments for both personal saving and personal income that are based on the actual NIPA interest income measure. The inflation component incorporated in personal saving is calculated as:

$$SPREM = (1 - TXINT)(RINTSAV - RINTSAV50)ASAV, \qquad (4.4)$$

where *ASAV* represents the stock of net household fixed-income assets at the beginning of the period,[5] *RINTSAV* represents the ratio of the relevant personal interest income to *ASAV*, *RINTSAV50* is the 1950 value of *RINTSAV*, and *TXINT* is the assumed tax rate on interest income.[6] This procedure allocates any increase in interest income (adjusted for the growth in net financial assets) to our inflation component measure. It is likely that the inflation component in 1950, if any, was extremely small. To the extent that it was nonzero, our measure differs from the true component by a small constant but still accurately reflects its movements. We have implicitly assumed that the real interest rate built into interest income was constant during the 1950–82 period.[7] The inflation-component adjustment to saving reaches $59 billion (in real 1972 dollars) by 1981.

The calculation of the inflation premium embedded in NIPA disposable income is similarly calculated:

$$YPREM = (1 - TXINT)(RINTYD - RINTYD50)AYD, \tag{4.5}$$

where *RINTYD* is now the ratio of the sum of the two interest income categories used to calculate *SPREM* and the imputed interest paid to persons by financial institutions to *AYD*. *RINTYD50* is its 1950 value, and *AYD* is all fixed-income assets. *AYD* differs from *ASAV* in that we do not subtract nonmortgage fixed-income liabilities of individuals because the inflation component in *INTPD* is relevant only to the calculation of *SPREM*. *TXINT* may slightly overstate the tax liabilities on interest income because it includes nontaxable imputed interest paid to persons by depository institutions, life insurance companies, and private noninsured pension funds, as well as monetary interest payments to persons. However, the imputed component is small relative to the total and probably accounts for a less than proportionate share of the inflation premium. Moreover, *TXINT* does not reflect state and local taxes. The adjusted personal saving rate can then be calculated as:

$$RSAVADJTX = \frac{SNIA - SPREM}{YD - YPREM} \tag{4.6}$$

Table 4–1 contains four personal saving rates. *RSAVNIA* is conventional *NIPA* personal saving, *RSAVADJ* is our adjusted saving rate with *TXINT* = 0, *RSAVADJTX* includes the tax adjustment, and *RSAVJUMP* represents the personal savingrate using Jump's method.[8] Our tax-adjusted personal saving rate is relatively stable through 1975. It does not rise in the late 1960s and early 1970s as does the official rate. While it does decline substantially after 1975, it remains positive. In sharp contrast, Jump's measure begins to decline after 1967, becomes negative after 1974, and is sharply negative in the early 1980s. The decline from 1967 to 1980 is 13 percentage points, 8 more than the decline in our series. About one-third of the excess decline can be attributed to the overstatement of the inflation premiums and two-thirds to the ignoring of taxes.

Adjusted Personal Saving Rates

We can now calculate our adjusted personal saving series. This series incorporates the four adjustments to NIPA personal saving described above: (1) net investment in consumer durable goods, (2) the treat-

Table 4-1. Alternative Measures of the Saving Rate (percentage).

Year	*RSAVNIA*	*RSAVADJ*	*RSAVADJTX*	*RSAVJUMP*
1950	5.77	5.77	5.77	7.84
1951	7.11	6.97	7.01	3.28
1952	7.31	7.22	7.25	5.49
1953	7.34	7.31	7.32	8.03
1954	6.61	6.42	6.47	7.60
1955	5.98	5.85	5.89	5.98
1956	7.28	7.15	7.19	6.82
1957	7.22	6.81	6.93	6.20
1958	7.39	6.75	6.93	7.15
1959	6.25	5.56	5.76	5.43
1960	5.59	4.78	5.01	4.48
1961	6.29	5.39	5.65	5.60
1962	6.02	4.89	5.20	4.68
1963	5.39	4.10	4.46	4.14
1964	6.71	5.32	5.67	5.61
1965	7.07	5.58	5.95	5.68
1966	7.00	5.33	5.75	5.13
1967	8.09	6.26	6.74	5.67
1968	7.07	5.20	5.73	3.83
1969	6.35	4.18	4.83	2.95
1970	8.02	5.52	6.23	3.96
1971	8.07	5.45	6.20	3.76
1972	6.49	3.92	4.68	2.70
1973	8.63	5.98	6.78	4.64
1974	8.53	4.97	6.09	2.21
1975	8.60	4.91	6.07	-0.03
1976	6.91	3.29	4.45	-0.46
1977	5.94	1.95	3.25	-0.93
1978	6.06	1.91	3.33	-1.85
1979	5.86	0.85	2.64	-3.19
1980	6.03	-0.49	1.99	-7.11
1981	6.61	-2.61	1.08	-7.77
1982	5.76	-3.38	0.31	-4.22

Data Sources: U.S. Bureau of Economic Analysis (1981), *The National Income and Product Accounts for the United States, 1929–76*, and (various issues) *Survey of Current Business;* Board of Governors of the Federal Reserve System (1983), Balance Sheet Accounts; U.S Internal Revenue Service (various years), *Statistics of Income, Individual Income Tax Returns.* Federal Reserve Bank of Philadelphia provided Livingston Survey expected inflation rate. Calculations described in text.

Table 4-2. Various Saving Adjustments (millions of 1972 dollars).

Year	*SNIA*	*SGPEN*	*SDUR*	*STAX*	*SPREM*	*SADJ*
1952	28030.7	3271.0	13925.8	3738.70	294.3	48671.8
1953	29302.2	3050.6	16034.8	2914.55	208.4	51093.8
1954	26659.4	2522.8	11166.4	2136.58	689.1	41796.0
1955	25534.2	2838.5	18925.5	1250.00	568.0	47980.2
1956	32522.9	3719.5	13006.1	1699.70	657.1	50291.0
1957	32870.2	3240.4	11340.7	2274.34	1655.7	48070.0
1958	34054.9	3988.4	5179.2	1552.02	2467.7	42306.8
1959	29939.1	4134.5	10383.9	-253.54	2711.0	41493.0
1960	27364.4	4395.0	9791.4	3310.14	3227.2	41633.7
1961	31691.5	4669.4	5900.8	666.67	3699.2	39229.1
1962	31605.2	4713.7	11564.5	2208.96	4787.0	45305.3
1963	29268.7	5149.7	15783.4	1311.50	5585.0	45928.3
1964	38943.4	5787.9	19786.6	-1517.79	6760.0	56240.0
1965	43602.3	6143.8	26123.1	2007.77	7842.9	70034.1
1966	45279.6	7035.2	29102.0	3167.50	9072.9	75511.4
1967	54436.1	6742.0	25934.9	1757.99	10339.6	78531.3
1968	49570.9	7260.0	31883.0	-173.76	10451.8	78088.3
1969	45914.0	8001.1	29727.4	5566.74	12083.2	77126.0
1970	60308.1	9600.0	21626.0	5463.77	15115.8	81882.1
1971	62850.8	9811.4	26924.4	426.94	16268.1	83745.4
1972	52610.0	11636.0	35213.0	9352.99	16001.2	92810.7
1973	74703.9	11154.2	38236.5	1495.74	18098.5	107492.0
1974	73125.5	10782.7	24421.0	2478.52	23021.5	87786.1

1975	75247.5	12053.5	21116.5	3773.34	24468.1	87722.6
1976	62635.6	13407.8	30346.3	-195.14	23906.2	82288.1
1977	55990.8	16176.6	35606.7	2103.38	26695.9	83181.4
1978	59941.0	18711.0	38009.4	600.94	28584.4	88677.9
1979	59501.6	15014.8	32312.7	6824.61	34076.9	79576.8
1980	61559.3	19708.4	18126.8	1373.19	42390.2	58377.3
1981	69690.9	19312.2	19670.3	3685.21	59137.4	53221.1
1982	61100.4	21090.1	16096.5	7276.18	58052.8	47510.3

Data Sources: See Table 4–1. SGPEN furnished by FOF section of Board of Governors. Calculations described in text.

ment of contributions to government insurance and pensions as household saving, not taxes, (3) the conversion of household taxes to an accrual basis, and (4) the inflation component incorporated in interest income. The first three adjustments are added to NIPA saving, while the inflation component is subtracted. The adjusted personal saving measure is thus:

$$SADJ = SNIA + SDUR + SGPEN + STAX - SPREM. \qquad (4.7)$$

Table 4–2 presents this measure and its components. Table 4–3 lists the same variables as a percentage of disposable labor income. Disposable labor income is used rather than total disposable income because the former avoids the serious measurement problems associated with property income during inflationary periods.

The saving rate including all adjustments was in the 13 to 16 percent range in the early to middle 1950s before sliding into the 10 to 12 percent range in the 1958–63 span. For the years 1965 to 1975, the rate again assumed the high values of the middle 1950s. From there, the rate fell to the 11 to 13 percent range in the second half of the 1970s and then down to the 7 to 8.5 percent level in the early 1980s.

THE MODEL[9]

The model is developed in three parts. We begin with planned wealth accumulation, then consider actual accumulation and its implication for the saving relation, and finally consider the likely impact of different capital gains components.

Planned Wealth Accumulation

Planned wealth accumulation is assumed to arise from the desires of individuals to smooth their patterns of consumption over their lifetimes and to leave bequests. Because human capital cannot be carried over into retirement years, some of it must be transformed into nonhuman wealth to allow consumption after retirement or to permit bequests. In addition, a precautionary motive arising from the existence of unforeseen fluctuations in income (and perhaps needs) would lead to the holding of a nonzero stock of nonhuman wealth by indi-

Table 4-3. Various Saving Rate Adjustments (percentage).

Year	*RSNIA*	*RSGPEN*	*RSDUR*	*RSTAX*	*RSPREM*	*RSADJ*
1952	9.05	1.06	4.50	1.21	0.10	15.72
1953	9.12	0.95	4.99	0.91	0.06	15.90
1954	8.35	0.79	3.50	0.67	0.22	13.09
1955	7.57	0.84	5.61	0.37	0.17	14.22
1956	9.17	1.05	3.67	0.48	0.19	14.18
1957	9.18	0.91	3.17	0.64	0.46	13.43
1958	9.61	1.13	1.46	0.44	0.70	11.94
1959	8.11	1.12	2.81	-0.07	0.73	11.23
1960	7.26	1.17	2.60	0.88	0.86	11.05
1961	8.28	1.22	1.54	0.17	0.97	10.25
1962	7.91	1.18	2.89	0.55	1.20	11.33
1963	7.13	1.25	3.84	0.32	1.36	11.19
1964	8.86	1.32	4.50	-0.35	1.54	12.80
1965	9.30	1.31	5.57	0.43	1.67	14.93
1966	9.17	1.42	5.89	0.64	1.84	15.29
1967	10.69	1.32	5.10	0.35	2.03	15.43
1968	9.35	1.37	6.02	-0.03	1.97	14.74
1969	8.38	1.46	5.42	1.02	2.20	14.07
1970	10.75	1.71	3.86	0.97	2.69	14.60
1971	10.98	1.71	4.70	0.07	2.84	14.63
1972	8.72	1.93	5.83	1.55	2.65	15.38
1973	11.90	1.78	6.09	0.24	2.88	17.13
1974	11.97	1.76	4.00	0.41	3.77	14.37
1975	12.35	1.98	3.46	0.62	4.01	14.39
1976	9.90	2.12	4.80	-0.03	3.78	13.00
1977	8.45	2.44	5.37	0.32	4.03	12.55
1978	8.70	2.71	5.51	0.09	4.15	12.87
1979	8.40	2.12	4.56	0.96	4.81	11.23
1980	8.94	2.86	2.63	0.20	6.16	8.48
1981	10.16	2.81	2.87	0.54	8.62	7.76
1982	9.02	3.11	2.38	1.07	8.57	7.02

Data Sources: See Table 4-1. SGPEN furnished by FOF section of Board of Governors. Calculations described in text.

viduals even if anticipated future consumption and income were equal.

Given an intertemporal utility function with current and future levels of consumption (as well as any final bequest) as arguments, an individual determines a desired consumption path by maximizing utility subject to his or her perceived lifetime resources. Given an expected labor income path, the interest rate, and the length of the retirement span, this desired consumption path implies an associated wealth accumulation path. At any given time, the end-of-period wealth required would be the level that would just allow the individual to meet his future planned consumption path, assuming his expectations of the future are realized. Consistency requires that each period's desired wealth level must be attainable if expectations about the other variables are realized. Thus, the planned change in wealth in any period is simply the difference between the level of desired end-of-period household nonhuman wealth consistent with the desired consumption path, W^d, and actual household nonhuman wealth at the end of period $t-1$ (beginning of period t), W_{t-1}. The simultaneous determination of the desired wealth and consumption paths requires this complete adjustment of actual to desired wealth within the period because failure to attain the desired wealth stock by the end of the period means that the future planned consumption path cannot be realized.

Desired wealth is assumed to depend on total resources (proxied by expected disposable labor income (YDL_t^e), expected transfer payments (YTR_t^e), beginning-of-period nonhuman wealth (W_{t-1}), and expected capital gains (G_t^e)), the gap between potential and actual real GNP (GAP_t), the real after-tax interest rate ($RRAT_t$), and the share of the population that is over age 65 (AGE_t), where the last two variables are scaled by YDL_t^e to allow their real dollar impacts to grow with the level of real economic activity.

$$W_t^d = w_0 + w_1 YDL_t^e + w_2 YTR_t^e + w_3 W_{t-1} + w_4 G_t^e + w_5 GAP_t + w_6 RRAT_t YDL_t^e + w_7 AGE_t YDL_t^e. \quad (4.8)$$

The resources coefficients w_1 through w_4 should be positive.[10] We would expect w_5, the coefficient on GAP, also to be positive because a cyclical increase in expected labor income would represent a smaller rise in perceived total resources (and hence W^d) than would an increase representing an upward shift in the time path of expected labor income. Thus, w_1 would represent the effect on desired wealth of such a noncyclical rise in YDL^e (that is, unaccompanied by a decline in GAP). Owing to offsetting income and substitution effects, w_6 could have either sign. The age composition variable is intended to reflect any changes over time in the proportion of individuals in the retirement (dissaving) stage of their lifetimes; thus w_7 should be negative.

Derivation of the Saving Relation

Actual wealth accumulation, ΔW_t, is the sum of planned, $W^d_t - W_{t-1}$, and unplanned, ΔW^u_t, accumulation:

$$\Delta W_t \equiv W^d_t - W_{t-1} + \Delta W^u_t. \tag{4.9}$$

The latter is assumed to be related to the unexpected components of disposable labor income (YDL^u_t), transfer income (YTR^u_t), and capital gains (G^u_t):

$$\Delta W^u_t = b_1 YDL^u_t + b_2 YTR^u_t + b_3 G^u_t. \tag{4.10}$$

The fractions of the unexpected components that are saved, b_1, b_2, and b_3, are assumed to be near unity. Virtually all of any unexpected increments to purchasing power would be added to wealth during the period in which they occur because individuals are unable to incorporate these unknown increments into their current expenditure plans. However, the longer the length of the time period taken as the unit of analysis, the more opportunity there is to adjust expenditure behavior within the current period and, therefore, the smaller would be the b's.

As emphasized in the previous chapter, there are two ways in which household nonhuman wealth can change: (1) net purchases of assets by individuals (personal saving) and (2) the net change in the real value of household assets previously held (capital gains). We can state this identity as:

$$\Delta W_t \equiv S_t + G_t. \tag{4.11}$$

With respect to current wealth, the source of its value is unimportant. Accrued capital gains embedded in an asset (less any accrued income tax liability)[11] are indistinguishable from an equal amount of personal saving that has been invested in a similar asset. Recognizing that accrued capital gains in equation (4.11) are composed of expected and unexpected components,

$$G_t \equiv G_t^e + G_t^u, \tag{4.12}$$

we can substitute equation (4.10) into (4.9), the result and equation (4.12) into (4.11), and solve for saving as:

$$S_t = W_t^d - W_{t-1} + b_1 YDL_t^u + b_2 YTR_t^u - (1 - b_3)G_t^u - G_t^e. \tag{4.11$'$}$$

The final term ($-G_t^e$) represents a displacement, or deflection, effect of expected capital gains on personal saving.[12] The extent to which the displacement effect of expected capital gains on planned saving will be less than one-for-one depends on the magnitude of the response of total planned wealth accumulation to expected capital gains (w_4 in equation (4.8)).

Disaggregation of Capital Gains

The detailed discussion on capital gains in the previous chapter suggests that there are theoretical reasons to disaggregate total capital gains by asset groups. We can write total real capital gains as:

$$G_t = \lambda_1 GHLN_t + \lambda_2 GDUR_t + GSTK_t + GNFAP_t + \lambda_3 GNFAB_t, \tag{4.13}$$

where *GHLN* represents real capital gains on owner-occupied housing, land, and noncorporate equity; *GDUR* represents real capital gains on consumer durable goods; and *GSTK* represents real capital gains on corporate equities. Real capital gains on net financial assets have been separated into two components: *GNFAP* (real capital gains on net financial assets due to changes in the general price level)[13] and *GNFAB* (real capital gains on net financial assets due to nominal bond price changes). As discussed in the previous chapter, we would expect the λ's to be between zero and unity, with λ_1 larger than λ_2 because housing and land are longer lived than consumer durable goods. We would expect λ_3 to be closer to zero the longer the intended holding period of bond owners. A strict Hicks's prospective-income view would imply a value of zero for λ_3.

Each of the gains components in equation (4.13) can be partitioned into expected and unexpected components, where the expected component affects desired wealth accumulation through the w_4 coefficient in equation (4.8) and the unexpected component influences the unexpected change in wealth through b_3 in (4.10). However, the values of w_4 and b_3 could vary across asset categories. The effect of an expected capital gain on desired wealth would depend on its informational content, that is, the magnitude of its effect on the perceived value of total resources. This is related to how certain one is of the expected gain actually occurring and the extent to which current gains provide information about future gains. A capital gain expected to recur in the future would represent a larger increase in perceived total resources (and hence a higher level of current and future consumption) than a one-time gain. Thus, a nonrecurring gain would raise current consumption less and the end-of-period desired wealth level more. If we let w_{41} through w_{45} represent the w_4's for $GHLN^e$, $GDUR^e$, $GSTK^e$, $GNFAP^e$, and $GNFAB^e$, in that order, then we might expect w_{43} and w_{45} to be largest because stock and bond prices are more volatile than goods prices. For example, the standard deviations of $GSTK^e$ and $GNFAB^e$ are five and a half and four and a half times as large as their respective means. At the same time, the standard deviations of $GDUR^e$ and $GNFAP^e$ are roughly half and nine-tenths of their respective means. The standard deviation of $GHLN^e$ is just under one and a half times its mean. Based on relative volatility, we would expect to find $w_{43} > w_{45} > w_{41} > w_{44} > w_{42}$.

The b_3's, on the other hand, will tend to be smaller the quicker that individuals learn of unexpected gains and losses and can incorporate such information into their behavioral decisions. Because people trade houses, land, and durables less often than stocks and bonds (for which we have daily price quotes), we would expect b_{31} and b_{32} to exceed b_{33} and b_{35}. Moreover, while much attention is given to trades of comparable houses by others because houses constitute so much of one's wealth, little attention is apparently accorded durable trades. Because changes in general price indices are published with relatively short lags, b_{34} should lie between the two extremes.

Combining equations (4.8), (4.11′), and (4.13)—after restating the latter in terms of expected and unexpected components—we obtain:

$$\begin{aligned} S_t = {} & A_0 + A_1 YDL_t^e + A_2 YTR_t^e + A_3 W_{t-1} + A_4 GAP_t + A_5 RRAT_t YDL_t^e \\ & + A_6 AGE_t YDL_t^e + A_7 YDL_t^u + A_8 YTR_t^u + A_9 GHLN_t^e + A_{10} GDUR_t^e \\ & + A_{11} GSTK_t^e + A_{12} GNFAP_t^e + A_{13} GNFAB_t^e + A_{14} GHLN_t^u \\ & + A_{15} GDUR_t^u + A_{16} GSTK_t^u + A_{17} GNFAP_t^u + A_{18} GNFAB_t^u, \end{aligned} \tag{4.14}$$

where

$$A_0 = w_0 \qquad A_6 = w_7 \qquad A_{13} = \lambda_3(w_{45} - 1)$$
$$A_1 = w_1 \qquad A_7 = b_1 \qquad A_{14} = -\lambda_1(1 - b_{31})$$
$$A_2 = w_2 \qquad A_8 = b_2 \qquad A_{15} = -\lambda_2(1 - b_{32})$$
$$A_3 = w_3 - 1 \qquad A_9 = \lambda_1(w_{41} - 1) \qquad A_{16} = -(1 - b_{33})$$
$$A_4 = w_5 \qquad A_{10} = \lambda_2(w_{42} - 1) \qquad A_{17} = -(1 - b_{34})$$
$$A_5 = w_6 \qquad A_{11} = w_{43} - 1 \qquad A_{18} = -\lambda_3(1 - b_{35}).$$
$$A_{12} = w_{44} - 1$$

We would expect to find $A_3<0$ and $1>A_7 \sim A_8>A_1>A_2$. While we expect A_7, A_8, and A_1 to be positive, as discussed earlier, A_2 could take on a small negative value. Similarly, we would expect A_4 to be positive, A_6 to be negative, and are uncertain about the sign of A_5 *a priori.* Given the preceding analysis, we would expect all ten capital gains coefficients to be negative.

An important characteristic of the expected capital gains coefficients is that the larger the effect of an increase in expected capital gains on desired wealth, the smaller the expected capital gains coefficient in the saving equation. This is related to the deflection effect discussed earlier. The more the expected capital gain raises desired wealth, and thus planned wealth accumulation, the less it deflects (or reduces) saving. Consequently, a large behavioral effect on desired wealth would be associated with a relatively small effect on personal saving. However, the interpretation of the expected capital gains coefficients is complicated by the presence of the λ's in A_9, A_{10}, and A_{13}. A value of λ less than unity, indicating that the capital gains are only partially viewed as additions to wealth, would further reduce (in absolute value) the expected capital gains coefficients. In fact, the less the capital gains are viewed as additions to wealth, the nearer to zero are the values of A_9, A_{10}, and A_{13}. Thus, relatively large effects on desired wealth or relatively small effects on the perceived actual change in wealth will both result in values of A_9, A_{10}, and A_{13} very near zero. Of the unexpected capital gains coefficients, we would expect to find A_{14} and A_{15} very near zero, and A_{16}, A_{17}, and A_{18} having values between zero and A_{11}, A_{12}, and A_{13}, respectively.

EMPIRICAL ANALYSIS

This section is divided into four parts. After discussing the data, we present estimates of the basic model and of an extended model. An interpretation of the preferred estimated relationship concludes the section.

Data Specification

Estimation of the saving equation requires proxies for each of the relevant variables. The saving, income, wealth, and capital gains variables are all per capita constant 1972 dollar magnitudes. The dependent variable, *SAV*, is the sum of the NIPA personal saving measure (*SNIA*) and net investment in consumer durable goods (*SDUR*). This is consistent with the theoretically appropriate measurement of consumption as service flows rather than as expenditures. The measurement error terms (*SGPEN, STAX,* and *SPREM*) have been described above. They, too, are divided by population. Population and the share aged 65 or older (*AGE*) are from the U.S. Council of Economic Advisors 1983 *Economic Report of the President.*

The beginning-of-period value of household wealth (*W*) is taken from the Board of Governors of the Federal Reserve System (1983) *Balance Sheet Accounts.* Thus it does not include the real value of unfunded pension wealth, a series that rose markedly during the 1950–80 period. Our measure of the GNP gap (*GAP*), potential less actual GNP, relies on the potential GNP series calculated by the President's Council of Economic Advisors and the NIPA GNP measure. It is lagged one period to avoid simultaneity problems. The real after-tax interest rate (*RRAT*) is calculated as the after-tax yield on one-year Treasury bills less the Livingston survey measure of the one-year expected inflation rate. The Treasury bill yield is the average for the preceding December. The effective marginal tax rate is the *TXINT* series.

The income measures are based on NIPA data. To calculate disposable labor income, total personal tax liabilities must be allocated between labor and property income. Personal labor income is the sum of the NIPA measures of wages and salaries, other labor income, and a proportion of proprietor's income. Using SOI data on federal income tax liabilities and wage income and extending a series on federal income tax liabilities on wages and salaries provided by Charles Steindel, we were able to allocate SOI federal and NIPA state and local income tax liabilities between labor and property income. Personal social security contributions were included in labor's share of tax liabilities.

The calculation of the capital gains proxies from *Balance Sheet Account* data and the decomposition of the capital gains series into their expected and unexpected elements were described in the previous chapter. Disposable labor income and transfer payments are divided into their expected and unexpected components by a similar regression procedure.[14]

The mean, high, and low values for the variables and their scale are listed in Table 4–4. The saving, income, capital gains, wealth, and *GAP* variables are all 1972 dollars per capita. Both *AGE* and *RRAT* are measured in decimals (in the equations they are measured as deviations from their means). The minutes-to-midnight series will be discussed below.

Estimates for the Basic Model

Table 4–5 presents estimates of variants of equation (4.14). Although the specification differs somewhat, the estimates presented in column 1 are consistent with the general findings of Peek (1983). As predicted by our measurement error discussion, the tax liabilities adjustment (*STAX*) has an estimated coefficient that does not differ significantly from minus one (t-statistic = 0.69). The relative magnitudes of the income coefficients are as predicted. The *YTRE* coefficient does not exceed its estimated standard error. The unreasonably large estimated effect of *YTRU* may be related to several retroactive increases in social security benefit levels (see Modigliani and Steindel 1977). Because NIPA saving is measured as a residual, any retroactive and unexpected increase in disposable income is automatically forced into measured saving leading to an overstatement of the marginal response of saving to unexpected transfer payments. The coefficients on wealth and population over age 65 have the predicted negative sign. The GNP gap coefficient has the incorrect sign, but does not differ significantly from zero. The interest rate coefficient is negative and statistically insignificant.

Initially all ten capital gains proxies were included in the saving equation. To reduce the number of explanatory variables to a more manageable size, the capital gains proxies with estimated coefficients having *t*-statistics below unity were eliminated from the equation. Because there were a number of strong simple correlations between pairs of capital gains variables making it very difficult to pinpoint individual effects, the proxies were eliminated sequentially. First, *GHLNU* and *GDURU* (with *t*-statistics of -0.17 and -0.49, respectively) were eliminated. Their near-zero effects are consistent with our expectations. Next, *GNFABE* (with a *t*-statistic of 1.45) and then *GNFAPE* (with a *t*-statistic of 2.07) were eliminated. Although we were using a rule that estimated coefficients should exceed their estimated standard errors for retention of the capital gains variables in the equations, we eliminated *GNFAPE* and *GNFABE* because they had the wrong sign and always had *t*-statistics below unity (with the appropriate negative signs) in later specifications. Similarly, we retained *GNFAPU* and *GNFABU* for comparison purposes because they meet the criteria in our later key equations. Of the six remaining capital gains coefficients, two (*GDURE* and *GSTKU*) differ significantly from zero. Contrary to our predictions, however, unexpected capital gains on corporate equities have a larger (although not significantly so) effect on saving than do their expected counterpart. Furthermore, the coefficient on unexpected gains on net financial assets due to changes in the general price level has the wrong sign but is much less than its estimated standard error.

The rather high correlations between pairs of explanatory variables make it very difficult to pinpoint the individual effects of the explanatory variables on personal saving. For example, the pairwise correlations between *W*, *YDLE*, *YTRE*, and *AGE* range (in absolute value) between 0.89 and 0.98. Furthermore, the pairwise correlations of *RRAT* and *GDURE* with these variables range from 0.61 to 0.79. First-differencing the data substantially reduces the collinearity between pairs of explanatory variables, thereby making it easier to disentangle the separate influences of each explanatory variable.[15] Column 2 presents the results of reestimating the basic saving equation using changes rather than levels of the data. While many of the estimated coefficients are little changed from their column 1 values, there are a number of notable exceptions.

Table 4–4. Data Summary.

	Mean	*Low*	*High*	*Standard Deviation*
Saving and Adjustments to It				
SAV (personal saving)	341.3	204.6	533.0	88.9
SADj (adjusted personal saving)	326.7	204.8	507.3	78.1
STAX (tax adjustment)	12.7	-7.9	44.6	11.1
SGPEN (government pension adjustment)	42.7	15.5	90.9	22.7
SPREM (inflation premium adjustment)	70.0	1.3	257.3	68.0
Income Variables				
YDLE (expected disposable labor income)	2515.0	1954.8	3095.8	402.3
YTRE (expected transfer payments)	397.8	131.5	807.4	213.1
YDLU (unexpected disposable labor income)	-0.53	-66.4	64.3	29.3
YTRU (unexpected transfer payments)	0.44	-25.8	53.8	13.4
Expected Capital Gains Variables				
GHLNE (land, housing, and noncorporate equity)	133.3	-297.7	604.5	188.8
GDURE (consumer durable goods)	-52.6	-111.1	-2.1	29.3
GSTKE (corporate equities)	87.2	-1363.0	911.0	482.9
GNFAPE (bonds due to general price level changes plus SPREM)	-53.8	-141.8	45.2	47.9
GNFABE (bonds due to nominal bond price changes)	4.1	-33.4	48.1	18.4

Unexpected Capital Gains Variables				
GHLNU (land, housing, and noncorporate equity)	-2.1	-265.6	245.0	116.9
GDURU (consumer durable goods)	-0.3	-33.1	29.3	14.5
GSTKU (corporate equities)	-11.4	-911.6	719.8	349.1
GNFAPU (bonds due to general price level changes)	-2.4	-61.0	45.3	23.6
GNFABU (bonds due to nominal bond price changes)	0.5	-64.7	34.7	18.3
Other Variables				
W (beginning-of-period wealth)	14798.4	10524.2	19498.7	2586.4
GAP (GNP gap lagged one period)	82.3	-131.5	412.1	148.9
AGE (share of population age 65 or older)	0.0979	0.0838	0.1155	0.0088
RRAT (real after-tax one-year interest rate)	0.0045	-0.0269	0.0250	0.0152
MINMID (minutes to midnight)	7.24	2	12	3.64

Data Sources: See Table 4–1, U.S. Council of Economic Advisors (1983) *Economic Report of the President*, potential real GNP furnished by Council of Economic Advisors, MINMID furnished by Joel Slemrod. The calculation of the actual and expected capital gains measured are described in Chapter 3. The calculations of the remaining variables are described in the text.

Table 4-5. Estimated Saving Equations, 1952-82.[a]

	(1)[b]	(2)	(3)	(4)	(5)	(6)	(7)
Dependent *VAR*	*SAV*	*SAV*	*SAV*	*SADJ*	*SADJ*	*SADJ*	*SADJ*
Constant	-379	—	—	—	-6.9	-10.8[c]	-10.0[c]
	(125)				(5.1)	(4.7)	
STAX	-1.338	-0.989	-0.896	—	—	—	—
	(0.489)	(0.456)	(0.267)				
SGPEN	—	—	-1.054	—	—	—	—
			(0.402)				
SPREM	—	—	1.337	—	—	—	—
			(0.252)				
W	-0.0197	-0.0261	-0.0441	-0.0374	-0.0314	-0.0322	-0.0383
	(0.0147)	(0.0163)	(0.0105)	(0.0081)	(0.0077)	(0.0066)	(0.0061)
YDLE	0.374	0.574	0.604	0.587	0.597	0.641	0.615
	(0.170)	(0.159)	(0.094)	(0.089)	(0.052)	(0.053)	(0.045)
YTRE	0.196	-0.123	-0.120	-0.093	—	—	—
	(0.350)	(0.403)	(0.238)	(0.225)			
YDLU	0.572	0.623	0.597	0.602	0.597	0.641	0.615
	(0.138)	(0.124)	(0.074)	(0.065)			
YTRU	1.165	0.735	0.765	0.807	0.948	0.922	0.877
	(0.443)	(0.426)	(0.264)	(0.240)	(0.178)	(0.161)	(0.166)
AGE	-3.41	-3.39	-4.57	-4.29	-3.59	-3.05	-1.50
	(1.69)	(2.66)	(1.59)	(1.47)	(1.36)	(1.17)	
GAP	-0.0729	0.1047	0.0724	0.0747	0.0900	0.0942	0.0773
	(0.1029)	(0.1056)	(0.0619)	(0.0568)	(0.0330)	(0.0297)	(0.0284)

RRAT	-0.039 (0.276)	-0.154 (0.281)	0.097 (0.172)	0.079 (0.135)	0.090 (0.112)	0.081 (0.103)	0.085 (0.107)
GHLNE	-0.0928 (0.0669)	-0.1118 (0.0552)	-0.0168 (0.0363)	-0.0344 (0.0305)	-0.0530 (0.0215)	-0.0509 (0.0189)	-0.0408 (0.0187)
GDURE	-0.777 (0.282)	-0.277 (0.315)	-0.430 (0.186)	-0.380 (0.175)	-0.397 (0.121)	-0.352 (0.114)	-0.397 (0.112)
GSTKE	-0.164 (0.0120)	-0.0211 (0.0123)	-0.0272 (0.0073)	-0.0247 (0.0060)	-0.0215 (0.0044)	-0.0210 (0.0041)	-0.0241 (0.0038)
GSTKU	-0.0357 (0.0128)	-0.0228 (0.0125)	-0.0176 (0.0074)	-0.0201 (0.0063)	-0.0215	-0.0210	-0.0241
GNFAPU	0.128 (0.217)	-0.039 (0.190)	-0.157 (0.113)	-0.119 (0.088)	-0.164 (0.074)	-0.177 (0.069)	-0.154 (0.069)
GNFABU	-0.061 (0.264)	-0.041 (0.243)	-0.183 (0.145)	-0.183 (0.117)	-0.164	-0.177	-0.154
MINMID	—	—	—	—	0.00073 (0.00061)	0.00088 (0.00057)	0.00088 (0.00057)
R^2	0.979	0.830	0.949	0.939	0.942	0.951	0.941
SEE	18.60	22.54	13.16	12.71	11.74	10.83	11.25
D.W.	1.96	1.98	2.05	1.90	1.94	2.00	1.91

a. Standard errors in parentheses.
b. This equation is in level form; the others are in changes.
c. Truncated constant (zero after 1979).

The point estimate of the income-tax-liabilities-adjustment coefficient (−0.989) is now much nearer minus unity (t-statistic = 0.02). The effects of beginning-of-period wealth, expected disposable labor income, and unexpected disposable labor income have all increased. The estimated wealth effect is now slightly closer to the −0.03 to −0.05 value typically obtained. On the other hand, the 0.57 *YDLE* coefficient is somewhat larger than the 0.3 to 0.5 coefficient on disposable income cited in the literature.[16] However, because disposable labor income is only about 75 percent of total disposable income, an estimated coefficient in the range of 0.4 to 0.67 would be consistent with a disposable income coefficient in the range of 0.3 to 0.5. In fact, Juster and Taylor (1975), using a disposable labor income measure, found effects consistent with an estimate in the range of 0.4 to 0.5 in our specification.[17]

The estimated coefficient on expected transfer payments now has a small (statistically insignificant) negative value, while the estimated effect of unexpected transfer payments is now below unity as our theory predicts. The GNP gap coefficient has the predicted positive sign, although it is still statistically insignificant, and the real after-tax interest rate has a larger (and still statistically insignificant) negative effect. With respect to the capital gains coefficients, the *GNFAPU* coefficient now has the correct sign (although both *GNFAPU* and *GNFABU* still have estimated coefficients exceeded by their estimated standard errors). The estimated effects of expected capital gains on durables and unexpected gains on both corporate equities and on net financial assets due to nominal bond price changes have each declined, causing *GDURE* and *GSTKU* to lose their statistical significance. The effect of expected capital gains on housing, land, and noncorporate equity has increased and now differs significantly from zero. Due to the slight increase in the effect of *GSTKE* and the sharp decline in the *GSTKU* effect, the two coefficients are now almost identical.

As noted in the development of our model, the interpretation of the capital gains coefficients is rather complicated. The magnitude of the estimated coefficients represents a combination of effects: one related to the effect of capital gains on desired wealth (the w_{4i}'s) or on unplanned wealth accumulation (the b_{3i}'s) and one related to the extent to which the capital gains are perceived as additions to wealth (the λ_i's). Our earlier analysis suggested relative sizes for the w_{4i}'s and b_{3i}'s as well as the λ_i's. Based on the w_{4i}'s alone, we would expect to find *GDURE* and *GNFAPE* with the largest effects and *GSTKE* and *GNFABE* with the smallest. To the extent that the λ_i's are below unity, the effects of *GHLNE, GDURE,* and *GNFABE* would be reduced somewhat. In fact, we do find a relatively large effect of expected capital gains on durables due to their relatively small effect on desired wealth, even after incorporating the λ_2 effect which tends to reduce the extent of deflection. However, its estimated standard error is even larger. The much smaller estimated effects on saving of the other expected capital gains proxies are probably related to their relatively larger effects on desired wealth (and hence smaller deflection effects). This is certainly the case with *GHLNE* relative to *GDURE* because our theoretical analysis suggests that $\lambda_1 > \lambda_2$. Again, the relatively smaller effect of *GSTKE* is consistent with our theory. The combination of a relatively large value of w_{45} and a value of $\lambda_3 < 1$ probably accounts for the absence of *GNFABE*.

The absence of unexpected gains on housing, land, and noncorporate equity and on consumer durables is consistent with our prior analysis suggesting values of b_{31} and b_{32} very near unity. This is reinforced to the extent that λ_1 and λ_2 are below unity. Small negative effects of *GSTKU, GNFAPU,* and *GNFABU* would be consistent with the relatively smaller values of b_{33}, b_{34}, and b_{35}. None of the three unexpected capital gains effects, however, differs significantly from zero.

We now turn to a consideration of the remaining two measurement error terms, *SGPEN* and *SPREM.* Column 3 presents the results of reestimating the column 2 equation with these two additional explanatory variables. We retain the first-differenced specification because the levels of both these variables are highly correlated with the other explanatory variables. The standard error of the equation drops dramatically (over 40 percent) from 22.54 to only 13.16. Most of this decline is due to the introduction of *SPREM*.[18] All three of the measurement error terms have coefficients that differ significantly from zero, but not from their predicted values. The t-statistic for the null hypothesis that the *STAX* coefficient is minus one is only 0.39. Similarly, the t-statistics for the *SGPEN* coefficient differing from minus one and for the *SPREM* coefficient differing from plus one are 0.13 and 1.34, respectively. Thus, we can not reject any of the hypothesized restrictions.

The primary differences between the coefficients on the other variables are: The wealth and *AGE* coefficients increase substantially, the *RRAT* coefficient becomes positive (but is still less than its standard error), the *GHLNE* coefficient drops sharply and loses its significance, and the coefficients on both *GDURE* and *GSTKE* increase and become significant. The *GSTKE* effect now exceeds that of *GSTKU* as our theory predicts. The coefficients on unexpected capital gains on net financial assets due to nominal bond price changes and due to changes in the general price level both rise (in absolute value) and exceed their estimated standard errors.

Column 4 imposes the hypothesized plus or minus unity restrictions on the measurement error terms. That is, the dependent variable is now our adjusted saving measure, *SADJ.* The standard error of the equation is reduced slightly from 13.16 to 12.71. Except for the doubling of the *GHLNE* effect, the estimated coefficients on the capital gains proxies are only slightly altered. The wealth and expected transfer payments effects also decline somewhat. (These reactions to the imposition of the coefficient restrictions may be related to the strong trend elements contained in *SGPEN, SPREM, W,* and *YTRE*).

The estimated effects of expected and unexpected capital gains on corporate equity are very similar to each other in each specification we have considered. This could be due to problems in separating total corporate equity capital gains into expected and unexpected components. Consequently, we also considered an alternative measure of expected gains on corporate equity based on the Livingston survey expectations of Standard and Poor's Industrial Stock Price index. The expected percentage increase (or decrease) was multiplied by the beginning-of-period value of household corporate equity holdings to calculate *GSTKE.* The difference between this measure and the actual stock market capital gains was taken as the unexpected component. Because the Livingston data are available only after 1952, the sample period for this regression is 1954–82. The results are very similar to those obtained when the specification in column 4 is reestimated over the same sample period, indicating that our results are robust with respect to quite different measures of expected stock market capital gains. The *SEE* of the equation with the alternative *GSTKE* measure is 12.19, slightly lower than our original specification when estimated over the same sample period (12.52). The Livingston *GSTKE* and *GSTKU* estimated coefficients are –0.0401 and –0.0214 with standard errors of 0.0191 and 0.0048, respectively. The similarity in the magnitudes of the effects may be due to individuals reacting similarly to both the expected and unexpected components because information on actual stock market capital gains and losses is available on a next-day basis. If that is the case, we lose very little by considering total stock market capital gains because the particular decomposition of total stock market capital gains is irrelevant.

Further Estimates

The one unappealing aspect of the coefficients in column 4 is the implied response of saving to changes in the age distribution of the population. The three percentage point increase in the share of population over age 65, together with the -4.29 coefficient, yields a decline in the personal saving ratio in the last thirty years of over 13 percentage points! One might contend that this response is five to ten times too great. On the other hand, one might argue that older households were not only growing in relative importance but that each was saving relatively less, possibly owing to a sharp rise in social security wealth and the certainty of this wealth (due to indexation in 1972).[19] Further, an increased tendency toward early retirement has occurred concurrently with the aging of the population; between 1954 and 1980, the labor force participation rate of males between the ages of 55 and 64 declined from 0.88 to 0.72. This could make a coefficient as large, in absolute magnitude, as -1.5 plausible. The remaining columns in Table 4-5 reflect attempts to reduce the age coefficient to a more reasonable value without losing the appealing aspects of column 4.

The major additions in column 5 are a constant term in our difference equation and Slemrod's (1984) minutes-to-midnight or nuclear-fear variable (scaled by expected labor income). In Slemrod's view, increased fear of a nuclear holocaust (decreased expected life span and ability to leave a bequest) would likely reduce the propensity to save. The equation also combines some like variables with similar impacts (expected and unexpected labor income, expected and unexpected stock market gains, and unexpected gains on net financial assets due to changes in the general price level and to changes in nominal bond prices) and deletes some variables with negligible impacts (expected transfer income, expected gains on net financial assets due to changes in the general price level, etc.). As can be seen, the constant and fear variable have *t*-ratios slightly above unity and reduce the age coefficient by nearly 20 percent. The coefficient on the nuclear-fear variable suggests that a ten minute increase in the clock, the largest observed variation, would raise the saving rate by almost a full percentage point.[20]

Not only is the constant term insignificantly different from zero, but it is difficult to interpret. One general interpretation is the negative impact of the growth in social security (and other unfunded pension) wealth on saving; this would be consistent with the large and significant negative impact of real nonhuman wealth (*t*-ratios over 4 in columns 4 and 5). However, social security wealth certainty has not been growing in the 1980s. To account for this, the constant in column 5 was replaced, in turn, by constants that were truncated (became zero) in 1974, 1977, and 1980. The best fit was obtained with the latter variable and is reported as column 6 in the table. As can be seen, this truncated constant is significantly different from zero. Also, the *AGE* coefficient exhibits a further decline, although it is still at least double what we would consider a plausible magnitude.

While the truncated constant may reflect something other than the impact of unfunded pensions, we shall accept this interpretation. Because Feldstein (1982) is the most visible and vocal advocate of the negative unfunded-pensions effect, we compare our results with his. He concludes that personal saving was reduced by $58 billion in 1976, his last year of analysis, when NIA personal saving was $69 billion (p. 636). Moreover, three-quarters of this reduction was due to the increase in social security wealth since 1951, the year our analysis begins; that is, the growth in social security wealth between 1951 and 1976 reduced personal saving in 1976 by $43.5 billion. To obtain our 1976 impact on the *level* of personal saving per capita, we multiply the 10.8 coefficient in our change equation by 25. The result of $270 is then compared with the 1976 NIA measure of personal saving per capita of $426. This ratio, 0.63, is the same as that computed by dividing Feldstein's $43.5 by $69. The two estimates, then, are compatible, suggesting both specifications may be capturing the same phenomenon.[21]

In our final estimates, we arbitrarily halved the age coefficient to −1.5, its maximum plausible value. The result was a sharp increase in the coefficient on the truncated constant to −15 (*t*-ratio of 4). In order not to overstate the unfunded-pensions effect, we then constrained the constant to −10, roughly the value in column 6. Column 7 contains the estimates of such a relation. Note the small decline in the overall explanatory power from column 6 and the general correspondence between the coefficients in column 7 and those in columns 4, 5, and 6. In addition to the enormous significance of labor income, coefficients on wealth, stock market gains, and unexpected transfer income have *t*-ratios above 5, and those on expected housing et al. and durable gains, unexpected net financial asset gains, and temporary economic slack (the GNP gap) are in the 2 to 3.5 range. The nuclear fear variable has a *t* of 1.5. The real after-tax interest rate continues to have a small, insignificant positive coefficient.

Interpretation of the Estimates

Short-run capital gains, unexpected transfer payments and the GNP gap have only a temporary impact on household saving. The largest stock market losses occurred in 1973–74, sandwiched in between relatively large gains in both 1971–72 and 1975–76. As a result, household saving was about 10 percent higher in 1973–74 than in the surrounding years. Large expected gains on housing, land and noncorporate equity in 1977–78 reduced personal saving by over 5 percent; systematic large losses on durables raised saving by a like amount in the late 1970s and early 1980s. More generally, the GAP variable and its coefficient suggest that household saving is about 10 percent greater in the early stages of economic recoveries than in the late stages of economic booms. Finally, unexpected transfers only rarely have affected saving by 5 percent, although a large jump in government unemployment insurance benefits in 1975 associated with legislation to extend both the duration and coverage of benefits increased saving by over 10 percent.

Determinants of longer term, major shifts in the saving ratio are probably of more interest. The adjusted saving rate, as computed in Table 4–3, is reproduced at roughly seven-year intervals in the top row of Table 4–6. The ratio fell sharply in the 1950s, reversed itself in the 1960s, held constant through the middle 1970s and has since plummeted. The second row contains the major determinant of changes in the saving ratio, the wealth/disposable labor income ratio. The general inverse relationship between rows one and two is obvious. The next two rows contain the percentage changes in real disposable labor income and wealth per capita, the determinants of changes in the wealth/income ratio. In three of the four intervals, real wealth grew at a roughly 21 percent rate, the first two being dominated by

Table 4–6. Explanation of Broad Swings in the Saving Ratio.

	1953–54		*1960–61*		*1968*		*1974–75*		*1981–82*
Saving Rate (%)	14.5		10.6		14.7		14.4		7.4
W/YDL	5.36		6.21		5.95		5.60		6.55
%ΔW		21.8		21.4		1.3		21.7	
%ΔYDL		6.5		26.6		7.6		4.0	
Change in Saving Rate		-3.9		4.1		-0.3		-7.0	
Due to									
W/YDL		-3.2		1.0		1.3		-3.7	
AGE and Unfunded Pensions		-4.3		-2.5		-3.0		-2.8	
Real Income Growth		1.3		5.2		1.4		0.7	
GAP and Transfers		1.4		-1.2		1.5		-0.5	
Minutes to Midnight		0.1		0.7		0.0		-0.5	
Other		0.8		0.9		-1.5		-0.2	

Data Sources: For underlying variables, see Table 4–4. Other data are authors calculations.

equity gains and the last by the land-housing surge; the negligible real gains in the 1968–74 period were the result of equity losses offsetting land-housing gains (see Chapter 3 for a full discussion of these real wealth changes). Real disposable labor income grew less rapidly on average and was more volatile, with enormous real growth in the 1960s and minimal growth since the middle 1970s. The wealth/income ratio rose in the first and last intervals owing to large wealth growth and declined in the middle two intervals, first because of the incredibly large income growth and then because of the stock market debacle.

The remainder of the table indicates the changes in the saving ratio between periods and the sources of the changes. The dominant role of the wealth/income ratio in the major declines in the saving ratio in the 1950s and late 1970s is clear. Also contributing to these declines, and causing declines generally, was the aging of the population and the growth in unfunded pensions (the truncated constant). Acting to offset the strong negative impact of these variables was the growth in real income; because the marginal propensity to save is greater than the average, increases in income raise the average saving rate.[22] The real growth effect was particularly prominent in the 1960s and explains the sharp increase in the saving rate in that period. Also listed in the table are the effects of the GNP gap and unexpected transfers, the nuclear-fear variable and other, which is largely an error term. Some of the rise in the saving ratio in the 1960s is explained by the relaxation of international tensions following the solution of the Cuban missile crisis and passage of the Partial Test Ban Treaty in the early 1960s, and part of the recent decline in the rate owes to increased tensions between the United States and the Soviet Union.

While the real after-tax interest rate has a negligible direct impact on household saving, this variable appears to have a major indirect effect. As one might expect, real cumulated gains on housing, land, and noncorporate equity (which are related to land) and the real after-tax interest rate exhibit a statistically significant negative correlation. An increase in the interest rate leads to a downward revaluation of the assets and a decrease to an upward revaluation. These gains (or losses) then feed into the level of household wealth which has a negative influence on personal saving.

The real after-tax interest rate (*RRAT*) declined from 0.0183 in 1970 to -0.0210 in 1980–81. To obtain an impact of this decline on wealth (and then on saving), we estimated a relationship between cumulated real gains on housing, land and noncorporate equity (*TGHLN*) and *RRAT* over the 1952–82 period, obtaining (standard errors in parentheses):

$$TGHLN = \underset{(38)}{438} - \underset{(2419)}{17489}RRAT \qquad \begin{aligned} R^2 &= .643 \\ DW &= 0.88 \\ SEE &= 204 \\ \text{Mean} &= \$359 \text{ billion.} \end{aligned}$$

Multiplying 17489 by 0.0393 (the change in *RRAT*) gives an induced increase in *TGHLN* (and hence wealth at the beginning of the 1981–82 period) of \$688 billion or \$2992 per capita (in 1972 dollars). Using the estimated wealth coefficient of -0.0383 from column 7 of Table 4–5, we obtain a reduction in saving between 1970 and 1981–82 of \$114.6 per capita (in 1972 dollars). Thus, in the absence of the sharp reduction in *RRAT* (and the associated surge in *TGHLN* and wealth), the average value of our adjusted personal saving measure in 1981–82 would have been \$332.8 rather than \$218.2 per capita (in 1972 dollars). The 1981–82 saving rate then would have been 11.27 percent, or 50 percent more than the observed 7.39 percent value. This calculation overstates the effect because a lower level of wealth in the earlier years due to the absence of cumulated gains on housing, land, and noncorporate equity would have induced additional saving. Allowing for this feedback, the 1980–81 saving ratio still would have been about 10 percent or 2.5 percentage points higher than the observed ratio.

SUMMARY

The NIPA measurement of personal saving is incorrect in a number of important respects. These include the treatment of net purchases of consumer durables as consumption instead of saving, the treatment of net contributions to government life insurance and retirement funds as taxes instead of saving, and the measurement of personal taxes on a cash-payment rather than liability-accrual basis. Finally, because inflation converts part of fixed-income wealth into an interest income flow (some of the inflation premium in new issue interest rates is built into recorded after-tax interest income), the NIPA measure overstates saving in an inflationary period. We have computed an adjusted saving variable to correct for all of these errors, and we have obtained empirical support for the validity of our corrections.

Our adjusted saving rate exhibits some major movements in the 1951–82 period. The rate declines from over 15 percent in the early 1950s to around 11 percent in the early 1960s and then rebounds to over 14 percent by the middle 1960s. After approximately a decade of relative stability, the rate plummets in the second half of the 1970s to under 8 percent in the early 1980s.

The most important variables explaining longer-run swings in the saving rate are real wealth and income. Large real gains on equities and on housing and land in the second halves of the 1950s and 1970s, respectively, account for most of the sharp declines in the saving ratio in these periods. While wealth also grew rapidly during most of the 1960s, again owing largely to stock-market gains, the saving ratio actually increased because of unparalleled real income growth. This growth raised the saving ratio both directly, because the marginal propensity to save out of income exceeds the average propensity, and indirectly, because the wealth/income ratio was lowered.

Acting almost continuously to depress the saving ratio throughout the 1951–80 period was a marked increase in the retired portion of the population and rapid growth in unfunded pension wealth (both social security and pensions for government employees). The former resulted from both a three percentage point increase in the share of the population over age 65 (from 8 percent to 11) and a doubling of males below age 65 choosing early retirement. The precise role of these two factors is uncertain, but together they would have reduced the saving rate to zero in the absence of real income growth (the marginal greater than average phenomenon).

The real after-tax interest rate (which obviously measures the returns to savers with some imprecision) does not have a direct influence on the saving ratio. However, an indirect channel of influence exists, namely a strong significant negative relationship between the market value of housing, land, and noncorporate equity and the real after-tax interest rate. In fact, the sharp decline in this rate underlies the fall in the saving ratio attributable to the housing and land boom in the second half of the 1970s.

Short-run movements in the saving ratio are caused by the volatility of the stock market and of economic activity generally. The GNP gap variable indicates that the saving rate is higher in the early stages of an upswing than in the late stages. Finally, there is some weak evidence that heightened fear of nuclear war lowers the saving ratio and relaxation of international tensions raises the ratio.

NOTES

1. Interest payments on mortgage and home improvement loans are not included in interest paid by consumers to business. Because homeowners are treated as business operators in the NIPA, these payments are counted as interest paid by business to business and are not included in personal income.
2. Net personal transfer payments to foreigners are also subtracted from personal income in calculating SNIA. We have ignored this term in our theoretical analysis because of its relatively small magnitude and because it is not central to our analysis.
3. For a discussion of the flow of funds treatment, see Board of Governors of the Federal Reserve System (1975:31–33). The data on SGPEN were supplied by their flow of funds section.
4. The inflation adjustment was first addressed by Poole (1972). His measure of the inflation premium in disposable income was constructed as:

$$YPREM = \frac{\pi}{RCB} YINT,$$

where π, *RCB*, and *YINT* represent the anticipated inflation rate, the corporate bond rate, and net interest income.
5. Fixed-income assets are measured net of consumer credit, but mortgage debt is not subtracted. This is because interest payments on consumer credit are subtracted from personal income in constructing personal saving while interest payments on mortgages are not (see note 1).
6. The *TXINT* series is constructed from the SOI data supplemented with tables provided by Charles Hicks. Following Wright (1969), the tax rate is calculated as a weighted average of the marginal personal income tax rate for each adjusted gross income class. The weight for each class is equal to its share of the total interest received by all income classes.
7. This is not meant to suggest that we think the real interest rate was constant over this period. In fact, there is ample empirical evidence that the real rate has varied cyclically (Hendershott and Huang 1984, for example). However, that variation has been on the order of only two percentage points. Moreover, the variation in the rate built into interest income is substantially less given the lags with which this income reflects rate movements. In contrast, interest income incorporated a major (six to eight percentage point) trend increase in expected inflation between 1950 and 1981.
8. This series is calculated as $(SNIA - \pi ASAV)/(YD - \pi AYD)$, where π is the one-year expected inflation rate at the end of the previous year from the Livingston survey data supplied by the Federal Reserve Bank of Philadelphia.
9. The model is similar to that of Peek (1983).

10. While an increase in expected transfer payments would tend to raise W^d by increasing the perceived value of total lifetime resources, it would at the same time discourage the accumulation of wealth for retirement to the extent that it leads to the expectation of a higher retirement income (e.g., social security benefits). Similarly, an increase in unemployment benefits could reduce the need for precautionary wealth held to carry an individual through a period of less than normal earnings. If these influences more than offset the positive total resources effect, w_2 would be negative.
11. We will ignore any accrued income tax liabilities on accrued capital gains. Such taxes are paid only upon realization, if ever, and are based on nominal rather than real capital gains. Bailey (1969) found that the effective tax rate on accrued capital gains was very small, perhaps as low as 5 to 10 percent.
12. Nichols (1970) investigates some implications of this deflection issue whereby real capital gains crowd out asset accumulation in satisfying wealth accumulation motives.
13. Recall that the adjustment to personal saving for the inflation premium component in interest income requires a compensating adjustment to (the expected component of) *GNFAP*. Consequently, in the equations that follow, our measure of the expected component of *GNFAP* will be the sum of our original (Chapter 3) measure of *GNFAPE* and *SPREM*. This is equivalent to reducing expected capital losses by the inflation premium component in net interest income.
14. The estimated equation for disposable labor income is (estimated standard errors in parentheses):

$$\underset{}{YDL} = \underset{(270)}{980} + \underset{(.141)}{.908YDL1} - \underset{(.139)}{.373YDL2} + \underset{(.195)}{.870G} + \underset{(.0603)}{.0955GAP}$$

$$- \underset{(8.4)}{45.3RNT} - \underset{(357.1)}{1091.2\,TXRT} + \underset{(43.4)}{106.1DKW} - \underset{(.757)}{.818DSCR}$$

$R^2 = .995$ $\quad$ $SEE = 34.16$ $\quad$ Durbin $h = -1.374$

Annual observations for 1951–82 are used. The explanatory variables are (in addition to two own lagged values) one lagged value each of government expenditures (*G*), the GNP gap (*GAP*), the one-year after-tax nominal Treasury bill yield (*RNT*), and an index of marginal personal income tax rates (*TXRT*). The equation also includes dummy variables for the Korean War period (*DKW*) and the 1968–70 temporary personal income tax surcharge and the 1975 income tax rebate (*DSCR*). The transfer payments equation is:

$$YTR = \underset{(115)}{238} + \underset{(.055)}{.802YTR1} + \underset{(.038)}{.124G} + \underset{(.0407)}{.0565GAP} + \underset{(4.1)}{14.7RNT} + \underset{(.083)}{.134M}$$

$R^2 = .996$ $\quad$ $SEE = 14.89$ $\quad$ Durbin $h = .271$

where *M* represents the lagged value of the *M*1 definition of the money supply.

15. Plosser and Schwert (1978) suggest differencing as a crude test of model specification. The results from the levels regression of a correctly specified model should be confirmed by the results from the reestimation of the equation using the first differences of the data.
16. Tobin and Dolde (1971:101) suggest that a consumption function specification containing disposable income and wealth would have coefficients on these variables in the ranges of 0.5 to 0.7 and 0.03 to 0.05, respectively. This implies a disposable income coefficient between 0.3 and 0.5 for the corresponding saving equation.
17. When the equation is reestimated omitting some of the variables that are highly correlated with *YDLE* (*W, AGE,* and *GHLNE*), as well as *GAP,* the estimated coefficient on *YDLE* drops to only 0.28, while the estimated coefficient on *YDLU* (0.59) is little affected.
18. When only *SPREM* was added to the specification in column 2, its estimated coefficient was 1.28 (*S.E.* = 0.30) and the *SEE* was reduced from 22.54 to 15.51.
19. Kane (1985) suggests this effect.
20. This estimate, which is obviously measured with some imprecision, is slightly less than half the impact on the NIA private saving rate obtained by Slemrod (1984). We obtained a much larger impact when the NIA personal saving rate, rather than our corrected rate, was employed as the dependent variable.
21. A similar estimate, again employing a different data set and methodology, was recently obtained by Carmichael (1984). See Feldstein (1982) for references to numerous studies, micro and macro, on the saving impact of social security.
22. There is an implicit constant term in the saving-levels equation of −500. Given the −10 coefficient on the truncated constant in the changes equation, the "constant" in the levels equation rises, in absolute value, by 10 each year through 1979. If expected real labor income per capita were to increase by 2 percent the first year and then by slightly decreasing amounts in later years, the unfunded pensions effect on the average saving rate would precisely offset the effect of real income growth (higher marginal than average rate) leaving the average saving rate unchanged. Of course, real income per capita grew by far less than 2 percent per year except in the 1960s when the growth rate was nearly 3 percent.

REFERENCES

Auerbach, Alan J. 1985. "Saving in the United States: Some Conceptual Issues." In *The Level and Composition of Household Saving,* edited by Patric H. Hendershott, pp. 15–37. Cambridge, Mass.: Ballinger Publishing Company.

Bailey, Martin J. 1969. "Capital Gains and Income Taxation." In *The Taxation of Income from Capital,* edited by Arnold C. Harberger and Martin J. Bailey, pp. 11–49. Washington, D.C.: The Brookings Institution.

Blades, Derek W., and Peter H. Sturm. 1982. "The Concept and Measurement of Savings: The United States and Other Industrialized Countries." In *Saving and Government Policy.* Conference Series No. 25. Boston, Mass.: Federal Reserve Bank of Boston, pp. 1–30.

Board of Governors of the Federal Reserve System. 1975. *Introduction to Flow of Funds.* Washington, D.C.: U.S. Government Printing Office.

Board of Governors of the Federal Reserve System. 1983. *Balance Sheets for the U.S. Economy 1945–82.* Washington, D.C.: U.S. Government Printing Office.

———. Various issues. *Federal Reserve Bulletin.*

Boskin, Michael J. 1983. "Saving Incentives: The Role of Tax Policy." In *New Directions in Federal Tax Policy for the 1980s,* edited by Charls E. Walker and Mark A. Bloomfield, pp. 93–111. Cambridge, Mass.: Ballinger Publishing Company.

Carmichael, Jeffrey. 1984. "Pitfalls in Testing the Ricardian Equivalence Theory." Mimeo.

Feldstein, Martin S. 1977. "National Saving in the United States." In *Capital for Productivity and Jobs,* pp. 124–54. Englewood Cliffs, N.J.: Prentice-Hall, Inc.

———. 1982. "Social Security and Saving: A Reply." *Journal of Political Economy* 90 (June):630–42.

Hendershott, Patric H., and Roger Huang. 1985. "Debt and Equity Yield: 1926–80." In *Corporate Capital Structure in the United States,* edited by Benjamin Friedman, pp. 117–63. Chicago: University of Chicago Press.

Jump, Gregory V. 1980. "Interest Rates, Inflation Expectations, and Spurious Elements in Measured Real Income and Saving." *American Economic Review* 70 (December):990–1004.

Juster, F. Thomas, and Lester D. Taylor. 1975. "Towards a Theory of Saving Behavior." *American Economic Review* 65 (May):203–09.

Kane, Edward J. 1985. "Microeconomic Evidence on the Composition of Household Savings in Recent Years." In *The Level and Composition of Household Saving,* edited by Patric H. Hendershott, pp. 101–49. Cambridge, Mass.: Ballinger Publishing Company.

Modigliani, Franco, and Charles Steindel. 1977. "Is a Tax Rebate an Effective Tool for Stabilization Policy?" *Brookings Papers on Economic Activity* (no. 1):175–203.

Nichols, Donald A. 1970. "Land and Economic Growth." *American Economic Review* 60 (June):332–40.

Peek, Joe, 1982. "Personal Saving and the Measurement of Income Tax Liabilities." *Review of Economics and Statistics* 64 (February):143–47.

———. 1983. "Capital Gains and Personal Saving Behavior." *Journal of Money, Credit and Banking* 15 (February):1–23.

Plosser, Charles I., and G. William Schwert. 1978. "Money, Income, and Sunspots: Measuring Economic Relationships and the Effects of Differencing." *Journal of Monetary Economics* 4 (November):637–60.

Poole, William. 1972. "The Role of Interest Rates and Inflation in the Consumption Function." *Brookings Papers on Economic Activity* (no. 1):211–20.

Slemrod, Joel. 1984. "Saving and the Fear of Nuclear War." Mimeo.

Tobin, James, and Walter C. Dolde. 1971. "Wealth, Liquidity and Consumption." In *Consumer Spending and Monetary Policy: The Linkages,* Conference Series No. 5, pp. 99–146. Boston, Mass.: Federal Reserve Bank of Boston.

U.S. Bureau of Economic Analysis. 1981. *The National Income and Product Accounts of the United States, 1929–76.* Washington, D.C.: U.S. Government Printing Office.

———. *Survey of Current Business.* Washington, D.C.: U.S. Government Printing Office, various issues.

U.S. Council of Economic Advisors. 1983. *Economic Report of the President.* Washington, D.C.: U.S. Government Printing Office.

U.S. Internal Revenue Service. *Statistics of Income, Individual Income Tax Returns.* Washington, D.C.: U.S. Government Printing Office, various years.

Wright, Colin. 1969. "Saving and the Rate of Interest." In *The Taxation of Income from Capital,* edited by Arnold C. Harberger and Martin J. Bailey, pp. 275–300. Washington, D.C.: The Brookings Institution.

5 MICROECONOMIC EVIDENCE ON THE COMPOSITION OF HOUSEHOLD SAVINGS IN RECENT YEARS

*Edward J. Kane**

This chapter employs survey data on consumer balance sheets to describe mean differences in effective savings rates and in the allocation of accumulated savings across financial and real estate assets for households in different demographic circumstances. Adopting a balance-sheet perspective, effective saving is defined as the net increase between survey dates in the amount of wealth a household holds in the particular assets and liabilities for which survey data are collected. Effective saving is an ex post and data-determined concept. It differs from anticipated saving not only because of income and expenditure surprises but also by the amount of the unanticipated capital gain or loss that accrues on a respondent's overall portfolio position. In that it includes the effect of revaluations of existing assets, it differs also from the concept of ex post saving that is embodied in the national income and product accounts.[1]

*The author wishes to thank Alexander Shumay for four years of painstaking research assistance, Patricia Akison for manuscript typing, and the U.S. Department of Housing and Urban Development and the American Council of Life Insurance for financial support. Valuable criticism was received from Patric Hendershott, Paul Wachtel, Douglas Diamond, and members of the 1983 NBER Summer Institute. Opinions expressed in the paper are those of the author and should not be construed to represent those of either the NBER or the project's sponsors.

Three surveys conducted by the Survey Research Center (SRC) of the University of Michigan serve as our principal source of data. Because survey instruments did not regularly include questions about the value of pension claims, claims against insurance reserves, and tangible assets other than real estate, these assets are neglected in our study. To assign a name to the wealth concept that corresponds to the net-worth account of these truncated survey balance sheets, we introduce the term *net transactable wealth.*

In this paper, household savings are cumulated as increases in net transactable wealth observed across three benchmark dates: January/February 1962, the first half of 1970, and August/September 1977. These time intervals are chosen because in each of them the SRC conducted a comprehensive national survey of household balance sheets. Because data were collected from over 2,000 households in each instance, the samples are large enough to support some analysis of cross-classified data.

Our goal is to develop and to interpret data on cross-sectional differences in wealth trajectories through time. Our unifying hypothesis is that changes in the economic and financial environment seldom lead individuals in different demographic circumstances to effect parallel adjustments either in their saving rate or in the composition of their equilibrium portfolios. This hypothesis implies that class-level differences in the rate of wealth accumulation reflect returns from active portfolio management as well as the passive realignment of portfolio shares occasioned by unpredictable fluctuations in the prices of individual assets. We strive to show that, over 1962–77, wealth redistribution had an active as well as a passive dimension.

The analysis can be likened to examining the slopes of line segments drawn triangularly through three data points. For most partitions of survey respondents, we concern ourselves mainly with differences in the orientations of the 1962–70 and 1970–77 legs of the triangle. However, for specified age cohorts, we look also at data covering the longer 1962–77 segment.

A PRELIMINARY LOOK AT THE DATA

Although the 1962 and 1970 Surveys of Consumer Finances record holdings to the nearest dollar (that is, asked respondents for point estimates), most of the balance-sheet data collected in the 1977 Consumer Credit Survey sponsored by the Federal Reserve Board are in interval form. To aggregate 1977 observations across asset classes to estimate an individual household's transactable wealth, it is first necessary to convert the interval estimates into point estimates. Detailed aggregation procedures, which draw on mean values recorded for various asset-holding intervals in the 1962 and 1970 surveys, are explained in Shumay and Kane (1983).

Because the accuracy and representativeness of survey data are always in doubt, a responsible researcher must endeavor as far as possible to collate survey measurements with comparable figures from other data sets. Reported percentage allocations of consolidated transactable wealth to financial assets and real-estate equity differ greatly between SRC surveys of households and institutionally derived Federal Reserve Flow-of-Funds (FOF) data. Averaged across survey years, SRC portfolio weights for financial assets are roughly 3/8; this is just over one-half of their average weight in FOF data. For real-estate equity, the situation is reversed: SRC weights range between 60 and 65 percent, while FOF weights vary between 25 and 35 percent. These discrepancies have many sources. First, in sample surveys, respondents have both a tendency to forget and an understandable reluctance to disclose sensitive economic information. This leads respondents to misreport (and on average to underreport) their positions in various financial assets (Ferber et al. 1969a, 1969b; Goldsmith 1982). Shumay and Kane (1983) describe the error-detection and error-correction procedures to which the 1962, the 1970, and particularly the 1977 data sets were subjected. Answers to straightforward questions of fact such as whether a household is a homeowner or has mortgage debt should be more reliable than value estimates. In an interview situation, a household that owns a wide variety of stocks and bonds may easily overlook its position in particular securities. Second, valuation skills may differ across respondents, especially for real-estate assets. Third, valuation principles, intrayear timing, and reporting categories differ between the SRC and Flow-of-Funds accounts. In the Flow-of-Funds accounts, the household sector includes personal trusts and nonprofit organizations, and a category of miscellaneous assets exists. A fourth complication is that the interviewing unit in SRC surveys shifted after 1964 from the "spending unit" to the "family unit."

In view of these discrepancies, this chapter does not produce unbiased estimates of consolidated balance sheets for the household sector as a whole but instead examines differences in saving and portfolio behavior across households partitioned by age and family composition. To assess the representativeness of SRC samples and of our aggregation procedures vis-à-vis patterns of *incremental* wealth accumulation, Table 5–1 compares cumulative movements shown for the pooled cross-section sample between survey dates with time-series changes reported in FOF data covering approximately the same intervals. SRC and FOF estimates of cumulative growth rates for deposits and savings bonds and for owner-occupied real estate are similar in both periods, but especially for 1962–70 other categories diverge considerably. In part this is because in an effort to compensate for the greater nonreporting of financial information by high-income households, SRC surveys oversample high-income households (Katona et al. 1971:3–4; Durkin and Elliehausen 1978:97–99). Measured against Census data, the concentration on high-income households increased from the 1970 to 1977 survey. In Table 5–1, the divergences are greatest for assets favored by wealthy households: for corporate equities, for marketable bonds (where, by recording increases in par values without respect to ongoing price depreciation, SRC surveys seriously overstate value growth in an era of rising interest rates), and for the category of investment real estate (which has no strict counterpart in the Flow-of-Funds accounts). In addition, these same assets bulk large in the portfolios of personal trusts and nonprofit organizations. Goldsmith (1982) reports that nonprofit organizations greatly reduced the weight of bonds and stocks in their portfolios between 1964 and 1975. Except for corporate equities, the alternative estimates of cumulative growth in net transactable wealth prove closer for the 1970–77 period (which makes use of the same concept of interviewing unit at both end dates) than for 1962–70.

For equity in homes, it proved impossible to maintain complete comparability between 1977 and earlier survey data. First, fully 6.6 percent of 1977 respondent households reported themselves as homeowners without revealing either the value of their home or information about the terms of their mortgage. Second, unlike the 1962 and 1970 survey instruments, the 1977 questionnaire did not ask for the value of outstanding mortgage debt. Fortunately, in all but fifty-seven cases (2.2 percent of sample respondents and 5.2 percent of the 1,099 mortgagors in the sample) it proved possible to estimate the book value of mortgage debt from information concerning the terms of the mortgage. In the sample analyzed in this study, the homeownership

Table 5-1. Comparison of Survey and Time-Series Estimates of Cumulative Growth Rates between Survey Dates in the Mean Value of Components of Net Transactable Wealth (percentage).

	1961–1969 Cumulative Growth for F.R. Data	*1962–1970 Survey Estimates of Cumulative Growth*	*1969–1976 Cumulative Growth for F.R. Data*	*1970–1977 Survey Estimates of Cumulative Growth*
Deposits and savings bonds	80.9	85.9	109.7	100.0
Marketable bonds	105.2	829.3	73.2	78.7
Corporate equities	49.0	97.2	3.5	54.8
Owner-occupied real estate	73.2	65.8	118.2	108.0
Investment real estate	48.9	132.2	67.1	26.9
Home mortgages	84.7	59.6	95.5	61.2
Other mortgages	92.2	57.4	43.3	50.3
Net transactable wealth	63.8	88.4	68.5	79.8

Sources: Board of Governors of the Federal Reserve System (1982) and calculations made from data tapes of the 1977 Consumer Credit Survey and of the 1962 and 1970 Surveys of Consumer Finances. In the Flow-of-Funds accounts, the household sector is consolidated with personal trusts and nonprofit organizations.

Note: Survey data record savings bonds, marketable bonds, and mortgages at par value. From the Flow-of-Funds accounts, the sum of miscellaneous assets and mortgage assets is treated as a loose proxy for the SRC concept of "investment real estate."

rate falls short of the 64.8 percent Census estimate for 1977 reported by Carliner (1982), even though the unedited survey sample showed a homeownership rate of 68.9 percent. Moreoever, the deletion bias does not fall uniformly across various demographic partitions. In particular, because families that have undergone some form of breakup or have occupied a home for a long time are more likely to fail to report the value of their home as well as to forget relevant information or to report inconsistent mortgage terms, the cases deleted include a disproportionately large number of older mortgagors. The edited sample's lack of representativeness can be assessed from Table 5-2, which compares homeownership rates in our 1977 sample with two-age class partitions published in Carliner (1982). The percentage of homeowners deleted increases steadily with the age of a household's head (as may be seen in Table 5-9 below).

FACTORS DIFFERENTIALLY AFFECTING HOUSEHOLD SAVINGS PATTERNS IN THE 1960s AND 1970s

Modern theories of consumption emphasize that for a representative household savings behavior differs as it moves through the life cycle. Life-cycle theories of saving (Modigliani and Brumberg 1954; Ando and Modigliani 1963) hold that over its lifetime a household accumulates and decumulates wealth to smooth the timestream of its consumption expenditures by offsetting the effects of anticipated and unanticipated variation in income receipts and in spending goals. Spending goals include predictable and partly controllable bulges in expenditure, such as those occasioned by retirement, college expenses, vacations, and downpayments on big-ticket items such as cars and houses. They also include provisions for bequests and unpredictable (and often uncontrollable) bulges in expenditure such as for household repairs and health emergencies. If it could ignore complications due to uncertainty about the age of death, this theory would predict that as a household approached the end of its expected life span, it would plan to decumulate wealth to the level of intended bequests.

Because differences in implicit and explicit transactions charges and in securities' minimum denominations affect the liquidity of various assets, the existence of a life cycle in saving patterns suggests the likelihood of a corresponding life cycle in patterns of asset hold-

Table 5-2. Comparison of Homeownership Rates for Married Households and One-Person Households in the Edited 1977 SRC Sample with Census Estimates for the Same Year (percentage).

Age of Household Head (in years)	*One-Person Households*		*Married Households*	
	Homeownership Rate in Our Sample	*Homeownership Rate in Census Data*	*Homeownership Rate in Our Sample*	*Homeownership Rate in Census Data*
Under age 25	3.0	7.6	33.3	35.3
25 to 34	20.4	19.2	73.2	69.5
35 to 44	25.8	27.0	82.4	82.1
45 to 54	51.2	41.4	80.1	86.9
55 to 64	47.6	52.3	80.0	86.5
65 and over	53.1	57.1	76.7	83.1
Subset of respondents classified	38.4	42.2	74.5	77.1

Source: Census estimates from Carliner (1982).

ing. In this second life cycle, we may expect differences in age-class transactions costs, tax structure, and portfolio risks to play an important role. Historically, securities dealers and brokers have priced their services in ways that discourage small individual trades: imposing odd-lot fees, transactions minima, and per-trade charges. Calculated as a percentage of the value of a trade, explicit transactions charges fall as the dollar amount increases. Although we may presume that this schedule of charges mirrors underlying broker costs, it predisposes financial investments by low-wealth households toward small-denomination retail assets such as deposits and U.S. savings bonds. At the same time, households must worry about the exposure of their accumulated wealth to implicit and explicit taxation and to various kinds of risk. Differential changes between survey dates in age-class transactions costs, tax structure, and portfolio risk-return loci should lead to a change in the equilibrium composition of age-class portfolios. For convenience, we may call this the portfolio-churning hypotheses.

Of course, the distribution of wealth across age classes may change without active churning of household balance sheets. Passive churning occurs when the prices of assets held to a disproportionate extent by particular age classes appreciate or depreciate faster than the prices of other assets. Over any interest-rate cycle, passive churning occurs because the assets favored by low-wealth households (checking accounts and passbook savings accounts) are fixed in value, while the value of highly wealth-elastic assets such as stocks, bonds, and real estate fluctuate with market forces. As Table 5–3 shows, between the 1962 and 1970 survey dates, savings accounts and U.S. Treasury bills both returned about 12.5 percent after inflation while common stock and single-family homes both appreciated 28 percent. However, in the 1970–77 period, while liquid investments in Treasury bills held their real value only slightly better than savings accounts did, stocks and houses appreciated at greatly divergent rates. As stock prices rose less than 8 percent, the value of single-family homes increased 85.4 percent. Even ignoring the implicit or shelter services a house provides, over 1970–77 housing investments far outperformed financial assets.

Real-estate and stock prices move in response to private economic forces such as exogenous movements in construction costs, to demographic pressures, and to government taxes and subsidies. In particular, much of the active and passive churning observed in the 1960s and 1970s was driven by the interaction of unanticipatedly accelerating

Table 5-3. Estimates of Cumulative Price Appreciation and Cumulative Inflation-Adjusted Total Returns on Selected Assets between Survey Dates (percentage).

	Cumulative Percentage Price Appreciation			*Inflation-Adjusted Cumulative Price Appreciation in Constant-Quality Houses*	*Inflation-Adjusted Cumulative Total Returns*			
	in Deflator for Personal Consumption Expenditures	*in Prices of Common Stock*	*in Price of Constant-Quality House*		*on Common Stock*	*on Long-Term Government Bonds*	*on U.S. Treasury Bills*	*on Savings Accounts at S&L's*
February 1962 to March 1970	25.7	28.1	27.8	1.7	32.2	-16.8	12.5	12.3
March 1970 to September 1977	52.5	7.7	85.4	21.6	-6.5	11.4	-1.1	-3.4
February 1962 to September 1977	91.7	38.0	137 0	23.6	23.7	-7.4	11.3	8.5

Source: *Business Cycle Developments* (monthly) for PCE Deflator. Ibbotson and Sinquefield (1979) for price appreciation and nominal total returns on stocks, bonds, and bills. C-27 Construction Reports for Second Quarter 1981 for appreciation in constant-quality houses. *Savings and Loan Fact Book* (Annual) for yields on savings accounts at S&L's.

Notes: Appreciation in PCE deflator and housing prices are calculated from the first quarter of 1962 to the first quarter of 1970 and from the latter quarter to the third quarter of 1977. Yields on savings accounts are compounded using annual figures for 1962–69 and 1970–76. During the 1970s, due to growing role of certificate accounts, these yields moved increasingly above ceiling rates on passbook accounts. Every inflation-adjusted return is calculated from the ratio of one plus the cumulative nominal return in source data to one plus the cumulative rate of appreciation in the PCE deflator over the same period.

inflation with the inherited structure of deposit-rate ceilings, deposit insurance, federal income taxes, and housing subsidies. Households also responded to changes in taxes and regulations that authorities made, after a lag, to adapt taxes and regulatory policies to ongoing inflation.

For households, the federal income tax is nonneutral with respect to inflation in two principal ways. First, capital-gains taxes (though set typically at only a fraction of tax rates on ordinary income) are levied even when purely nominal price increases are realized in the sale of physical assets. Second, federal taxes are levied progressively on *nominal* incomes. For both reasons, inflation tends over time to push given levels of real personal income into potentially higher and higher tax brackets. Bracket drift simultaneously puts pressure on Congress to lower statutory tax rates and raises the incentive for households to engage in tax-avoidance activity. Estimates of average marginal tax rates on personal income show a small upward drift between survey dates (Barro and Sahasakul 1983). Moreover, the changing *structure* of tax rates, particularly on explicit capital income as documented by Estrella and Fuhrer (1983), ought to have affected various types of households differently.

During 1970–77, effective tax rates on capital gains were increased in several ways. First, over 1970–72, the maximum tax rate on long-term capital gains was increased in three steps to 35 percent. However, until 1978 the tax rate on the first $50,000 of an individual's capital gains was capped at 25 percent. Second, the holding period necessary to qualify a capital asset for preferential long-term capital-gains treatment was raised from six months to nine months in 1977 and to one year in 1978. Third, beginning in 1970, net long-term capital losses of $1,000 or less could no longer be deducted *in full* against ordinary income. Henceforth, only 50 percent of these losses could be deducted, again up to a maximum deduction of $1,000 (now $3,000) in any tax year.

It is widely believed that because service returns and capital gains from investments in owner-occupied housing continued to be treated preferentially throughout the 1970s, unanticipated increases in inflation and inflation risk tended to raise the price of owner-occupied homes relative to stock prices (DeLeeuw and Ozanne 1979; Summers 1981; Hendershott and Hu 1983).[2] Tax preferences accorded owner-occupied housing include nontaxation of the value of the services provided by an owner-occupied home, the capacity for repeated deferrals of capital gains due on changes in residence, and a once-in-a-lifetime forgiveness of some of the capital-gains taxes that would otherwise be due on the sale of a principal residence once the seller has attained a designated age. Before July 26, 1978, gains on the sale of a principal residence with an adjusted sales price of $35,000 or less were not taxable for sellers who were age 65 or older and who had occupied the residence for five of the eight years preceding the sale. In cases where the adjusted sales price exceeded $35,000, sellers who met the age and occupancy tests could still exclude a portion of the gain from taxation. In 1978 the critical age was lowered to 55, the occupancy rule shortened to three of five years, and the excludable amount raised to $100,000. (While not strictly indexed with inflation, the maximum exclusion has since been raised to $125,000.) Although the alteration in the capital-gains tax forgiveness on sales of homes occurred after the 1977 survey date, it would not have found a place on the legislative agenda unless households who were in or approaching the 55–64 age range were fighting for it politically during the preceding years. The cost of mobilizing political resources to extract a new tax advantage suggests that during the 1970s many so-called empty-nest households must have been contemplating the sale of what had become in terms of its size or implied burden of school taxes an inappropriate house.

It should be clear that the value of the in-kind services a house performs for its occupants varies with the composition of the household residing in it. Because these services are not taxed for owner-occupants, changes in the structure of explicit taxes differentially affect implicit rates of return on rental and owner-occupied types of housing.

Leveraged investments in housing financed with regulatorily subsidized fixed-rate mortgages benefited additionally from unanticipated inflation. Unanticipated inflation lowers the real burden of fixed-rate mortgage debt (see Hendershott and Hu 1981). With returns on financial instruments distorted by deposit-rate ceilings and multiple regulatory subsidization of homeownership and home financing (see Kane 1981), no other easily available financial transaction offered established or growing households of low or average wealth as high an anticipated real after-tax rate of return or as favorable a hedge against unanticipated inflation.

Extended to savings-and-loan associations in 1966, ceilings on nominal interest rates payable on deposits discriminated against low-wealth households. Regulators selectively relaxed these ceilings in the 1970s by tying differences in ceiling rates on certificate accounts to differences in maturity and minimum denominations. This helped deposit institutions to discriminate more effectively between interest-sensitive and interest-insensitive low-wealth customers. As Table 5–3 shows, this discrimination pushed inflation-adjusted explicit returns in the 1970s on savings accounts below those on Treasury bills and left them sharply negative for passbook savings.

Opportunities to counterbalance the negative real after-tax rates of explicit returns on deposit assets differed with the level of household wealth. For wealthy households, they differed also between the 1960s and 1970s. In either era, wealthy households could better extract a compensating stream of implicit returns from deposit institutions and move wealth more efficiently into stocks and bonds. Transactions costs and the risks of being underdiversified made these avenues less feasible for low-wealth households. Similarly, when money-market mutual funds (whose rate of growth first surged in 1974) and the variety of high-rate certificate-of-deposit (CD) accounts expanded in the 1970s, financial-market opportunities improved for households of moderate and high wealth. But these changes did little for low-wealth investors. Throughout the period of observation, while wealthy households could reallocate their portfolios to escape most of the ex ante burden that anticipated inflation and deposit-rate regulation would otherwise place on them, poor households were more tightly constrained. Two principal avenues of adjustment were open to low-wealth households: (1) to make highly leveraged investments in housing and durable goods and (2) to cut back their overall rate of saving.

This study focuses on transactable and noncontractual savings, forms of household wealth that are not administered by outside parties such as insurance companies, pension funds, and the Social Security System. However, we must recognize that wealth accumulated in contractual arrangements should, as explained in Munnell (1981), condition a household's decisions about how to accumulate and to manage transactable wealth. Whatever life cycle in portfolio structure we observe must be interpreted in the light of the lifetime pattern of simultaneous and partly exogenous growth in the risk-adjusted present value of households' pension-fund and social security claims.[3] In 1972 the decision to increase real social security benefits and to double-index them to an upwardly biased consumer price index may be interpreted as a governmental redistribution of wealth from younger to older households. This redistribution, which also reduced older households' exposure to inflation risk, might have altered each group's need for transactable saving.

Focal Hypotheses Concerning Differential Savings Behavior

We hypothesize that a household's effective saving rate over any period varies with its place in the life cycle, its size, and the marital status of its head. We further hypothesize that as the economic and financial environment changes, class-level saving rates and portfolio structures vary actively as well as passively. Passively, any class of households tends to gain or lose wealth relative to other classes whenever assets in which that class historically maintains a disproportionately large position experience an unanticipated increase or decrease in value. This hypothesis implies that on average windfall gains and losses on particular assets impact saving as well as consumption. Asset revaluation is only partly offset by readjustments in the level and composition of new savings. (In fact, using longitudinal data, Jianakoplos (1983, 1984) is unable to reject the hypothesis that no readjustment takes place at all.) Actively, households in any class adapt their portfolios to differential movements in the net after-tax risk-adjusted real returns anticipated on different assets. Because anticipated returns were not observed for survey respondents, the institutional facts developed in the previous section are used along with the ex post returns listed in Table 5-3 as proxies for the set of information on which a rational respondent would have conditioned his or her rate-of-return forecasts. Particular stress is placed on the roles played by three factors: differential changes in implicit returns on owner-occupied housing, the 1966 expansion of deposit-rate regulation and its subsequent decline in effectiveness, and the level of a household's wealth as a restraint on incentives to engage in disintermediation.

To examine what we may call the life-cycle, family-size, and marital-status hypotheses, we develop a series of statistical tables. The first two tables present evidence on differences in propensities to save and in patterns of real wealth accumulation. These tables are reported for every sample partition we examine. Other tables track differences in class-level positions in particular assets. These tables throw light on the extent to which active and passive portfolio churning may be observed at the class-level.

Although portfolio churning is examined in detail only for age classes, we compare summary distributions for all sample partitions of class-level positions in selected financial and real-estate assets with the percentage of sample families in each class. These tables amount to a series of Lorenz curves for assets.

For age classes and age cohorts, various additional tables are developed. Two of these disaggregate percentage and dollar changes in class-level wealth across specific financial and real-estate opportunities. These tables support inferences about the allocation of new saving. A third table reports mean wealth and homeownership and mortgagor rates for each class. Finally, for age classes only, wealth-based Engels curves are estimated for four types of financial and real-estate investments. Differences in Engels-curve coefficients are tested both across survey dates and across age classes at each date. This analysis provides additional evidence on the extent of active and passive portfolio churning.

Observed Shifts in Life-Cycle Savings Patterns

Tables 5–4 through 5–9 compare households at identical stages of the life cycle across time. Table 5–4 focuses on mean savings in dollars and on ratios of real (that is, inflation-adjusted) saving to real income. The ratios reported in the table tend to overstate the magnitude of age-class average propensities to save because incomes reported by survey respondents tend to be understated. Survey responses are subject to deliberate underreporting and omit imputed income such as unrealized capital gains, the services of owner-occupied housing, and implicit interest received as subsidized accountholder services from deposit institutions.

This error in measurement tends to raise reported saving-to-income ratios for all groups. If we ignore possible differences in measurement errors across demographic classes, Table 5–4 indicates that during the 1960s households whose heads were at least age 55 saved a much larger percentage of their real incomes than younger persons did. Moreover, unless it reflects age-related reporting bias in 1977 home equity or

Table 5-4. Incremental Mean Savings and Per-Year Real Saving Rates between Survey Dates, for Households in Specific Age Classes.

	1962 to 1970		1970 to 1977		
Age of Household Head (in years)	*Dollar Increment in Mean Transactable Wealth*	*Real Increment Per Year as a Percentage of Mean Real Income in the Two Survey Years*	*Dollar Increment in Mean Transactable Wealth*	*Real Increment Per Year as a Percentage of Mean Real Income in the Two Survey Years*	*Difference in Real Savings Rate between Eras (percentage)*
Under age 25	–607	-2.6	6,316	8.3	10.9
25 to 34	2,074	1.0	13,414	8.4	7.4
35 to 44	9,140	6.9	23,670	8.8	1.9
45 to 54	6,030	2.0	37,437	17.8	15.8
55 to 64	21,566	24.5	22,717	2.4	-22.1
65 and older	22,250	44.8	3,068	-29.2	-74.0
All respondents	10,683	10.5	18,178	5.6	–4.9

Note: Calculated from data tapes of the 1977 Consumer Credit Survey and of the 1962 and 1970 Surveys of Consumer Finances. Real values are calculated by multiplying base-date wealth and income by one plus the cumulative rate of change between survey dates in the deflator for personal consumption expenditures.

unanticipated passive appreciation of existing portfolio holdings, the high rate of accumulation observed in the 1960s for households in the age 65-and-over category is hard to reconcile with the life-cycle theory. But increased life-cycle decumulation by older households and the hypothesized redistributive impact of social security indexing is consistent with the turnaround between the 1960s and the 1970s in effective patterns of life-cycle saving reported in the table. This pattern pivots like a mirror image around the breakpoint observed at age 55. Below this age, households increased their effective saving rates substantially during the 1970s. However, over the same period, older households greatly reduced their effective saving rates. Comparing 1972–73 with 1962 behavior in an income-expenditure data set, Lieberman and Wachtel (1980) report a similarly sharp decline in the savings rate of older households that predates the 1972 adjustment in social security benefits.

Table 5–5 reports cumulative growth rates for mean nominal wealth and mean real wealth. As explained in the note to the table, the cumulative rate of increase in real wealth is calculated from the ratio of mean end-date wealth to inflation-adjusted base-date wealth. The table provides further evidence that age-group wealth trajectories differed sharply between the two periods. During the 1960s, wealth accumulation by households whose heads were age 55 and older greatly outpaced the savings growth achieved by younger households. In the 1970–77 period, the reverse proves true. Although two-thirds of the population of sample households were on balance net savers during the 1970s, these households were the youngest ones. Because the proportion of transactable wealth controlled by households in the designated age classes rises on average with the age of the household head, the pooled growth rate in real saving fell by almost two-thirds.

Table 5–6 shows means dollar increments experienced in three broad components of net transactable wealth: retail financial assets (deposits and savings bonds), wholesale financial assets (stocks and bonds), and equity in real estate (value of real-estate assets less mortgage debt). To allow readers to unravel the effect of mortgage leverage, an additional column describes the cumulative increase in the market value of real-estate assets. The table indicates that for households above and below age 55 differential rates of wealth accumulation spread across portfolio categories during the 1970s but (in keeping with the wealth constraint on opportunities for disintermediation)

Table 5-5. Cumulative Percentage Change in the Real and Nominal Value of Accumulated Mean Savings between Survey Dates, by Age of Household Head (percentage).

Age of Household Head (in years)	*Cumulative Percentage Change in Mean Net Wealth between 1962 and 1970*		*Cumulative Percentage Change in Mean Net Wealth between 1970 and 1977*	
	Nominal Wealth	*Real Wealth*	*Nominal Wealth*	*Real Wealth*
Under age 25	-28.5	-43.1	413.8	237.0
25 to 34	41.4	12.5	189.2	89.6
35 to 44	77.4	41.1	113.0	39.7
45 to 54	37.4	9.1	168.0	75.7
55 to 64	131.0	83.8	59.7	4.8
65 and older	121.5	76.2	7.6	-29.5
All respondents	88.4	49.9	79.8	17.9

Note: Percentage changes in real wealth employ base-date wealth that has been inflated by cumulative growth in the implicit deflator for personal consumption expenditures (PCE) figured from either the first quarter of 1962 to the second quarter of 1970 or from the latter quarter to the third quarter of 1977, as appropriate. Let c represent cumulative growth in the deflator for PCE between survey dates and W_0 and W_1 represent mean base-date and end-date wealth, respectively. The cumulative percentage growth rate in real wealth is calculated as $[W_1 - (1 + c)W_0]/(1 + c)W_0$.

that differences observed during the 1960s were dominated by differences in the flow of new savings into wholesale financial assets.

Table 5-7 illustrates the proportionate weight carried by real-estate investment as a vehicle of household wealth accumulation. Real-estate equity is defined as the difference between the market value of real estate owned and the book value of mortgage debt secured by these holdings.[4] This variable is dominated by equity in homes. For survey respondents in the 1960s and 1970s, real-estate equity carried roughly 60 percent of the overall increase in mean household wealth.

For each survey date, Table 5-8 shows the distribution across age classes of retail financial assets (deposits and savings bonds), wholesale financial assets (stocks and marketable bonds), real-estate equity, net transactable wealth, and the value of owner-occupied housing. This table presents something like a Lorenz curve for age classes. It lets us see that the age structure of the population interacts with life-

Table 5-6. Dollar Increments between Survey Dates in the Mean Values of Real-Estate Assets and Three Components of Net Transactable Wealth, by Age of Household Head (dollars).

Age of Household Head (in years)	*Between 1962 and 1970*				*Between 1970 and 1977*			
	Retail Financial Assets	*Wholesale Financial Assets*	*Real-Estate Equity*	*Real-Estate Assets*	*Retail Financial Assets*	*Wholesale Financial Assets*	*Real-Estate Equity*	*Real-Estate Assets*
Under age 25	272	-1,098	218	1,348	1,732	1,595	2,988	3,848
25 to 34	458	-35	1,652	3,916	2,339	2,535	8,542	14,539
35 to 44	1,471	694	6,981	11,429	4,020	2,995	16,665	21,936
45 to 54	1,135	-929	5,830	8,678	5,982	10,873	20,664	24,387
55 to 64	3,550	7,522	10,538	12,095	5,283	4,051	13,537	15,092
65 and older	3,664	8,176	10,409	11,167	4,182	-6,338	5,279	5,079
All respondents	1,880	2,439	6,372	8,518	4,068	2,684	11,464	14,441

Source: Author's calculations.

Table 5-7. Distribution of Cumulative Changes in the Nominal Value of Mean Transactable Wealth between Survey Dates, by Age of Household Head (percentage).

Age of Household Head (in years)	*Percentage of 1962–70 Increase Attributable to:*			*Percentage of 1970–77 Increase Attributable to:*		
	Retail Financial Assets	*Wholesale Financial Assets*	*Real-Estate Equity*	*Retail Financial Assets*	*Wholesale Financial Assets*	*Real-Estate Equity*
Under age 25	-44.8[a]	180.9[a]	-36.0[a]	27.4	25.3	47.3
25 to 34	22.1	-1.7	79.6	17.4	18.9	63.7
35 to 44	16.1	7.6	76.4	17.0	12.7	70.4
45 to 54	18.8	-15.4	96.7	16.0	29.0	55.2
55 to 64	16.5	34.9	48.9	23.3	17.8	59.6
65 and older	16.5	36.7	46.8	136.3	-206.6	172.1
All respondents	17.6	22.8	59.6	22.4	14.8	63.1

a. Because nominal wealth declined for this age class during the 1962–70 period, the signs of the percentage allocations are the reverse of observed portfolio movements. In fact, holdings of wholesale assets declined while the other two portfolio components increased.

Table 5–8. Distribution of Selected Assets and Respondent Population across Age Classes at 1962, 1970, and 1977 Survey Dates (percentage).

Age of Household Head (in years)	*Retail Financial Assets*	*Wholesale Financial Assets*	*Real-Estate Equity*	*Net Transactable Wealth*	*Value of Homes*	*Respondent Population*	*Number of Respondents*
1962 Survey							
Under age 25	1.7	5.1	0.6	1.6	0.6	9.1	192
25 to 34	8.5	5.5	8.7	8.1	13.5	19.5	413
35 to 44	16.5	25.6	23.9	22.8	29.3	23.4	495
45 to 54	21.2	29.3	26.8	26.2	26.6	19.5	413
55 to 64	17.6	17.9	18.3	18.1	15.1	13.3	281
65 and older	34.4	16.5	21.8	23.1	14.9	15.3	323
All respondents	99.9	99.9	100.1	99.9	100.0	100.1	2,117
1970 Survey							
Under age 25	1.7	0.3	0.5	0.7	1.5	10.0	257
25 to 34	6.4	2.3	6.6	5.7	12.5	18.3	471
35 to 44	14.0	12.6	20.0	17.4	24.3	18.9	488
45 to 54	17.3	10.1	23.3	19.5	24.9	20.0	514
55 to 64	26.1	37.5	24.8	27.6	19.6	16.5	426
65 and older	34.6	37.2	24.8	29.0	17.2	16.3	420
All respondents	100.1	100.0	100.0	99.9	100.0	100.0	2,576

1977 Survey							
Under age 25	2.6	2.1	1.3	1.7	1.5	8.8	225
25 to 34	10.6	9.8	12.3	11.5	17.8	23.0	587
35 to 44	13.7	13.1	19.4	17.2	22.1	15.8	402
45 to 54	19.9	31.0	24.9	25.0	23.4	17.1	437
55 to 64	24.0	33.4	22.8	24.9	18.8	16.8	429
65 and older	29.1	10.6	19.3	19.7	16.3	18.5	472
All respondents	99.9	100.0	100.0	100.0	99.9	100.0	2,552

cycle patterns of asset accumulation to determine the share of national wealth controlled by a given age group. To assess the degree of wealth redistribution occurring across age classes between survey dates, it is useful to focus on changes in what we may call the *control ratio*: the percentage of net transactable wealth held per each 1 percent of respondents in a given age class. For this purpose, it is convenient to consolidate households into three age classes: under age 35, age 35 to 54, and age 55 and older. In 1962 older households held the greatest percentage control of transactable wealth. Their control ratio stood at 1.44, as against 1.14 for middle-aged households and 0.34 for young ones. Between 1962 and 1970, and in keeping with the savings rates shown in Tables 5-4 and 5-5, older households improved their control ratio even further, to 1.73 as against declines to 0.95 and 0.23 for middle-aged and young households, respectively. However, the high saving rates maintained by young and middle-aged households during the 1970s improved their 1977 ratios. In 1977 the control ratios were 0.42, 1.28, and 1.26, respectively. If these changes were due only to passive portfolio churning, percentage control of component assets would not change at all. Contrary to the temporal variation shown in the data underlying Table 5-8, control ratios for individual asset categories (such as for the value of homes) would have to remain constant over time.

Table 5-9 shows that at each survey date mean wealth, homeownership rates, and use of mortgage leveraging differed across age groups. For the first of these variables, the table also reports the standard error of the mean. Even allowing for age-level differences in leverage, variation in the percentage of wealth allocated to leveraged investments in housing across age-group portfolios made *passive* opportunities to benefit from unanticipated inflation in 1962 lowest for very young households and highest for middle-aged ones. This table provides evidence that unanticipated returns on accumulated wealth cannot account fully for the turnaround in the age profile of effective savings performance during the 1970s. New saving by young households is suggested by their establishing a steadily higher percentage of homeownership. Even allowing for the bias in our estimates of age-class homeownership rates, the table suggests that during the 1970s, some empty-nest housing was bid away from households in the 55-and-over age group.[5] Given young families' typically high use of leverage in their housing investments, their expanded homeownership rates repositioned them to realize portfolio gains from anticipated and unanticipated inflation.

Table 5-9. Homeownership Rate, Mortgage Status, and Mean Dollar Value of Net Transactable Wealth in 1962, 1970, and 1977, by Age of Household Head.

Age of Household Head (in years)	1962			1970			1977		
	Mean Dollar Value of Transactable Wealth	*Percentage Owning Home*	*Percentage of Homeowners with Mortgage Debt*	*Mean Dollar Value of Transactable Wealth*	*Percentage Owning Home*	*Percentage of Homeowners with Mortgage Debt*	*Mean Dollar Value of Transactable Wealth*	*Percentage Owning Home*	*Percentage of Homeowners with Mortgage Debt*
Under age 25	2,133 (934)	5.2	80.0	1,526 (192)	11.7	90.0	7,843 (1,652)	20.0 (20.9)	80.0 (80.9)
25 to 34	5,015 (564)	43.1	84.3	7,090 (735)	47.8	90.2	20,504 (2,147)	54.3 (56.5)	88.4 (88.0)
35 to 44	11,807 (1,913)	63.4	81.2	20,948 (2,167)	70.9	86.4	44,618 (3,688)	72.9 (77.9)	84.6 (83.1)
45 to 54	16,258 (1,288)	68.5	61.1	22,288 (1,338)	73.7	64.6	59,726 (5,159)	74.6 (81.0)	73.3 (70.3)
55 to 64	16,459 (1,551)	68.3	40.1	38,025 (5,352)	77.0	32.9	60,743 (5,223)	71.1 (79.0)	45.9 (42.8)
65 and older	18,312 (1,835)	63.2	15.2	40,563 (5,023)	71.2	16.4	43,631 (3,093)	64.4 (79.4)	15.5 (13.6)
All respondents	12,083 (646)	55.8	58.8	22,766 (1,334)	62.4	57.9	40,944 (1,613)	62.4 (69.0)	62.3 (58.8)

Note: The U.S. Bureau of the Census estimates that the aggregate homeownership rate was 62.9 percent in 1970 and 64.8 percent in 1977 (Carliner 1982). In the mean-wealth columns, the standard error of mean wealth is given in parentheses. In the percentage ownership and mortgagor columns for 1977, the figures in parentheses report corresponding values for the unedited sample. For age-class homeownership rates, the standard error of the mean rounds to 0.1 percent in all but two instances, where it rounds to 0.2 percent.

TESTING FOR SHIFTS IN WEALTH-HOLDING PATTERNS

Survey data show that wealth-holding patterns differ both across age groups and across time. This section fits these patterns into a framework of optimal choice.

Modern portfolio theory portrays balance-sheet choices as allocating wealth in response to variation in the mean vector and covariance matrix of asset returns (Friedman 1982). In this application, these choices should be conditioned by unobserved differences in the composition of an individual's holdings of nonmarketable assets such as pension claims and human capital (Mayers 1973). Taxes and transactions costs may (at least as an interpretive first approximation) both be presumed to vary with portfolio size. However, the means and covariances of asset returns (although not necessarily the marginal risks) should be the same for all households at each date. Hence, a particularly straightforward way to explain differences in asset-holding patterns is to estimate for every age group at each survey date a set of wealth-based Engels curves for the main components of transactable wealth. We may interpret each curve as showing how the increment in wealth that a household desires to place in a particular portfolio component varies with the level of household wealth.

Using a quadratic approximation, we estimated wealth-based Engels curves for retail financial assets, wholesale financial assets, home equity, and equity in investment real estate. To conserve space, we merely summarize the results here. Because reported portfolio positions in these assets never fall below zero, a Tobit limited-dependent-variable estimation procedure was employed. Respecting individual balance-sheet constraints, when the censored-regression equations for any age class are summed across the four portfolio opportunities, the wealth coefficients must sum to one, while the intercepts and wealth-squared terms must each sum to zero. Except for the 65-and-over age class in 1977, mean wealth rises with age. To show how much the first derivative of the mean portfolio position with respect to wealth departs from the regression coefficient for wealth, we defined an "adjusted coefficient" equal to the product of the wealth-squared coefficient with twice mean wealth. The sum of this adjusted coefficient and the regression coefficient for wealth represents the marginal proportion of mean wealth allocated to the asset class in question.

Although deviations between the mean marginal proportion and the wealth coefficient range up to 0.125 in magnitude, the median adjustment is less than 0.05. Of course, for very wealthy households deviations are much larger.

This evidence shows that across age groups and dates, portfolio positions in all four portfolio categories generally increase with household wealth. The major differences concern life-cycle differences in allocation patterns and the sensitivity of incremental allocation rates to the level of wealth. For most age groups, what we may call the marginal propensity to hold retail financial assets and real-estate equity decreases with wealth. On the other hand, the marginal propensity to hold wholesale financial assets increases with wealth.

Estimated differences in the wealth sensitivity of the various marginal propensities accord broadly with conventional wisdom about the role of transactions costs, minimum denominations, and difficulties in arranging credit as barriers to investment by low-wealth households in wholesale financial assets and investment real estate (Kane 1980). As compared to low-wealth households, high-wealth households should hold retail financial assets more for liquidity and diversification purposes than as vehicles for maximal accumulation of expected future wealth.

For retail financial assets, wholesale financial assets, and (to reduce the number of computer runs) the sum of the two kinds of equity in real-estate, formal tests were conducted of differences in coefficient estimates across age classes and across survey dates. These tests apply one-zero dummy variables for specific dates and age classes to all three parameters in the model.

Differences in Engels coefficients across time may be attributed to differences in the mean vector and covariance matrix of anticipated risk-adjusted after-tax returns on the component assets at different dates, to differences in the range of wealth observed, and to sampling error as well. Differences in coefficients across age groups reflect differences in life-cycle status, effective transactions costs, and range of wealth observed, as well as sampling error once again.

Coefficient Differences across Age Groups

On a cross-section basis, we are interested at each survey date in the significance of differences in coefficient estimates across age classes.

If significant differences did not exist, studying age-class Engels curves for assets would have no statistical justification.

Although the detailed results are not reported here, we used slope and intercept dummy variables to test the significance of differences between coefficient estimates for every age-class pair. For all equations, in both 1962 and 1977 significant differences prove to be the rule rather than the exception. On average in these years, two-thirds of the slope coefficients and 40 percent of the intercepts differ significantly from the corresponding estimates for other classes. In 1970 only about one-fifth of the coefficient pairs differ significantly, with significant differences particularly rare in the equation for real-estate equity. We interpret the similarity of coefficient pairs in 1970 as evidence that wealth-related constraints on a household's ability to engage in disintermediation temporarily became a more important force in portfolio allocation than life-cycle considerations.

Coefficient Differences over Time

Tobit estimates indicate that for retail financial assets, wholesale financial assets and real-estate equity, more than half of the estimated slope coefficients differ significantly across survey dates. The significance of coefficient differences is somewhat more frequent for the quadratic than for the linear term. This is important because an individual's marginal allocation to a given asset deviates from the wealth coefficient by the product of the coefficient for the quadratic term and twice the individual's level of wealth.

The pattern of differences observed is consistent with the hypothesis that the benefits of financial disintermediation increase with household wealth. Although importantly constrained by the evolving structure of taxes and transactions costs, households actively reallocated their portfolios to protect themselves against the interaction of ceilings on explicit nominal rates of interest on deposit assets with rising market rates of interest.

Between 1962 and 1970 older households increased their propensity to hold wholesale assets and decreased their propensity to hold retail assets and home equity. Although households in the under-45 group increased their marginal propensity to hold retail assets, this propensity to hold financial assets of either kind became more sensitive to increases with wealth. Older and wealthier households showed a reduced disposition to hold retail financial assets and a higher propensity to invest in more-volatile wholesale securities. The resulting increase in the demand for brokerage services drove up transactions costs in wholesale markets, especially for small trades (Kane 1980). These transactions-cost increases reinforced the attractiveness to very-young families of leveraged investments in homes, bringing about a reverse shift in wealth propensities for younger households.

Schemes for paying implicit interest on household deposits (such as "free" checking) proliferated in the 1970s, and the regulatory strategy shifted to one of letting the ceiling rate on a deposit account more closely approach its market level the larger the account's minimum denomination and the longer its stated maturity. In addition, as shown in Table 5-3, 1970-77 holding-period returns on stocks and Treasury bills proved negative in real terms. For at least some of these reasons, as our data show, between 1970 and 1977 retail assets regained their former attractiveness to older households, while wholesale assets lost some of their luster. Young and middle-aged families generally increased their propensity to allocate wealth to real estate, while this propensity declined significantly for (nonmarried) households in the 65-and-over age group.

ACCUMULATIONS BY AGE COHORTS

Another way to look at patterns of life-cycle saving is to study how the mean net worth of a particular age cohort behaves as members of the cohort grow older. Here, the focus falls on transitions through a prolonged preretirement phase of average wealth accumulation into a hypothesized phase of planned wealth decumulation.

Table 5-10 pushes forward the age cohorts reported in Table 5-4 and 5-5 for the 1962 and 1970 surveys to develop comparable data for appropriately older respondents in the 1970 and 1977 surveys. The table deletes the wealth of household heads that were under age 18 in 1962 and 1970 and therefore too young to be sampled. Following age classes through time provides something akin to a panel perspective on patterns of life-cycle saving. We see that in all cohorts households managed to increase their mean real net worth from 1962 to 1970. However, the second panel shows that during the 1970s the per-year rate of real accumulation increased dramatically for the

Table 5-10. Changes in the Real and Nominal Value of Accumulated Mean Savings between Survey Dates, by Age Cohorts Determined by the Age of a Household Head in 1962 and 1970 (percentage).

Age of Household Head at the Later Survey Date (in years)	*Dollar Increment in Mean Transactable Wealth*	*Cumulative Percentage Change in Mean Net Wealth*		*Accumulated Mean Real Saving Per Year as a Percentage of Mean Survey-Date Real Incomes*
		Nominal Wealth	*Real Wealth*	
1962 age cohorts in 1970				
26 to 33	3,928	184.1	126.1	9.6
33 to 42	12,643	252.1	180.1	13.3
43 to 52	11,478	97.2	56.9	9.6
53 to 62	19,745	121.4	76.2	18.7
63 to 72	24,207	147.1	96.6	33.8
73 and older	20,092	109.7	66.8	43.8
All cohorts	13,484	111.6	68.3	14.0
1962 age cohorts in 1977				
33 to 40	35,713	1,673.8	825.6	16.7
40 to 49	43,841	874.1	408.2	15.4
50 to 59	49,863	422.3	172.5	15.5
60 to 69	42,679	262.5	89.1	13.4
70 to 79	24,989	151.8	31.4	6.8
80 and older	14,276	78.0	-7.2	-2.8
All cohorts	38,568	319.2	118.7	12.8
1970 age cohorts in 1977				
25 to 31	15,226	997.4	619.9	16.8
32 to 41	32,390	456.8	265.1	22.2
42 to 51	31,207	149.0	63.3	13.8
52 to 61	41,102	184.4	86.5	21.8
62 to 71	16,321	42.9	-6.3	-3.9
72 and older	-4,287	-10.6	-41.4	-44.2
All cohorts	21,378	93.9	27.2	8.2

Note: See notes to Tables 5-4 and 5-5.

youngest 1962 cohort, decreased for the fourth cohort (some of whom were passing into the retirement stage), and turned negative for the two oldest cohorts. The third panel, which compares post-sample accumulation rates for 1962 and 1970 cohorts, shows a similar picture.

Economic theory treats changes in saving rates as adaptive responses to changing requirements for consumption smoothing. In the 1970s the two oldest cohorts experienced consumption-expanding windfall gains in wealth from two sources: the double-indexing of social-security benefits and unanticipated appreciation in real housing prices. For these cohorts, the desirability of decumulating transactable wealth may have been further enhanced by the structure of capital-gains taxes and declines in reported mean real incomes of 20 and 30 percent, respectively. If the two youngest cohorts' sharply higher savings rates represents consumption smoothing too, it may be due mainly to unanticipated increases in the capitalized real value of fulfilling their lifetime housing needs. We show in the next section that families with three or more children (for whom the average implicit return on housing space is greatest) greatly increased their mean saving rate in the 1970s, while smaller families drastically reduced theirs. Given the secularly rising divorce rate, in the 1970s some small-sized families may have been adapting to a reduction in family size.

To carry out plans to increase their mean rate of homeownership in the 1970s, many young households may have postponed the consumption of other goods and services. Although SRC data do not bear on this issue, young households may also have perceived secular growth in the size of government transfer programs as increasing the discounted real value of their lifetime tax bills.

Tables 5–11 and 5–12 provide evidence on the composition of age-cohort savings across different survey dates. Mean dollar increments in the values of real-estate assets and of three components of net transactable wealth are shown in Table 5–11. Data on real-estate assets are included to permit the interested reader to decompose increases in real-estate equity into price-appreciation, portfolio-rebalancing, and debt-expansion elements. Although component-by-component growth rates vary widely across age classes and asset categories (from -61.2 percent to 5,181.5 percent), Table 5–12 clarifies that for every age class whose mean nominal wealth increased (that is, all but the age 72-and-older group in 1970–77), real-estate equity served in both periods as the major vehicle for carrying increased wealth across time.

Table 5-11. Dollar Increments between Survey Dates in the Mean Value of Real-Estate Assets and Three Components of Net Transactable Wealth, by Age Cohorts Determined by the Age of a Household Head in 1962 and 1970 (dollars).

Age of Household Head (in years)	*Retail Financial Assets*	*Wholesale Financial Assets*	*Real-Estate Equity*	*Real-Estate Assets*
1962 age cohorts in 1970				
26 to 33	846	-842	3,928	9,516
33 to 42	1,891	2,107	8,647	13,315
43 to 52	1,744	235	9,505	12,458
53 to 62	3,170	5,789	10,823	11,175
63 to 72	5,546	7,298	11,362	11,326
73 and older	4,298	7,890	7,902	7,952
All cohorts	2,324	3,029	8,141	10,727
1962 age cohorts in 1977				
33 to 40	5,522	4,705	25,486	40,554
40 to 49	6,815	6,455	30,628	38,718
50 to 59	9,940	11,189	28,937	31,953
60 to 69	9,668	8,485	24,622	23,885
70 to 79	11,259	826	12,902	11,715
80 and older	4,079	3,665	6,531	6,392
All cohorts	7,882	6,828	23,931	28,863
1970 age cohorts in 1977				
25 to 31	2,212	1,989	11,031	21,325
32 to 41	4,564	5,941	21,894	30,464
42 to 51	5,932	6,526	18,788	19,671
52 to 61	7,954	11,958	21,387	22,410
62 to 71	6,796	-1,965	11,560	10,428
72 and older	3,140	-6,436	-991	-1,929
All cohorts	4,624	3,222	13,578	17,097

Lorenz distributions for age cohorts are displayed in Table 5-13. For each asset category, percentage control ratios are reported in parentheses. These control percentages show the relative position that a representative household takes in each type of wealth as it ages. For most assets and dates, the control percentage follows a humped or inverted-U curve. The typical curve reaches its maximum in middle

Table 5-12. Distribution of Cumulative Percentage Change in the Nominal Value of Mean Transactable Wealth between Survey Dates, by Age of Cohorts Determined by the Age of Household Head in 1962 and 1970 (percentage).

Age of 1962 Cohorts in 1977 (in years)	*Percentage of 1962–77 Increase Comprised by:*			*Age of 1970 Cohorts in 1977 (in years)*	*Percentage of 1970–77 Increase Comprised by:*		
	Retail Financial Assets	*Wholesale Financial Assets*	*Real-Estate Equity*		*Retail Financial Assets*	*Wholesale Financial Assets*	*Real-Estate Equity*
33 to 40	15.5	13.2	71.4	25 to 31	14.5	13.1	72.4
40 to 49	15.5	14.7	69.9	32 to 41	14.1	18.3	67.6
50 to 59	19.9	22.4	58.0	42 to 51	19.0	20.9	60.2
60 to 69	22.7	19.9	57.7	52 to 61	19.4	29.1	52.0
70 to 79	45.1	3.3	51.6	62 to 71	41.6	-12.0	70.8
80 and older	28.6	25.7	45.8	72 and older	-73.3	150.1	23.1
All cohorts	20.4	17.7	62.1	All cohorts	21.6	15.1	63.5

Table 5-13. Percentage Distribution of Selected Assets and of Respondent Population across Age Cohorts of the 1962 and 1970 Age Classes, at the 1970 and 1977 Survey Dates.

Age of Household Head (in years)	*Retail Financial Assets*	*Wholesale Financial Assets*	*Real-Estate Equity*	*Net Transactable Wealth*	*Percentage of Cohort Respondents*
1962 age cohorts in 1970					
25 to 33	4.2 (.28)	1.1 (.07)	4.2 (.28)	3.5 (.23)	14.9
33 to 42	13.1 (.63)	10.9 (.52)	15.9 (.76)	14.4 (.69)	20.8
43 to 52	16.9 (.73)	11.6 (.50)	25.4 (1.09)	21.1 (.91)	23.2
53 to 62	24.0 (1.22)	34.1 (1.74)	26.5 (1.35)	27.6 (1.41)	19.6
63 to 72	24.1 (1.88)	25.2 (1.97)	17.8 (1.39)	20.4 (1.59)	12.8
73 and older	17.7 (2.06)	17.0 (1.98)	10.3 (1.20)	13.0 (1.51)	8.6
Totals	100.0	99.9	100.1	100.0	99.9
1962 age cohorts in 1977					
33 to 40	10.4 (.59)	11.6 (.66)	14.4 (.82)	13.1 (.75)	17.5
40 to 49	16.3 (.77)	16.6 (.79)	22.7 (1.08)	20.3 (.96)	21.1
50 to 59	28.4 (1.13)	37.8 (1.51)	29.2 (1.16)	30.6 (1.22)	25.1
60 to 69	24.1 (1.19)	26.4 (1.31)	22.5 (1.11)	23.5 (1.16)	20.2
70 to 79	17.3 (1.42)	5.1 (.42)	9.1 (.75)	10.0 (.82)	12.2
80 and older	3.5 (.92)	2.6 (.68)	2.1 (.55)	2.5 (.66)	3.8
Totals	100.0	100.1	100.0	100.0	99.9

1970 age cohorts in 1977					
25 to 31	6.2 (.34)	5.0 (.27)	7.8 (.42)	7.0 (.38)	18.4
32 to 41	13.3 (.69)	16.1 (.83)	18.8 (.97)	17.3 (.90)	19.3
42 to 51	17.4 (1.03)	20.7 (1.22)	20.5 (1.21)	20.0 (1.18)	16.9
52 to 61	26.2 (1.30)	36.6 (1.82)	27.4 (1.36)	28.8 (1.43)	20.1
62 to 71	22.9 (1.53)	16.3 (1.09)	17.8 (1.19)	18.5 (1.23)	15.0
72 and older	14.0 (1.36)	5.4 (.52)	7.6 (.74)	8.5 (.83)	10.3
Totals	100.0	100.1	99.9	100.1	100.0

Note: The figures recorded in parentheses report the percentage of outstanding balances in each portfolio category controlled per each 1 percent of respondent population occupying the cohort.

age. Compared to financial assets, real-estate equity shows higher values for young cohorts and generally peaks at an earlier age. The control percentage for wholesale financial assets rises relative to retail assets as households move through their thirties and forties. Households in their fifties and early sixties hold the maximal percentage of wholesale assets, but this percentage falls off rapidly when they reach retirement age. Although for comparable age classes the percentage level of control varies across survey dates (presumably with differences in the economic environment), the qualitative association with the life cycle does not.

Table 5–14 focuses on changes in the homeownership rate and use of mortgage debt across time. Allowing for the extent to which the understatement of 1977 homeownership rates rises with age, the table provides time-series confirmation of cross-section evidence on life-cycle patterns of homeownership and mortgage repayment. Both within and across survey dates, homeownership rates are seen to rise into late middle age and to fall off thereafter, while the use of mortgage debt declines steadily as a household ages.

DIFFERENCES IN ACCUMULATION RATES FOR HOUSEHOLDS OF DIFFERENT SIZES

For many households, family size rises and falls over the life cycle in a humped pattern that parallels the rise and fall of age-class homeownership rates. This cycle in the size of the typical nuclear family reflects corresponding cycles in the market value of its human capital, in marginal in-kind rates of return on given amounts of housing space and school taxes, and in the household's detailed expenditure goals.

One-person households consist of bachelors, divorced and separated individuals, and widowed persons. The age distribution of this group may have distinct modes for each component class. The above-average age and high standard deviation shown for one-person households in Table 5–15 supports this presumption of multimodality.

Two-person households consist of childless couples, older "empty-nest" couples, widowed, divorced, and single parties with one child, and various combinations of unmarried adults. The high (though falling) average age reported for heads of two-person households in Table 5–15 is consistent with the hypothesis that the mean number of children in these households is small

Tables 5–16 and 5–17 show a sharp change in effective savings propensities between the 1960s and the 1970s paralleling the age-class

Table 5-14. Homeownership Rate and Mortgage Status in 1962, 1970, and 1977, by Age Cohorts Reflecting the Age of a Household Head in 1962 and 1970 (percentage).

Age of Household Head at Indicated Survey Date (in years)	1962			1970			1977		
	Number of Households	*Percentage Owning Home*	*Percentage of Homeowners with Mortgage Debt*	*Number of Households*	*Percentage Owning Home*	*Percentage of Homeowners with Mortgage Debt*	*Number of Households*	*Percentage Owning Home*	*Percentage of Homeowners with Mortgage Debt*
1962 age cohorts									
All under age 25	192	5.2	80.0	339	30.9	91.0	325	50.4	87.8
25 to 34	413	43.1	84.3	473	70.6	85.9	391	75.7	81.1
35 to 44	495	63.4	81.2	526	72.4	71.7	466	71.7	59.6
45 to 54	413	68.5	61.1	445	77.5	36.8	374	69.0	31.4
55 to 64	281	68.3	40.1	291	71.1	24.2	227	64.3	11.0
65 and older	323	63.2	15.2	196	71.9	9.2	71	59.2	7.1
All respondents	2,117	55.8	58.8	2,270	62.4	57.9	1,854	62.4	62.3
1970 age cohorts									
18 to 25				257	11.7	90.0	428	52.8	89.8
25 to 34				471	47.8	90.2	449	67.9	86.2
35 to 44				488	70.9	86.4	393	74.6	77.8
45 to 54				514	73.7	64.6	467	71.9	55.4
55 to 64				426	77.0	32.9	350	67.7	27.0
65 and older				420	71.2	16.4	240	62.5	8.0
All respondents classified				2,576	62.4	57.9	2,327	66.5	61.8

Table 5-15. Age of Heads of Households of Different Sizes in 1962, 1970, and 1977 (years).

Number of Persons in Household	*1962 Survey*		*1970 Survey*		*1977 Survey*	
	Mean Age	*Standard Deviation*	*Mean Age*	*Standard Deviation*	*Mean Age*	*Standard Deviation*
One	48.9	20.7	51.7	20.7	53.6	21.1
Two	54.4	16.2	53.8	17.5	51.8	18.1
Three or more	40.0	11.0	40.8	11.7	40.9	12.0
All respondents	45.5	16.1	46.5	16.5	46.9	17.3

Table 5-16. Accumulated Mean Savings in Dollars and Savings Per Year as a Percentage of Mean Survey-Date Incomes, for Households in Different Size Classes.

	1962 to 1970		*1970 to 1977*		
Number of Persons in Household	*Dollar Increment in Mean Transactable Wealth*	*Real Increment Per Year as a Percentage of Mean Real Income in the Two Survey Years*	*Dollar Increment in Mean Transactable Wealth*	*Real Increment Per Year as a Percentage of Mean Real Income in the Two Survey Years*	*Difference in Real Savings Rate between Eras (percentage)*
One	9,202	19.2	9,354	0.3	-18.9
Two	14,858	14.7	15,786	-1.4	-16.1
Three or more	7,736	5.8	23,319	10.1	4.3
All respondents	10,681	10.5	18,155	5.6	-4.9

Note: Same as Table 5-4.

Table 5-17. Cumulative Percentage Change in the Real and Nominal Value of Accumulated Savings between Survey Dates, for Households in Different Size Classes (percentage).

Number of Persons in Household	*Cumulative Percentage Change in Mean Net Wealth between 1962 and 1970*		*Cumulative Percentage Change in Mean Net Wealth between 1970 and 1977*	
	Nominal Wealth	*Real Wealth*	*Nominal Wealth*	*Real Wealth*
One	111.2	68.0	53.5	0.7
Two	82.3	45.0	48.0	-3.0
Three or more	70.9	36.0	125.1	47.6
All respondents	88.4	49.9	79.8	17.9

Note: As in Table 5-4, percentage changes in real wealth are calculated from base-date wealth figures that have been inflated by the cumulative growth rate in the implicit deflator for personal consumption expenditures figured from survey quarter to survey quarter of the years in question.

reversals reported earlier. Households of three or more persons were much more effective savers in the 1970–77 period than in the 1962–70 era. Correspondingly, while smaller households grew wealthier during the 1960s, on average they drew down their real wealth during the 1970s.

These patterns may be explained as adaptations to changes observed between survey dates in tax structure, financial transactions costs, and risk-return opportunities. As risk-adjusted real after-tax returns on financial assets fell, the relatively constant real in-kind return on housing space for large households made it optimal for them to expand their housing investments more than a smaller household would. Interacting with the life cycle, the proportion of households owning their home rises sharply with household size, as does the use of mortgage leverage. For households with three or more persons, ownership and mortgagor rates are twice as high as for smaller households. Table 5-18 shows that positions in real-estate equity and owner-occupied housing also increase with household size. Although two-person households have higher per-capita wealth than the other categories at all three survey dates, during the 1970s larger households narrowed the gap considerably. In contrast, the relative posi-

Table 5–18. Distribution of Selected Assets and Respondent Population across Household Size Classes at 1962, 1970, and 1977 Survey Dates (percentage).

Number of Persons in Household	*Retail Financial Assets*	*Wholesale Financial Assets*	*Real-Estate Equity*	*Net Transactable Wealth*	*Value of Homes*	*Respondent Population*
1962 survey						
One	24.6 (1.12)	15.5 (.70)	12.2 (.55)	15.0 (.68)	7.9 (.36)	22.0
Two	42.5 (1.73)	36.2 (1.48)	35.1 (1.43)	36.6 (1.49)	28.7 (1.17)	24.5
Three or more	32.9 (.61)	48.3 (.90)	52.7 (.99)	48.3 (.90)	63.4 (1.19)	53.5
All respondents	100.0	100.0	100.0	99.9	100.0	100.0
1970 survey						
One	18.7 (1.14)	11.6 (.71)	11.1 (.68)	12.6 (.77)	8.3 (.51)	16.4
Two	48.6 (1.61)	55.0 (1.82)	38.6 (1.28)	43.7 (1.45)	30.4 (1.01)	30.2
Three or more	32.6 (.61)	33.4 (.63)	50.3 (.94)	43.7 (.82)	61.3 (1.15)	53.4
All respondents	99.9	100.0	100.0	100.0	100.0	100.0
1977 survey						
One	21.6 (1.04)	14.7 (.71)	10.7 (.52)	13.6 (.66)	9.0 (.43)	20.7
Two	40.3 (1.30)	35.9 (1.16)	36.2 (1.17)	36.9 (1.19)	30.6 (.99)	31.0
Three or more	38.1 (.79)	49.3 (1.02)	53.1 (1.10)	49.5 (1.03)	60.4 (1.25)	48.2
All respondents	100.0	99.9	100.0	100.0	100.0	99.9

Note: The figures recorded in parentheses report the percentage of outstanding balances in each portfolio category controlled per each 1 percent of the respondent population occupying the cohort.

tions of one-person households change little across dates. Differential savings performance across size classes in the two eras does not merely reflect the passive interaction of increasing real-estate prices with the positive association between prior real-estate holdings and household size. During the 1970s large families increased their holdings of financial assets even more rapidly than their real-estate equity. This increased financial saving may have two sources. First, it may reflect the efforts of households still occupying rental housing to accumulate a sufficient downpayment to support a planned house purchase. Second, it may reflect the use of mortgage credit (which to most households represents the low-cost form of credit available) to support financial investments.

DIFFERENCES IN ACCUMULATION RATES FOR DIFFERENT TYPES OF HOUSEHOLDS

Table 5–19 explores the relationship between household size and marital status. During the 1960s, all types of large households were less-effective savers than smaller ones. Moreover, the 1970–77 increase in savings propensities for large households was limited to married and other nonsingle (that is, widowed, separated, and divorced) households. This provides further support for the view that movements in the expected value and variance of implicit returns on owner-occupied housing explain a good part of the divergent movements in saving propensities during the 1970s. These families' future housing requirements may be presumed to be more stable than those for single households. During the 1970s large single households dissaved at a high rate.

Table 5–20 shows the effect of changing savings propensities on the real rate of accumulation of transactable wealth. In the 1970–77 period, except for large households in the married and other categories, no household type much improved the real value of its mean transactable wealth. Table 5–21 shows that in 1977 the mean age of the heads of accumulating large households in the married and other categories was in the forties. The mean ages of the heads of the four low-accumulation types of households all prove significantly older or younger than this. Particularly remarkable is the downward trend in the age of heads of single families with two or more members. This reflects growth in the number of couples living together without

Table 5-19. Dollar Increment in Mean Wealth and Ratio of Accumulated Mean Saving Per Year to Average Survey-Date Incomes, by Type of Household.

Type of Household	1962 to 1970		1970 to 1977		Difference in Real Savings Rate between Eras (percentage)
	Dollar Increment in Mean Transactable Wealth	*Real Increment Per Year as a Percentage of Mean Real Income in the Two Survey Years*	*Dollar Increment in Mean Transactable Wealth*	*Real Increment Per Year as a Percentage of Mean Real Income in the Two Survey Years*	
Single, one in household	7,068	13.1	7,429	0.5	-12.6
Single, two or more	5,866	6.5	806	-9.7	-16.2
Married, two only	17,672	17.3	19,495	0.2	-17.1
Married, three or more	8,376	6.0	25,820	10.8	4.8
Other, one only	9,796	21.6	10,372	-0.2	-21.8
Other, two or more	2,495	1.6	11,316	9.4	7.8
All households classified	10,698	10.5	18,285	5.7	-4.8

Note: Real savings rates are constructed as explained in the note to Table 5-4. A few observations (seven in 1962 and three in 1970) coded as "married, one only" are assumed to be miscoded. They are included in the "married, two only" class.

Table 5-20. Cumulative Percentage Change in the Real and Nominal Value of Accumulated Mean Savings between Survey Dates, by Type of Household Head (percentage).

	Cumulative Percentage Change in Mean Net Wealth between 1962 and 1970		*Cumulative Percentage Change in Mean Net Wealth between 1970 and 1977*	
Type of Household	*Nominal Wealth*	*Real Wealth*	*Nominal Wealth*	*Real Wealth*
Single, one in household	109.2	66.4	54.9	1.6
Single, two or more	58.1	25.8	5.0	-31.1
Married, two only	93.3	53.7	53.2	0.5
Married, three or more	72.8	37.4	129.8	50.7
Other, one only	95.8	55.8	51.8	-0.4
Other, two or more	35.6	7.9	119.0	43.6
All households classified	88.5	50.0	80.3	18.2

Note: As in Table 5-5, percentage changes in real wealth are calculated from base-date wealth figures that have been inflated by the observed cumulative growth rate in the implicit deflator for personal consumption expenditures, calculated from survey quarter to survey quarter of the years in question.

benefit of marriage. For these households, unsettled property rights and uncertainty about the couple's commitment to a shared future may erect substantial disincentives to homeownership and saving.

Data on portfolio shares (not reported here) show that the turnaround between 1962–70 and 1970–77 in savings performance by large nonsingle families was an across-the-board one. During the 1970s, relative to their initial wealth, these families expanded their holdings of retail assets, wholesale assets, and real-estate equity all at above-average rates. As they cut their savings rate, single families markedly shifted the composition of their wealth accumulations. One-person single households, which had concentrated on amassing real-estate equity in the 1960s, accumulated their wealth in financial assets in the 1970s. Larger single households (people living with friends and relatives) had reallocated wealth from real-estate equity into financial assets during the 1960s but reversed the pattern in the 1970s, apparently in response to improved implicit returns on owner-occupied housing.

Table 5-21. Age of Heads of Different Types of Households in 1962, 1970, and 1977 (years).

Type of Household	*1962 Survey*		*1970 Survey*		*1977 Survey*	
	Mean Age	*Standard Deviation*	*Mean Age*	*Standard Deviation*	*Mean Age*	*Standard Deviation*
Single, one in household	35.5	17.6	33.8	17.6	36.2	18.2
Single, two or more	43.8	19.0	40.4	16.8	35.4	17.6
Married, two only	54.6	15.9	54.8	17.5	53.6	17.5
Married, three or more	40.0	10.9	40.7	11.4	41.0	11.7
Other, one only	62.3	13.9	62.7	13.6	62.2	16.7
Other, two or more	46.5	15.0	46.4	15.3	45.4	15.3
All households classified	45.5	16.1	46.5	16.5	46.8	17.2

Note: A few observations (seven in 1962 and three in 1970) coded as "married, one only" are thrown into the "married, two only" class.

Table 5-22 clarifies the role of home equity in the saving behavior of households of different type by tracking trends in homeownership and mortgage financing by household type. The most marked trends are the continued high use of leverage by large married households, its increasing use by single and other nonmarried households, and the increased rate of homeownership for one-person households. For so-called small savers—households not wealthy enough to invest directly in wholesale financial assets—these trends may be interpreted as a form of disintermediation. Small savers with large and stable households found it profitable to shift some of their deposit balances into housing. These investments offered untaxed implicit returns, protection against unanticipated inflation, a better anticipated real after-tax explicit return than small-demonination accounts, and a regularized and partially subsidized arrangement for borrowing against small accumulations of wealth. Even for wealthy households, some of these advantages apply. In particular, changes in the level and structure of federal capital-gains tax rates enacted during the 1970s enhanced the tax advantages of owner-occupied housing relative to stock-market investments.

SUMMARY AND CAUTION

Our analysis of SRC data supports three broad inferences. First, life-cycle patterns of accumulation and asset holdings shift importantly with such changes in the economic environment as inflation risk, tax structure, and transactions costs. Perhaps because of such shifts, consistent evidence of average postretirement decumulation emerged only for cohorts of advanced age. Second, between the 1960s and 1970s a sharp turnaround occurred in the profiles of household saving and homeownership. Households whose heads were age 55 and older were strong savers in the 1960s, but younger households proved to be the principal accumulators of the 1970s. A parallel shift in savings propensities occurred between large married or previously married households and other families, suggesting that movements in the expected value and variance of the implicit return on owner-occupied housing may have evoked the adjustment. During the 1960s, all age groups increased their homeownership rates. In the 1970s large nonsingle households and households whose heads were under age 45 accentuated the trend, while most other households merely

Table 5-22. Homeownership Rate and Mortgage Status in 1962, 1970, and 1977, by Household Type (percentage).

Type of Household	*1962*		*1970*		*1977*	
	Percentage Owning Home	*Percentage of Homeowners with Mortgage Debt*	*Percentage Owning Home*	*Percentage of Homeowners with Mortgage Debt*	*Percentage Owning Home*	*Percentage of Homeowners with Mortgage Debt*
Single, one in household	10.2	17.4	15.6	28.0	18.2 (21.0)	46.9 (43.2)
Single, two or more	33.3	25.0	32.8	40.0	27.6 (33.7)	48.1 (39.4)
Married, two only	65.7	37.9	67.7	36.4	70.0 (77.4)	44.6 (42.3)
Married, three or more	66.2	76.2	70.9	77.8	77.3 (81.5)	79.9 (78.1)
Other, one only	43.7	19.8	59.8	23.2	48.7 (60.2)	27.9 (24.5)
Other, two or more	47.1	49.2	43.7	47.9	44.1 (54.2)	62.9 (56.6)
All households classified	55.8	58.7	62.3	58.1	62.5 (69.0)	62.4 (58.9)

Notes: Figures in parentheses report the homeownership and mortgagor rates in the unedited 1977 sample. A few observations (seven in 1962 and three in 1970) coded as "married, one only" are included in the "married, two only" class.

continued it. Third, the compositions of 1962 and 1977 portfolios end up far closer to each other than to 1970 values. This suggests that some of the portfolio churning observed in SRC data reflects disintermediation that was reversed during the 1970s as deposit institutions made ceilings on explicit interest less effective by broadening their product line to develop less-restricted liability instruments and to expand the ways in which they could pay implicit interest on regulated accounts. Combined with a capital-gains tax structure that taxed nominal as well as real price appreciation, these ceilings made the implicit and explicit tax rate on financial savings rise with the rate of inflation. This lowered the saving rate for many households and distorted the allocation of transactable wealth between financial and real-estate assets for everyone.

Because the hypotheses of differential behavior and portfolio churning are such straightforward ones, this paper emphasizes statistical description over statistical testing and interpretation. By conventional Chi-square tests, saving and asset-holding behaviors *reported* by respondents differ significantly across demographic categories. But we must keep in mind two problems in drawing inferences from SRC data. First, observations taken at only three points in time cannot discriminate closely among plausible alternative explanations for observed differences in class-level behavior. Second, in a survey context the ultimate meaningfulness of statistical tests depends on the validity of joint hypotheses about the appropriateness of the sampling frame and the accuracy of respondent reports. Validation studies (Ferber et al. 1969a, and 1969b) indicate that noncooperation, especially among high-income groups, leads to a systematic understatement of sample variances. Ascertaining the ways in which the three survey observations of cross-section data on respondent wealth management are each, in fact, representative of the population of U.S. households is a herculean task. This task can be accomplished only by carefully examining sampling frames and respondent behavior in alternative data sets and tirelessly endeavoring to reconcile whatever differences emerge.

NOTES

1. Peek (1983) explores the link between capital gains and saving as measured by the national income and product accounts. Friend and Lieberman (1975)

use 1963 Federal Reserve Survey data to estimate the effect of capital gains on what they call saving net of depreciation on owned homes.

2. In equilibrium, some of the benefit would be shifted backwards to specialized construction labor and materials (Diamond 1983).
3. Using Canadian data, Dicks-Mireaux and King (1982) investigate the effect of pension wealth on the composition of household portfolios.
4. On the grounds that a mortgage is obviously a financial instrument, we might have chosen to categorize mortgage debt as a negative financial asset. Our approach has the advantage of incorporating the portfolio restriction that mortgage loans are limited to owners of real estate. Programming difficulties persuaded us to defer our efforts to estimate the market value of mortgage debt.
5. Detailed analysis of 1977 survey data indicate that a decrease in the home-ownership rate for older households was recorded only for nonmarried households, especially households whose heads were separated, divorced, or widowed.

REFERENCES

Ando, Albert, and Franco Modigliani. 1963. "The 'Life-Cycle' Hypothesis of Savings: Aggregate Implications and Tests." *American Economic Review* 53 (March):55–84.

Barro, Robert J., and Chaipat Sahasakul. 1983. "Measuring the Average Marginal Tax Rate From the Individual Income Tax." *Journal of Business* 56 (October):419–52.

Board of Governors of the Federal Reserve System, Division of Research and Statistics, Flow of Funds Section, *Balance Sheets for the U.S. Economy, 1945–81*, Washington, D.C., 1982.

Carliner, Michael. 1982. *The Future of Bank Financial Services for Housing.* Washington, D.C.: American Bankers Association.

DeLeeuw, Frank, and Larry Ozanne. 1979. "The Impact of the Federal Income Tax on Investment in Housing." *Survey of Current Business* 59 (December): 50–61.

Diamond, Douglas B. 1983. "The Impact of Inflation on New House Prices." Unpublished paper. Washington, D.C.: Department of Housing and Urban Development.

Dicks-Mireaux, Louis, and Mervyn A. King. 1982. "Portfolio Composition and Pension Wealth: An Econometric Study." Working Paper No. 903. Cambridge, Mass.: National Bureau of Economic Research.

Durkin, Thomas A., and Gregory E. Elliehausen. 1978. *1977 Consumer Credit Survey.* Washington, D.C.: Board of Governors of the Federal Reserve System.

Estrella, Arturo, and Jeffrey C. Fuhrer. 1983. "Average Marginal Tax Rates for

U.S. Household Interest and Dividend Income, 1954–80." Working Paper No. 1201. Cambridge, Mass.: National Bureau of Economic Research.

Ferber, Robert; John Forsythe; Harold W. Guthrie; and E. Scott Maynes. 1969a. "Validation of Consumer Financial Characteristics: Common Stock." *Journal of the American Statistical Association* 64 (June):415–32.

———. 1969b. "Validation of a National Survey of Consumer Financial Characteristics: Savings Accounts." *Review of Economics and Statistics* 51 (November):435–44.

Friedman, Benjamin. 1982. "Effects of Saving Patterns on Interest Rates and Economic Activity." *Journal of Finance* 37 (March):37–62.

Friend, Irwin, and Charles Lieberman. 1975. "Short-Run Asset Effects on Household Saving and Consumption: The Cross-Section Evidence." *American Economic Review* 65 (September):624–33.

Goldsmith, Raymond. 1982. *The National Balance Sheet of the United States, 1953–1980.* Chicago: University of Chicago Press for the National Bureau of Economic Research.

Hendershott, Patric H., and Sheng Cheng Hu. 1981. "Inflation and Extraordinary Returns on Owner-Occupied Housing: Some Implications for Capital Allocation and Productivity Growth." *Journal of Macroeconomics* 3 (Spring): 177–203.

———. 1983. "The Allocation of Capital between Residential and Nonresidential Uses: Tax, Inflation and Capital Market Restraints." *Journal of Finance* 38 (June):795–812.

Ibbotson, Roger G., and Rex A. Sinquefield. 1979. *Stocks, Bonds, Bills, and Inflation: Historical Returns (1926–1978).* Charlottesville, Va.: The Financial Analysts Research Foundation, second edition.

Jianakoplos, Nancy A. 1983. *Household Wealth Accumulation During Periods of Inflation: Some Evidence from Longitudinal Data.* Ph.D. dissertation, The Ohio State University.

———. 1984. "Inflation and the Accumulation of Wealth by Older Households, 1966 to 1976." In *The Level and Composition of Household Saving,* edited by Patric H. Hendershott, pp. 151–180. Cambridge, Mass.: Ballinger Publishing Company.

Kane, Edward J. 1980. "Accelerating Inflation and the Distribution of Household Savings Incentives." In *Special Study on Economic Change,* vol. 4, *Stagflation: The Causes, Effects and Solutions,* pp. 193–224. Washington, D.C.: U.S. Congress, Joint Economic Committee.

———. 1981. "Re-regulation, Savings-and-Loan Diversification and the Flow of Housing Finance." In *Savings and Loan Asset Management Under Deregulation,* pp. 80–109. San Francisco: Federal Home Loan Bank.

Katona, George: Lewis Mandell; and Jay Schmiedeskamp. 1971. *1970 Survey of Consumer Finances.* Ann Arbor: Survey Research Center, Institute for Social Research, The University of Michigan.

Lieberman, Charles, and Paul Wachtel. 1980. "Age Structure and Personal Savings Behavior." In *Social Security Versus Private Saving,* edited by George von Furstenberg, pp. 315–57. Cambridge, Mass.: Ballinger Publishing Company.

Mayers, David. 1973. "Nonmarketable Assets and the Determination of Capital Asset Prices in the Absence of a Riskless Asset." *Journal of Business* 46 (April):233–51.

Modigliani, Franco, and R. Brumberg. 1954. "Utility Analysis and the Consumption Function." In *Post-Keynesian Economics,* edited by Kenneth Kurihara, pp. 388–436. London: Allen and Unwin.

Munnell, Alicia. 1981. "Social Security, Private Pensions and Saving." In *Saving for Retirement: Report on a Miniconference on Saving Held for the 1981 White House Conference on Aging,* edited by Phillip Cagan, pp. 122–55. Washington, D.C.: American Council of Life Insurance.

Peek, Joe. 1983. "Capital Gains and Personal Saving Behavior." *Journal of Money, Credit, and Banking* 15 (February):1–23.

Shumay, Alexander J., and Edward J. Kane. 1983. "Consumer Finance Research Project Documentation." Revised working paper, Ohio State University.

Summers, Lawrence H. 1981. "Inflation, the Stock Market, and Owner-Occupied Housing." *American Economic Review (Papers and Proceedings)* 71 (May): 429–34.

U.S. Department of Commerce, Bureau of the Census. 1981. *Construction Reports C27, Second Quarter 1981.* Washington, D.C.

6 INFLATION AND THE ACCUMULATION OF WEALTH BY OLDER HOUSEHOLDS, 1966–1976

*Nancy Ammon Jianakoplos**

Accelerating inflation was a prominent feature of the economic environment in the United States between the early 1960s and late 1970s. While inflation has numerous economic impacts, the most interesting to us is its differential effect on real asset and liability prices. The prices of assets (and debts) fixed in dollar value, such as deposits, bonds, and mortgages, systematically decline (rise) in real terms; the prices of other assets, such as real estate and human capital, seem to adjust to maintain their real values; and the prices of still other assets, such as corporate equities, respond in a seemingly uncertain manner. Moreover, accelerating inflation unequivocally reduces the real rate of return on financial assets whose nominal yields are limited by interest-rate ceilings. Differences in the response of asset and liability real values and yields to inflation potentially altered individual-household real wealth accumulation in the 1966–76 period.

The principal finding of this study is that both anticipated and unanticipated inflation-related real capital gains and losses on accumulated assets and liabilities are significant factors explaining individual-household wealth accumulation in the mid-1960s through mid-1970s.

*The author wishes to thank Edward J. Kane, Donald O. Parsons, J. Huston McCulloch, and Patric H. Hendershott for helpful comments.

The significance of anticipated and unanticipated real capital gains emphasizes the importance of the composition of household wealth, as well as the total magnitude of wealth, in explaining individual-household saving behavior.

Most models of individual-household wealth accumulation omit real asset-price changes. Two studies that do include real capital gains effects in explanations of individual wealth accumulation (Bhatia 1983; Friend and Lieberman 1975) find this factor is significant. These analyses rely on survey data from the early 1960s, before the substantial acceleration of inflation in the United States. Recent estimates of capital-gains effects for the aggregate household sector (Peek 1983; Hendershott and Peek 1985) suggest that the magnitude of asset-price effects are relatively large. These results emphasize the importance of distinguishing between anticipated and unanticipated price changes. This distinction has not been made in investigations at the individual-household level.

THEORETICAL MODEL

This section develops a framework for examining the effects of inflation-realted real capital gains on individual-household wealth accumulation. The concept of real capital gains and losses is defined and then incorporated into a life-cycle model of changes in household wealth.

Capital Gains and Saving Defined

A *nominal* capital gain is the difference between the price paid by an investor for an asset and the current market value of the asset, net of depreciation. A *real* capital gain is the nominal gain in excess of the increase in the average level of prices. Real capital gains or losses accruing to the *i*th household over interval *t*, $G_{i,t}$, are represented algebraically as:

$$G_{i,t} = \sum_{k=1}^{K} (P_{k,t} - I_t) A_{k,t,i}. \tag{6.1}$$

In equation (6.1), $P_{k,t}$ is the net, per-unit rate of price change in the kth asset or liability over interval t. I_t is the rate of change in the average level of prices over interval t. $A_{k,t,i}$ represents the number of units of the kth asset or liability held by the ith household at the beginning of interval t.[1]

Expected real capital gains, $G^*_{t,i}$, equal the sum of the differences between the expected rate of change in asset or liability prices, $P^*_{k,t}$, and the expected rate of inflation, I^*_t, times the quantity of the asset or liability held by the ith household:

$$G^*_{i,t} = \sum_{k=1}^{K} (P^*_{k,t} - I^*_t) A_{k,t,i}. \tag{6.2}$$

Similarly, unexpected real capital gains, $G^o_{i,t}$, equal the sum of the differences between the unexpected change in asset or liability prices, $P^o_{k,t}$, and the unexpected rate of inflation, I^o_t, times the quantity of the asset or liability held:

$$G^o_{i,t} = \sum_{k=1}^{K} (P^o_{k,t} - I^o_t) A_{k,t,i}. \tag{6.3}$$

Equations (6.2) and (6.3) point out that the magnitude of capital gains, both anticipated and unanticipated, experienced by the ith household depends on three factors: the rate of anticipated or unanticipated price change for individual assets or liabilities, the rate of anticipated or unanticipated inflation, and the quantity of each asset or liability owned by the household. If the expected and observed rates of asset- and liability-price changes and general inflation are assumed to be the same for all households, differences in household asset and liability holdings are the only source of differences in real capital gains between households.

Household saving over interval t, $S_{i,t}$, is defined as the observed change in wealth (net worth) of the ith household from the beginning of period t, $NT_{i,t}$, to the beginning of the next period, $NT_{i,t+i}$:

$$S_{i,t} = NT_{i,t+1} - NT_{i,t}. \tag{6.4}$$

This definition of saving focuses on the change in the *stock* of household wealth. Alternative definitions describe saving in *flow* terms—as the net acquisition of assets out of current income. The stock definition of saving includes cpaital gains on existing assets, while the flow definition does not.

The observed change in household wealth over an interval is the sum of the planned change in household wealth, $S^*_{i,t}$, and the unplanned change, $S^o_{i,t}$. The former is the difference between expected labor earnings, $YW^*_{i,t}$, and desired consumption, $C^*_{i,t}$:

$$S^*_{i,t} = YW^*_{i,t} - C^*_{i,t}. \tag{6.5}$$

The latter consists of unexpected earned income, $Y^o_{i,t}$, and unexreal capital gains, $G^o_{i,t}$:

$$S^o_{i,t} = Y^o_{i,t} + G^o_{i,t}. \tag{6.6}$$

Both expected and unexpected earned income are assumed to be exogenously determined.[2] Differences in unancitipated real capital gains, as developed previously, center around differences in household portfolio composition, which are assumed to be predetermined at the beginning of the interval. The remaining element in the development of an explanation of changes in household wealth is a model of desired consumption.

Desired Consumption and Observed Saving

The life-cycle/permanent-income model of Modigliani and Brumberg (1954) and Friedman (1957) provides the structure of the model of desired consumption used here.[3] Households are assumed to maximize the utility derived from consumption activities over their remaining lifetimes in a world of certainty, subject to a lifetime wealth constraint. The utility of consumption is assumed to be homogenous with respect to household size. The possibility of a household bequest motive is not incorporated into the utility function.

Household utility per member depends on present and future consumption, $C_{i,t}$:

$$U_{i,t} = \mu(C_{i,t}, C_{i,t+1}, \ldots, C_{i,L^*}). \tag{6.7}$$

In equation (6.7), L^* is the expected remaining economic lifetime of the household. Uncertainty surrounding the expected lifetime of the household members is likely to affect the household's consumption-planning process. However, Levhari and Mirman (1977) demonstrate that the effect of this uncertainty on consumption at any point in the planning horizon is theoretically ambiguous for risk-averse consumers. Here we assume that households make their plans on the basis of the best point estimate of life expectancy available to them.

Given perfect capital markets, the individual's lifetime wealth constraint states that the present discounted value of consumption from the current period forward must equal the present discounted value of expected lifetime resources, $V^*_{i,t}$:

$$\sum_{j=t}^{L^*} C_{i,j}(1/D)^{j-t} = V^*_{i,t}. \tag{6.8}$$

In equation (6.8), D is one plus the real after-tax interest rate, assumed constant, which is used to convert dollars at time j to t-period dollars.

Assuming the utility function is homogenous with respect to consumption at different points in time and that households desire to consume at a constant rate over their expected lifetime, desired consumption, $C^*_{i,t}$, over an interval t takes the form:

$$C^*_{i,t} = V^*_{i,t}/L^*_{i,t}. \tag{6.9}$$

The assumption of equal rates of consumption over time intervals is the essence of the smoothing procedure that forms the basis of the life-cycle model.

The expected value of lifetime resources can be expressed as the sum of the value of nonhuman resources, $NT_{i,t}$, plus the average annual expected (permanent) income from human resources (including claims and transfers), $Y^*_{i,t}$, times the expected lifetime:

$$V^*_{i,t} = NT_{i,t} + (L^*_{i,t})\, Y^*_{i,t}. \tag{6.10}$$

$V^*_{i,t}$ and $NT_{i,t}$ collapse streams of income and earnings over time into single summary measures. The current real market value of net worth is assumed to appropriately discount the future stream of expected capital income, $YC^*_{i,t}$, and expected capital gains, $G^*_{i,t}$, that accrue to owners of these assets and liabilities,

$$NT_{i,t} = \eta(YC^*_{i,t}, G^*_{i,t}). \tag{6.11}$$

Average annual expected future income from human capital can be split into expected annual income, $YW^*_{i,t}$, earned over the expected work span, $W^*_{i,t}$, and expected annual income, $YR^*_{i,t}$, received over the expected retirement span, $R^*_{i,t}$. Lifetime resources from human sources can be expressed as:

$$(L^*_{i,t})Y^*_{i,t} = (W^*_{i,t})YW^*_{i,t} + (R^*_{i,t})YR^*_{i,t}. \tag{6.12}$$

Substituting equations (6.10) and (6.12) into equation (6.9) yields the household's consumption function:

$$C^*_{i,t} = (W^*_{i,t}/L^*_{i,t})YW^*_{i,t} + (R^*_{i,t}/L^*_{i,t})YR^*_{i,t} + (1/L^*_{i,t})NT_{i,t}. \tag{6.13}$$

The income and asset measures are multiplied by ratios based on the household's expected lifetime, work span, and retirement span. These ratios are marginal propensities to consume out of each source of spending power. The propensities change as the households age.

Substitution of equation (6.13), the desired consumption function, into equation (6.5) yields a model of planned household saving. The addition of unplanned saving, equation (6.6), leads to the expression for observed household saving upon which the empirical analysis is based:

$$\begin{aligned} S_{i,t} = {} & (R^*_{i,t}/L^*_{i,t})YW^*_{i,t} - (R^*_{i,t}/L^*_{i,t})YR^*_{i,t} \\ & - (1/L^*_{i,t})NT_{i,t} + Y^o_{i,t} + G^o_{i,t}. \end{aligned} \tag{6.14}$$

Saving, the change in household wealth, is hypothesized to depend on expected work income, expected retirement income, net worth, expected retirement and life spans, unexpected noncapital income, and unexpected real capital gains.

The parameters modifying the income and asset magnitudes are marginal propensities to save. Saving out of work income increases as the retirement span approaches and becomes a larger proportion of the remaining expected life span. The marginal propensity to save out of work earnings is modified by the existence of expected retirement income, which could reduce the need to save. However, Feldstein (1974) suggests that increases in retirement earnings induce earlier retirement, therefore increasing the expected retirement span and thus household saving. The net effect of retirement earnings on household saving is thus ambiguous.

Both transitory income and unexpected real capital gains are outside the consumption-planning process. Saving serves as a shock absorber, cushioning consumption from these unexpected events. All noncapital transitory income is assumed to be saved. Capital gains enter the model in two ways. Expected capital gains are incorporated into the household's nonhuman resources and, consequently, affect spending plans; higher expected capital gains decrease desire saving out of human resources. Unexpected capital gains, on the other hand, like transitory income, are initially saved.

The model developed here predicts that changes in household wealth accumulation depend on the magnitude of real capital gains induced by anticipated and unanticipated inflation. Inflation-related capital gains vary because the combination of assets and liabilities in household portfolios differ. When unanticipated inflation-related real capital gains are included in a life-cycle model of household saving behavior, the unanticipated real capital gains are expected to increase household saving. Anticipated real capital gains are predicted to reduce desired household saving.

EMPIRICAL MODEL

The hypothesized effects of inflation-related real capital gains are tested by deriving statistical estimates of the household saving function. This section describes the National Longitudinal Survey (NLS) data used in the estimation procedures, the selection of proxy variables, and the econometric specification of the saving function.

Data

Variables used to estimate the parameters of the household saving function empirically are constructed using data from the NLS panel of men in their preretirement years. These data are obtained from interviews with an initial panel of 5,020 men selected to be representative of the U.S. civilian noninstitutional population that was age 45 to 59 in 1966.[4] The surveys, sponsored by the U.S. Department of Labor, conducted in 1966, 1969, 1971, and 1976 provide dollar values of assets and debts held by the households in the panel. In addition to household net-worth data, the NLS contains information about household income, labor-market experience, retirement plans, composition, and geographic, demographic, and socioeconomic characteristics.

Like other survey-data sets, the NLS data are subject to sampling error, measurement error, and incomplete coverage. In addition, the longitudinal nature of the data poses the problem of sample attrition. Because no new members are added to the initial panel over the ten-year span of interviews, the sample size falls continually due to deaths, the inability to locate respondents over the years, and respondent refusals to participate in succeeding interviews.

The main benefit that the NLS data bring to this study is the ability to observe changes in individual household wealth over time. While these NLS data resemble cross-sectional data collected at several points in time, the distinctive feature of these data is that the observations are on the *same* households at each survey date. An investigation of how inflation alters saving behavior, by its very nature, is concerned with changes in household wealth over time. Limiting the sample to the same group of households over the period has the additional advantage of holding constant unobservable individual differences among households. In addition to the advantage of the longitudinal design, the NLS is a relatively rich source of household data. The scope and detail of the household data collected in the NLS allow construction of empirical measures that more closely approximate the conceptual variables of economic theory.

The empirical analysis uses three subsamples of the NLS households: 2,099 NLS respondents who reported all data necessary to construct proxy variables for the 1966–71 interval (the early reporters), 1,087 NLS respondents who reported all data necessary to construct proxy variables for the 1971–76 interval (the late reporters), and 856 NLS respondents who reported all data necessary to construct proxy variables for both intervals (the consistent reporters).

Empirical Specification of Theoretical Variables

All variables in the estimation procedures, except estimates of life expectancy and rates of price change, are constructed from the NLS data tapes.[5] Real values are expressed in terms of 1966 dollars. The GNP deflator for personal consumption expenditures (PCE) is used to convert nominal values into real terms.

Saving, Net-Worth, and Income Variables. The dependent variable in the equations is the average annual change in household net worth, *SAVE*, between two survey dates five years apart:

$$SAVE = (NET_{t+5} - NET_t)/5. \tag{6.15}$$

Net worth (*NET*) is the sum of all assets less debts reported. The measure of net worth used here deviates from a complete accounting of household net worth because it excludes the value of consumer durables, inventories, the cash value of life-insurance policies, annuities, claims to pensions and transfers, and investment in human capital. In the most disaggregate form available in the NLS data, assets and liabilities include deposits at banks, savings and loan associations, and credit unions (*DEP*), U.S. savings bonds (*USBOND*), stocks, bonds, and mutual funds (*STOCK*), personal loans made to others (*PLOAN*), residential housing (*HOUSE*), investment real estate (*REAL*), equity interest in farms (*FARM*), equity interests in business or professional practice (*BUS*), and unsecured personal debt (*DEBT*), plus debts incurred in conjunction with the ownership of residential housing, businesses, farms, and investment real estate.

For some aspects of the empirical analysis, assets with common characteristics are grouped together. The variable *NOM* equals the sum of *DEP, USBOND,* and *PLOAN,* the assets assumed to have fixed-nominal values. Ownership of tangible assets other than residential homeownership are aggregated into *OTAN,* the sum of *REAL, FARM,* and *BUS.*

Panel members were requested to report their income in the surveys conducted in 1966, 1967, 1969, 1971, 1973, and 1976. Income figures refer to income received in the calendar year prior to the survey year. An estimate of applicable federal personal income tax is made for each total income figure reported. The income concept in the saving function corresponds to the respondent's noncapital income. To construct a proxy for this concept of income, a proportion of the respondent's total federal tax liability equal to the ratio of his wage and transfer income to total income is subtracted from wage and transfer earnings. *Expected* disposable wage and transfer earnings, *EARN**, is the average real value of disposable income in the sample interval. *EARN** includes pension contributions, a form of capital accumulation that would be omitted from an ideal measure of noncapital earnings.

Typically, measures of transitory income are constructed by subtracting expected income from current income. The method used to construct expected wage earnings and transfer payments in this instance makes such a measure zero by definition. Consequently, an alternative proxy for transitory earnings, the standard deviation of wage and transfer payments over the sample interval, *VARY*, is employed instead. While transitory income can take both positive and negative values, *VARY* is always positive. The transition from theory to practice alters the interpretation of this variable. Larger values of *VARY* indicate greater variability of annual labor earnings. It is reasonable to expect that households would accumulate more for precautionary purposes the greater are the fluctuations in their annual income.

A dummy variable, *PEN**, is included in the regression equation because the measure of household net worth, *NET*, does not include accumulated pension wealth. *PEN** takes the value of one if the respondent indicates he is covered by a private pension plan at the beginning of the interval and zero otherwise. Another dummy variable, *SS**, takes the value of one if the respondent reports eligibility to receive social security benefits at the beginning of the interval and zero otherwise.

Real Capital-Gains Variables. Measures of the average expected and unexpected real capital gains for each household are constructed by combining the observed rate of asset-price change for each category of asset or liability, the observed, expected, and unexpected rates of inflation, and the dollar value of each asset and liability held by the household at the beginning of the interval as described in equations (6.2) and (6.3).

Although unexpected inflation is an unobservable variable, several ways to construct proxy measures are common in economic research (Chan-Lee 1980). Possible measures of unanticipated inflation include: the unexplained residual from economic models of inflation, the difference between the measured rate of inflation and the expected rate of inflation reported by survey respondents, and the difference between the measured rate of inflation and the Treasury-bill rate. Measures of anticipated inflation, I^**-SURVEY*, and unanticipated inflation, I^o*-SURVEY*, based on inflation forecasts collected in the Livingston Surveys are used in constructing the real capital gains variables. Survey-based measures are selected because of their comparability to the survey-nature of the NLS data. The observed rate of inflation is measured by the CPI because the participants of the

Livingston Surveys are requested to forecast the CPI. The average annual growth rates of these measures over the sample intervals are reported in Table 6–1.

The classification of assets and liabilities into those having fixed-nominal values and those having nominally variable values follows

Table 6–1. Rates of Price Change (percentage).

	Compound Annual Rates of Price Change (percentage)	
	1966–71	*1971–76*
Inflation measures		
CPI[a]	4.5	7.2
I-SURVEY*[b]	3.1	5.1
I°-SURVEY[b]	1.4	2.1
Asset categories		
DEP[c]	0.0	0.0
USBOND[c]	0.0	0.0
PLOAN[c]	0.0	0.0
STOCK[d]	6.2	4.6
HOUSE[e]	5.2	7.8
REAL[f]	4.1	6.9
FARM[g]	4.2	6.8
BUS[h]	3.0	5.5
DEBT[c]	0.0	0.0

a. Ibbotson and Sinquefield (1979: Exhibit A-5).

b. Carlson (1977).

c. By assumption.

d. Relative shares of equities, long- and short-term securities are from Cagan and Lipsey (1978: Table 2–6). Compound annual rates of return for stocks, corporate bonds, and Treasury bills are from Ibbotson and Sinquefield (1979: Exhibit A-1, Exhibit A-3, Exhibit A-4).

e. An index of existing single-family homes median sales price from Cagan and Lipsey (1978: Table 2–10).

f. Implicit price deflator for nonfarm residential structures from *Economic Report of the President* (1982: Table B–3).

g. Implicit price deflator for farm structures from *Economic Report of the President* (1982: Table B–3).

h. Deflator for gross domestic product of nonfinancial corporate business from *Economic Report of the President* (1982: Table B–13).

the assumptions made in previous research that simulated the consequences of inflation on asset and liability prices (Bach and Stephenson 1974; Budd and Seiders 1971; Hurd and Shoven 1982). Among the nine types of assets and liabilities, *DEP, USBOND, PLOAN,* and *DEBT* are assumed to have fixed nominal prices. The nominal prices of the remaining assets are assumed to be variable. This classification scheme is somewhat arbitrary because certain asset categories are a mix of asset types. Nevertheless, the assets included in *DEP, USBOND, PLOAN,* and *DEBT* can be reasonably regarded as claims to a fixed number of dollars.

The observed, expected, and unexpected rates of nominal price change for assets with fixed nominal prices are set equal to zero, as indicated in Table 6–1. Specific price indexes used to measure the observed average annual change in the nominal prices of the assets assumed to have nominally variable prices are reported in Table 6–1 also. The expected rate of asset-price change for variably priced assets is assumed to equal the expected overall rate of inflation. As a result the unexpected rate of asset-price change for these assets is the difference between the observed rate of asset-price change and the expected general rate of inflation.

Unanticipated real capital gains for each household, $GAIN^o$, are the sum of unanticipated real gains on each asset held by the household. Unanticipated real capital gains on each variably priced asset equal the quantity of the asset owned times the difference between the rate of observed asset-price change and the observed rate on inflation. The unexpected capital loss (gain) on fixed-price assets (debts) equals the unexpected rate of inflation times the quantity of the fixed-price asset (liability). Thus, unexpected real capital gains for the ith household for 1966–71 interval, when unanticipated inflation measured using I^o-*SURVEY* averaged 1.4 percent, equal:

$$\begin{aligned} GAIN_i^o = & -0.014\,(DEP_i + USBOND_i + PLOAN_i) + 0.017\,STOCK_i \\ & +0.007\,HOUSE_i - 0.003\,FARM_i - 0.015\,BUS_i \\ & -0.04\,REAL_i + 0.014\,DEBT_i. \end{aligned} \tag{6.16}$$

Over the 1971–76 interval, when unexpected inflation measured by I^o-*SURVEY* equaled 2.1 percent, unexpected real capital gains are constructed using the following formula:

$$GAIN_i^o = -0.021\ (DEP_i + USBOND_i + PLOAN_i) - 0.026\ STOCK_i$$
$$+0.006\ HOUSE_i - 0.004\ FARM_i - 0.017\ BUS_i$$
$$-0.003\ REAL_i + 0.021\ DEBT_i. \qquad (6.17)$$

The market value of household net worth is assumed to reflect expected real capital gains. Expected capital gains or losses on nominally fixed-priced assets and liabilities cannot be reflected in the nominally fixed market price of these assets. To allow for household expectations of real capital gains on these assets, $GAIN^*$, equal to the expected rate of inflation times the quantity of household liabilities less fixed-price assets, is included in the equations.

Demographic Variables. The age and race of the respondent are reported in thc 1966 survey data. Each respondent is assigned an estimate of the number of years of life remaining, $LIFE^*$, based on his race, age, and actuarial life expectancy (U.S. Bureau of the Census 1968, 1973, 1974). The life span is adjusted at the beginning of each sample interval.

The expected age of retirement reported by the respondent in the 1966 and 1971 surveys is used when available as a proxy for expected age at retirement ($RETIRE^*$). If the respondent does not expect to retire, expected age of retirement is set equal to expected age at death. If the respondent has already retired, this variable takes the value of the respondent's current age. If the respondent does not provide an estimated age of reitrement, the variable is arbitrarily set equal to 65. The length of the expected work span, $WSPAN^*$, is computed as the difference between the respondent's expected age at retirement and current age. The expected retirement span, $RSPAN^*$, is computed as the respondent's current age plus expected lifetime minus his expected age at retirement.

In the 1966, 1971, and 1976 surveys, each respondent reports the number of his dependents excluding his wife. The average number of family members, *SIZE,* over the intervals 1966 to 1971 and 1971 to 1976 for each household is based on these responses and the respondent's marital status.

Although the desire to leave a bequest to one's heirs is not formally incorporated into the saving model, it is reasonable to hypothesize that some additional saving is undertaken for this purpose. To test this proposition, a dummy variable, *BEQ,* takes the value of one if the panel member indicates a desire to leave an inheritance in response to a question posed in the 1971 survey, and a value of zero otherwise.

Econometric Specification of Estimating Equations

Empirical tests of the model of household saving behavior are confined to estimates that are linear functions of the parameters. The general specification of the estimation equation is:

$$\begin{aligned} SAVE = {} & a_0 + a_1\, EARN^* + a_2\, NET + a_3\, PEN^* + a_4\, SS^* \\ & + a_5\, VARY + a_6\, GAIN^o + a_7\, GAIN^* + a_8\, WSPAN^* \\ & + a_9\, RSPAN^* + a_{10}\, SIZE + a_{11}\, BEQ + e. \end{aligned} \tag{6.18}$$

The coefficients, a_0 to a_{11}, are the parameters of the model estimated. A stochastic error term, e, is included in equation (6.18) to indicate that the equation is not expected to hold precisely.

From the theoretical development of the equation, a_0 is not expected to differ significantly from zero. The expected value of a_1 is R^*/L^*, the marginal propensity to save out of anticipated work income. Both a_2 and a_7 are expected to equal $-(1/L^*)$, the marginal propensity to save out of capital assets including expected capital gains. The coefficient of unanticipated real gains, a_6, is predicted to equal unity.

As mentioned before, the sign and magnitude of a_3 and a_4 are theoretically ambiguous. The coefficient a_5 is expected to be positive. The expected value of a_8 is negative because longer expected work spans allow more time to accumulate the desired quantity of assets; the value of a_9 is predicted to be positive because the greater length of the expected retirement span requires more accumulated resources to finance future consumption. The predicted value of a_{10} is negative because large households put greater demands on household resources for consumption purposes. The coefficient a_{11} is expected to be positive because those respondents indicating a desire to leave a bequest to their heirs should accumulate more than those who do not, other factors held constant.

DESCRIPTIVE ANALYSIS OF THE SAMPLE

Several interesting observations about the sample households are revealed by examining the mean values of selected household characteristics (Table 6–2). The measure of annual saving represents about 3 percent of initial household net worth and 9 percent of household disposable noncapital income in each interval based on the values in the early- and late-reporter samples. The calculated measures of anticipated and unanticipated real capital gains are quite small—less than 1 percent of either net worth or permanent disposable income. Households, on average, incur both anticipated and unanticipated real capital *gains* in the first interval, but anticipated and unanticipated real capital *losses* in the second period.

As might be expected in the age category observed, family size decreases on average as the households age. Over 60 percent of the

Table 6–2. Means of Selected Household Variables.

Variable		*1966–71 Early Reporters*	*1971–76 Late Reporters*
SAVE	Average annual change in net worth	616.9	699.6
*EARN**	Average earnings	7,024.3	7,415.0
*PEN**	Pension eligibility dummy	0.6	0.6
*SS**	Social security eligibility dummy	0.9	0.9
NET	Initial net worth	19,053.2	19,966.7
VARY	Standard deviation of earning	1,653.4	2,219.0
GAIN^o	Unanticipated real capital gains	62.2	-35.6
*WSPAN**	Work span	13.7	9.0
*RSPAN**	Retirement span	8.0	10.1
SIZE	Family size	3.1	2.7
BEQ	Bequest intent dummy	0.6	0.6
*GAIN**	Anticipated real capital gains on nominally fixed price assets and liabilities	45.9	-23.4
AGE	Respondent's age	51.2	55.5
*LIFE**	Respondent's life expectancy	21.7	19.0
*RETIRE**	Respondent's expected age at retirement	64.8	64.5
N	Sample size	2,099	1,087

households indicate a desire to leave a bequest to their heirs. In the early sample interval the average household's expected work span exceeds the expected retirement span. In the later period this situation is reversed. Over half of the households expect to receive private pension benefits in retirement, while over 90 percent are eligible for Social Security benefits.

Table 6–3 shows the breakdown of household wealth by major asset and liability categories at five-year intervals for the consistent-reporter sample. Following Kane (1982), the percentage of household net worth in each category is computed in two ways to illustrate the concentration of ownership of some types of portfolio items. To compute household mean portfolio shares, the share of household net worth held in each asset or liability category is first computed. Then these shares are averaged over all households in the sample. This measure gives equal weight to each household and therefore reflects the portfolio composition of the typical household. Using the alternative method, the sample mean is calculated by dividing the average value of each portfolio item in the sample by the average value of household net worth in the sample. This figure gives each dollar equal weight, regardless of how ownership is distributed across households. Wealthier households have a larger impact on this measure than on the household means.

The difference in the two measures is most pronounced with respect to the share of portfolio devoted to investment-type financial assets, *STOCK*, and tangible assets other than residential housing, *OTAN*. Not surprisingly, ownership of these types of assets is more concentrated in the hands of wealthy individuals. Residential housing is the most important asset in the typical household portfolio. Over the ten-year interval the shares of both housing and debt decline, while the proportion of household net worth held in nominally fixed-price assets increases slightly.

The panel design of the NLS data provides an opportunity to appraise the assumption of unchanging portfolio composition underlying the construction of the real capital-gains variables. If additional saving is allocated across assets and liabilities in the same proportion as initially observed, the changes in portfolio shares result solely from changes in asset prices. Table 6–4 compares the observed mean household portfolio shares in 1971 and 1976, with the simulated shares based on asset holdings five years earlier and asset-price changes over the interval. The simulated values are computed by in-

Table 6-3. Observed Changes in Household Portfolio Composition, 1966-76 (percentage of household net worth[a]).

Portfolio Item	1966 Household Mean[b]	1966 Dollar Mean[c]	1971 Household Mean[b]	1971 Dollar Mean[c]	1976 Household Mean[b]	1976 Dollar Mean[c]
NOM	0.20	0.19	0.22	0.20	0.23	0.22
STOCK	0.04	0.11	0.05	0.15	0.04	0.08
HOUSE	0.91	0.74	0.80	0.65	0.66	0.61
OTAN	0.11	0.26	0.11	0.19	0.09	0.22
DEBT	0.35	0.30	0.26	0.18	0.10	0.12

a. The percentages are calculated from 854 observations in the consistent-reporter sample. Two observations that distorted the mean values are omitted.

b. The sum of assets less debt will not necessarily equal unity.

c. The sum of assets less debt may not equal unity due to rounding error.

Table 6-4. Observed versus Simulated Changes in Portfolio Composition, 1971 and 1976 (percentage of household net worth[a]).

Portfolio Item	Average Household Portfolio Share[b] 1966 Observed	1971 Observed	1971 Simulated	1976 Observed	1976 Simulated
NOM	0.20	0.22	0.18	0.23	0.19
STOCK	0.04	0.05	0.04	0.04	0.05
HOUSE	0.91	0.80	0.80	0.66	0.64
OTAN	0.11	0.11	0.14	0.09	0.09
DEBT	0.35	0.26	0.23	0.10	0.05

a. The percentages are calculated from 854 observations in the consistent-reporter sample. Two observations that distort the mean values are omitted.

b. The sum of assets less debt will not necessarily equal unity.

creasing each household's holding of assets and liabilities at the observed rate of nominal-price change shown in Table 6–1.

A comparison of the predicted portfolio shares with the observed shares, assuming the nominal-price-change measures are correct, provides some indication of how households rearranged their portfolios.

T-tests indicate that none of the pairs of simulated and observed portfolio shares is statistically different. Rather than actively rearranging their portfolios, the similarity in observed and predicted shares suggests that households in this sample passively accepted asset-price changes. This observation is consistent with the findings of Cagan and Lipsey (1978) based on analysis of household portfolio composition at the aggregate level.

REGRESSION ANALYSIS

Equation (6.18) is estimated initially using ordinary least squares (OLS). The equation is estimated for two intervals: 1966–71 and 1971–76. SAS computer programs are used for all computations in this paper. All data processing is carried out on the Amdahl 470 V/8 computer of the Instruction and Research Computer Center of The Ohio State University.

The OLS assumption of homoscedastic error terms—that is, constant residual variances—is likely to be violated in cross-sectional data. Violation results in inefficient estimates of the coefficients. In addition, the estimated variances of the estimated coefficients will be biased, invalidating the usual statistical tests of significance. A frequent assumption made in cross-sectional studies of household saving is that the residual variance is proportional to the square of household income (Intriligator 1978:156).

The equations are reestimated using weighted least squares (WLS) deflating the variables by $EARN^*$. However, the deflation procedure has its own pitfalls. In particular, the possibility of spurious correlation exists, caused by the presence of the deflator in the denominator of both the dependent and independent variables (Maddala 1977: 265–68). This provides a potential explanation for some of the observed differences between the OLS and WLS estimates, particularly with regard to the coefficients of $EARN^*$.

Evaluation of OLS and WLS Coefficient Estimates

The estimated OLS and WLS coefficients (Table 6–5) are evaluated by comparing the estimated values with the predicted values. The estimated coefficients of the real capital gains variables, $GAIN^*$ and

$GAIN^o$, are the primary focus of this research. In addition to the significance and magnitude of these estimated coefficients relative to their predicted values, both the sensitivity of the other coefficient estimates to the inclusion of these variables and possible measurement error are considered. The sensitivity of the coefficient estimates provides some idea of the validity of the model in general and of the degree of confidence attached to the coefficient estimates of the variables of principal interest.

Real Capital Gains. The theory developed earlier distinguishes between the effect of anticipated and unanticipated real capital gains on household wealth. Each dollar of unexpected real capital gains is expected to increase annual saving by one dollar. Anticipated real capital gains are predicted to reduce pressure to accumulate assets from other sources by the marginal propensity to save out of capital assets, approximately equal to 0.045 and 0.050 in the early and late sample period, respectively.

In six of the eight OLS and WLS regressions estimated using the three samples, the coefficient of $GAIN^o$ exceeds the predicted value of unity. Five of the eight estimates of the coefficient of $GAIN^*$ are significantly less than the predicted value. One estimate is significantly greater than expected. The deviations of the estimated coefficients of $GAIN^*$ and $GAIN^o$ from their predicted values may be an indication of measurement error. On balance, however, the estimates confirm the prediction that anticipated real capital gains reduce wealth accumulation, while unanticipated gains increase wealth.

The equation is reestimated based on all three samples but excluding $GAIN^o$ and $GAIN^*$ from among the explanatory variables. *F*-tests (available from the author) reject the hypothesis that both a_6 and a_7 equal zero; the addition of $GAIN^o$ and $GAIN^*$ improves the explanatory power of the equation.

Because the variables *NET*, $GAIN^*$, and $GAIN^o$ are closely related and some degree of collinearity possibly exists, the stability of the coefficient estimates of *NET* when $GAIN^*$ and $GAIN^o$ are omitted is of particular interest. A comparison of the coefficient estimates in the regression including $GAIN^o$ and $GAIN^*$ with regression coefficients when these variables are excluded (not reported here) show that the coefficients are virtually unchanged based on the early- and late-reporter samples. The estimates using the consistent-reporter sample are more sensitive to the exclusion of $GAIN^o$ and $GAIN^*$. The estimated coefficients of *NET* become smaller (a larger negative

Table 6-5. *OLS* and *WLS* Regression Results (dependent variable: average annual change in net worth).

	Coefficient Estimates (standard errors in parentheses)							
	1966–71				1971–76			
	Early Reporters		Consistent Reporters		Late Reporters		Consistent Reporters	
Variable[a]	*OLS*	*WLS*	*OLS*	*WLS*	*OLS*	*WLS*	*OLS*	*WLS*
INTERCEPT[b]	-31 (1682)	1,804 (1434)	1,974 (1181)	-685 (464)	-1,432 (1545)	-332 (789)	-835 (1252)	-638 (679)
*EARN**[c]	0.24 (0.06)	-0.01 (0.28)	0.11 (0.05)	0.19 (0.02)	0.31 (0.05)	0.15 (0.05)	0.09 (0.05)	-0.05 (0.04)
*PEN**	-968 (485)	-3,844 (445)	-930 (327)	-276 (150)	223 (404)	269 (233)	747 (336)	432 (206)
*SS**	-1,560 (820)	-2,975 (473)	-324 (530)	387 (182)	762 (628)	63 (303)	420 (500)	303 (246)
NET	-0.114 (0.004)	0.058 (0.007)	0.009 (0.008)	-0.066 (0.005)	-0.098 (0.006)	-0.088 (0.006)	0.004 (0.007)	0.008 (0.008)
VARY	0.87 (0.12)	-1.98 (0.65)	0.26 (0.09)	0.25 (0.06)	0.47 (0.09)	0.59 (0.08)	0.18 (0.07)	0.36 (0.07)
GAIN[o]	3.85 (0.38)	1.30 (0.96)	12.85 (0.77)	8.05 (0.62)	2.73 (0.33)	1.26 (0.64)	7.19 (0.31)	4.12 (0.64)
*WSPAN**	58 (67)	92 (66)	-92 (47)	0 (17)	-86 (70)	14 (34)	-17 (56)	38 (29)

*RSPAN**	83	618	-102	-1	65	30	21	29
	(83)	(59)	(60)	(25)	(83)	(37)	(68)	(31)
SIZE	-88	251	-250	-117	115	-84	-39	-40
	(131)	(110)	(80)	(24)	(136)	(72)	(112)	(63)
BEQ	772	-4,372	327	93	-302	-326	-299	-241
	(447)	(352)	(287)	(109)	(366)	(180)	(299)	(157)
*GAIN**	-5.00	2.07	-3.45	-4.30	-1.46	-0.03	-1.50	0.67
	(0.45)	(0.56)	(0.66)	(0.36)	(0.35)	(0.34)	(0.29)	(0.33)
N	2,099	2,099	856	856	1,087	1,087	856	856
R^2	0.4150	0.3106	0.3882	0.6345	0.5117	0.2275	0.6254	0.2021
SSE (billions)	198.9	185,163.5	13.5	109.3	35.3	520.5	14.6	248.5

a. Each variable in the *WLS* regressions is divided by *EARN**.

b. In the *WLS* regressions this variable equals *1/EARN**.

c. In the *WLS* regressions this variable equals a vector of ones.

number) and the coefficient of $EARN^*$ becomes a larger positive value. The estimated intercept and coefficients of the dichotomous variables tend to shift more between regression specifications than the coefficients of the continuous variables because these terms are more sensitive to omitted variables.

An additional indication of the sensitivity of the coefficients to measurement error can be obtained by reestimating the equation with *NETSAVE* as the dependent variable, where:

$$NETSAVE = SAVE + (1/L^*)NET + (1/L^*)\ GAIN^* - GAIN^o, \qquad (6.19)$$

and the variables *NET*, $GAIN^*$, and $GAIN^o$ are not included among the explanatory variables in this specification. The error associated with the measurement of household assets and liabilities is concentrated in the dependent variable, rather than spread across both independent and dependent variables as in the other specifications. The coefficients of the remaining continuously measured variables (not reported here) are of the same order of magnitude as obtained in the previously estimated regressions.

A possible explanation for a greater than dollar-for-dollar transformation of unanticipated real capital gains into saving is that households find it more difficult to rechannel increases in wealth from unanticipated asset appreciation or depreciation than increases in wealth from other sources. This idea is consistent with the smaller-than-predicted estimates of the effect of earnings and net worth on household savings, which are discussed later. According to this interpretation, which Peek (1983) labels the "displacement effect," households respond to inflation-induced wealth changes by substituting saving from the appreciation of existing assets for acquisition of new assets.

The greater-than-predicted coefficient on unanticipated real capital gains is also consistent with Wachtel's (1980) suggestion that households do not recognize changes in wealth generated by capital gains as quickly as changes in wealth resulting from the net acquisition of assets. Consequently, increases in wealth generated by asset-price changes are not quickly diverted to other uses.

In summary, the addition of the capital-gain variables improves the explanatory power of the life-cycle model, given the specification, estimation procedures, and subsamples used here. Unexpected capital gains significantly increase household saving, while expected inflation-related real capital gains on nominally fixed-priced assets reduce household wealth accumulation from other sources. The coefficient estimates do not appear to be unusually sensitive to measurement errors stemming from errors in household asset and liability data. The greater-than-predicted effect of real capital gains on household saving can be attributed in part to measurement error but is also consistent with the concepts of a displacement of saving out of labor earnings by asset appreciation and a recognition lag in household saving behavior.

Other Variables. A constant term is included in the estimation specifications to test the hypothesis that saving is proportional to household resources and to allow for the possibility of omitted variables. In the WLS regressions the estimate of the intercept equals the estimated coefficient from the variable that is the reciprocal of *EARN**. The estimated coefficients of the intercept term provide support for the hypothesis of proportionality. Seven of the eight OLS and WLS coefficient estimates are not significantly different from zero.

The propensity to save out of expected earnings is hypothesized to be a positive fraction equal to the ratio of the retirement span to the remaining life span. This ratio equals 0.37 and 0.53, on average, at the beginning of the early- and late-sample intervals, respectively. In both periods the OLS and WLS coefficients are positive or not significantly different from zero. However, all of the coefficient estimates are significantly less than the predicted values. These results suggest that households in the sample save significantly less of their expected earnings than predicted by the model. Underaccumulation of wealth by households is consistent with the findings of several other tests of the life-cycle model (White 1978; Blinder, Gordon, and Weiss 1983).

The estimated coefficients of the pension and Social Security dummies tend to be significantly negative in the early-sample interval but positive in the later period, suggesting that the influence of retirement income may change as the household ages. The dichotomous variables are admittedly imperfect proxies for expected retirement income. Both future pension and social security benefits are likely to be closely related to income earned during the work span. Attempts to interact the dummy variables with estimates of current and permanent labor income were not successful due to the high degree of collinearity. The coefficient associated with *EARN** is very sensitive to the addition of these interactive terms.

Accumulated net worth is hypothesized to reduce saving by a fraction equal to the reciprocal of the remaining life span. The OLS and WLS estimated coefficients of net worth are significantly less than their expected values in four of the eight regressions. The coefficients are significantly greater than zero in only one case.

The OLS and WLS estimated coefficients of earnings variability are significantly greater than zero in each of the regressions estimated except in the WLS regressions using the early-reporter sample; households that experience greater earnings variability save more than households with smoother earnings streams. The estimated coefficients generally range between values of zero and one.

The coefficients on the variables representing the expected remaining years in the work span and retirement span are not significantly different from zero in most of the OLS and WLS regressions in which they are included. Also, no consistent pattern of signs of significance is evident for the variables measuring average family size and the desire to leave a bequest.

Regression Estimates Employing First-Differenced Variables

OLS and WLS estimates are likely to be biased because unobserved differences in household preferences exist. Households having a high propensity to save are likely to have a large accumulation of assets. Estimates made using just one cross-section of data force the omitted variables into the error term. If the unobserved variables are correlated with the explanatory variables this leads to biased estimates of the coefficients of the included variables (Johnston 1972:169).

If these individual-specific effects are time invariant, then estimates of the equations in first-difference form, which is possible with panel data, purges the estimates of this bias. The random-error term in the first-differenced regression is a set of moving average error terms. Maddala (1977:326) suggests that OLS is an appropriate estimation procedure in this situation. Along with the unobserved household characteristics, the desire to leave a bequest and eligibility for pension and social security benefits are assumed to be constant over the ten-year span. Variable names prefixed by the letter *D* indicate the difference between the value of the variable in the 1971–76 interval minus the value in the 1966–71 period.

The coefficient estimates obtained from a regression estimated in first-difference form are reported in Table 6–6. The coefficient of $DGAIN^o$ is positive and greater than unity, while the coefficient of $DGAIN^*$ is significantly less than zero. The estimated coefficient of *DNET* is negative but still continues to indicate a greater reduction in saving resulting from existing holdings of assets than predicted. The coefficient associated with earnings variability is significantly positive, but less than one. The coefficient of the permanent-income variable, on the other hand, is not significant.

Table 6–6. *OLS* Regression Results Employing First Differences of Variables (dependent variable: *DSAVE*).

Variable	*Coefficient Estimates (standard errors in parentheses)*
INTERCEPT	-2,892 (1055)
*DEARN**	-0.05 (0.05)
DNET	-0.27 (0.01)
DVARY	0.11 (0.05)
$GAIN^o$	4.30 (0.23)
*WSPAN**	1.427 (332)
*RSPAN**	-1.430 (334)
SIZE	173 (169)
*GAIN**	-0.66 (0.32)
N	856
R^2	0.8696
SSE (billions)	13.4

Table 6-7. Regression Results Using Fuller–Battese Pooled Time-Series and Cross-Section Model (dependent variable: average annual change in net worth).

Variable	*Coefficient Estimates*	*Standard Error*
INTERCEPT	1,492	2,018
*EARN**	0.28	0.04
*PEN**	-90	276
*SS**	-162	422
NET	-0.04	0.01
VARY	0.27	0.06
*GAIN^o^*	7.90	0.22
*WSPAN**	-114	53
*RSPAN**	-94	62
SIZE	-208	91
BEQ	5.67	314
*GAIN**	-1.11	0.29
N	1,712	

Pooled Cross-Section and Time-Series Estimates

To obtain more efficient estimates of the parameters of the saving equations, observations available in both intervals, the consistent-reporter sample, are pooled and the equations reestimated using a variance-components model. In this model the intercept term for each observation is considered to consist of two random variables: a time-series variable and a cross-section variable. Both of these are assumed independent of the residual error, which, in turn, is assumed to be serially independent and independent across cross-section units. The error term for each observation consists of a cross-section component, a time-series component, and the usual least-squares error component. A generalized least-squares estimator must be used because the time-series and cross-section error terms are correlated, for the same observation, although residuals for different observations are independent. A two-stage procedure developed by Fuller and Battese (1974) is used to obtain parameter estimates of the pooled data under these assumptions. In the first stage, estimates of the time-series, cross-section, and combined variances are obtained from OLS estimates. In the second stage each observation is weighted by a function of its estimated variances.

Estimates obtained using the pooled data, presented in Table 6-7, are not dramatically different from the OLS and WLS estimates over the separate intervals. Most important, the estimated effect of unexpected real capital gains is significantly positive in both specifications, while expected real capital gains have a significantly negative effect on household saving.

SUMMARY AND CONCLUSIONS

One possible channel through which inflation can affect individual households is through changes in the real value of the assets and liabilities contained in household portfolios. This study focuses on the effect of inflation-related changes in asset and liability prices on the accumulation of real wealth by individual households. Within the life-cycle model of individual household saving behavior, households are assumed to incorporate expected asset-price changes, or real capital gains, in their consumption-planning process. Consequently, expected capital gains reduce household demands for wealth accumulation from other sources. Likewise, expected real capital losses are predicted to increase household savings. Unanticipated real capital gains do not enter into the household consumption-planning process. Therefore, unanticipated real capital gains are initially saved, adding to the household's accumulated wealth. On the other hand, unanticipated, inflation-related real capital losses are expected to reduce household saving.

This model is tested empirically by estimating a household saving function that incorporates measures of anticipated and unanticipated inflation-related real capital gains developed from individual-household balance-sheet data. Despite the small magnitude of both types of real capital gains, the regression estimates indicate that these variables have a significant impact on individual-household saving behavior. The results indicate that the addition of the capital-gains variables improves the explanatory power of the life-cycle model. In most of the regressions estimated, regardless of the subsample, sample period, or estimation techniques employed, unexpected inflation-related real capital gains significantly increase household saving. In fact, the increase is generally four to eight times greater than expected. In contrast, the results suggest that expected inflation-related real capital gains on nominally fixed-prices assets reduce household savings requirements as the model predicts.

The large impact of unexpected gains is consistent with the existence of a recognition lag and a displacement effect. According to this interpretation, wealth changes stemming from asset-price appreciation or depreciation are not quickly recognized and are not easily rechanneled into consumption spending. The greater-than-predicted wealth accumulation out of capital gains can be interpreted as partially offsetting the less-than-predicted saving out of expected earnings and net worth estimated in these regressions. Viewed from this perspective, the results suggest that households respond to inflation-induced wealth changes by substituting saving from the appreciation of existing assets for the acquisition of new assets.

The construction of the capital-gains variables emphasized the differences in the sensitivity of asset and liability prices to inflation. The results suggest that *how* households hold their wealth, as well as *how much* wealth they hold, is an important factor explaining household saving behavior. While these results provide some new insights into individual household saving behavior, the significance of real capital gains in determining household saving behavior points out the importance of the factors that cause the gains to differ across households, that is, the factors determining individual-household portfolio composition.

NOTES

1. This definition ignores changes in the quantity of assets and liabilities over interval *t*.
2. A richer model would take into account factors determining the household's labor-leisure choice.
3. The derivation of this model closely follows that of Munnell (1976).
4. For a complete description of the sampling procedures and survey design, see Center for Human Resource Research (1981).
5. A description of the decision rules and procedures used to construct variables from values recorded on the NLS tapes is available from the author.

REFERENCES

Bach, G.L., and James B. Stephenson. 1974. "Inflation and the Redistribution of Wealth." *Review of Economics and Statistics* 56 (February): 1–13.

Bhatia, Kul B. 1983. "Asset Effects and Household Saving: Estimates from Survey Data by Income Class." London, Ont.: University of Western Ontario, Department of Economics Research Report No. 8304.

Blinder, Alan S.; Roger Gordon; and Donald E. Wise. 1981. "Social Security, Bequests, and the Life Cycle Theory of Saving: Cross-Sectional Tests." In *The Determinants of National Saving and Wealth*, edited by Franco Modigliani and Richard Hemming, pp. 89–122. New York: St. Martin's Press.

Budd, Edward C., and David F. Seiders. 1971. "The Impact of Inflation on the Distribution of Income and Wealth." *American Economic Review* 61 (May): 128–38.

Cagan, Phillip, and Robert E. Lipsey. 1978. *The Financial Effects of Inflation.* Cambridge, Mass.: Ballinger Publishing Company.

Carlson, John A. 1977. "A Study of Price Forecasts." *Annals of Economic and Social Measurement* 6 (June):27–56.

Center for Human Resource Research. 1981. *National Longitudinal Surveys Handbook.* Columbus: The Ohio State University.

Chan-Lee, James H. 1980. "A Review of Recent Work in the Area of Inflationary Expectations." *Welwirtschliches Archiv* 116:45–85.

Economic Report of the President. 1982. Washington, D.C.: U.S. Government Printing Office.

Feldstein, Martin S. 1974. "Social Security, Induced Retirement, and Aggregate Capital Accumulation." *Journal of Political Economy* 82 (September/October):902–26.

Friedman, Milton. 1957. *A Theory of the Consumption Function.* Princeton: Princeton University Press.

Friend, Irwin, and Charles Lieberman. 1975. "Short-Run Asset Effects on Household Saving and Consumption: The Cross-Section Evidence." *American Economic Review* 65 (September):624–33.

Fuller, Wayne A., and George E. Battese. 1974. "Estimation of Linear Models with Cross-Error Structure." *Journal of Econometrics* 2 (May):67–78.

Hendershott, Patric H., and Joe Peek. 1985. "Real Household Capital Gains and Wealth Accumulation." In *The Level and Composition of Household Saving*, edited by Patric H. Hendershott, pp. 41–61. Cambridge, Mass.: Ballinger Publishing Company.

Hurd, Michael, and John B. Shoven. 1982. "Real Income and Wealth of the Elderly." *American Economic Review* 72 (May):314–18.

Ibbotson, Roger G., and Rex A. Sinquefield. 1979. *Stocks, Bonds, Bills, and Inflation: Historical Returns (1926–1978).* 2d ed. Charlottesville, Virg.: The Financial Analysts Research Foundation.

Intriligator, Michael D. 1978. *Econometric Models, Techniques, and Applications.* Englewood Cliffs, N.J.: Prentice-Hall.

Johnston, J. 1972. *Econometric Methods.* 2d ed. New York: McGraw-Hill.

Kane, Edward J. 1982. "How Household Portfolios Responded to Accelerating Inflation and Differential Savings Incentives in the Late 1960s." Final report for HUD contract no. 2987.

Levhari, D., and L.J. Mirman. 1977. "Saving and Consumption with an Uncertain Horizon." *Journal of Political Economy* 85 (April):265–81.

Maddala, G.S. 1977. *Econometrics.* New York: McGraw-Hill.

Modigliani, Franco, and Richard E. Brumberg. 1954. "Utility Analysis and the Consumption Function: An Interpretation of Cross-Section Data." In *Post-Keynesian Economics,* edited by Kenneth K. Kurihara, pp. 388–436. New Brunswick, N.J.: Rutgers University Press.

Munnell, Alicia H. 1976. "Private Pensions and Saving: New Evidence." *Journal of Political Economy* 84 (October):1013–32.

Peek, Joe. 1983. "Capital Gains and Personal Saving Behavior." *Journal of Money, Credit, and Banking* 15 (February):1–23.

U.S. Bureau of the Census. 1968. *Statistical Abstract of the United States: 1968.* 89th ed. Washington, D.C.: U.S. Government Printing Office.

———. 1973. *Statistical Abstract of the United States: 1973.* 94th ed. Washington, D.C.: U.S. Government Printing Office.

———. 1974. *Statistical Abstract of the United States: 1974.* 95th ed. Washington, D.C.: U.S. Government Printing Office.

Wachtel, Paul. 1980. "Inflation and the Saving Behavior of Households: A Survey." In *The Government and Capital Formation,* edited by George M. von Furstenburg, pp. 153–74. Cambridge, Mass.: Ballinger Publishing Company.

White, Betsy B. 1978. "Empirical Tests of the Life Cycle Hypothesis." *American Economic Review* 68 (September):547–60.

III HOUSEHOLD SAVING IN SPECIFIC VEHICLES

7 HOUSEHOLD FORMATIONS

*Patric H. Hendershott and Mark Smith**

Over a quarter of the nearly $10 trillion net worth of Americans at the end of 1982 was in the form of residential structures. When the value of the land on which the structures rest is included, the ratio was over a third. Surprisingly, these ratios have not declined since 1960. One might have anticipated declines for two reasons. First, there seems to have been widespread belief over much of the last decade that housing has been unaffordable.[1] Second, real income per capita doubled in the last quarter century, and the income elasticity of housing demand is generally taken to be less than unity (Rosen 1979).[2]

The primary force preventing declines in the ratios has been a sharp increase in the ratio of households (groups occupying separate housing units) to population. In 1960 household heads comprised 29.5 percent of the population; in 1980, 36.3 percent. Given a 1980 population of 218 million, this increase translates into nearly 15 million additional households. Substantial economies exist when people live together: A couple shares a kitchen, dining room, and so forth; living

*We wish to thank Robert Buckley, James Follain, and participants at seminars at the Department of Housing and Urban Development, a NBER Tax Program meeting, and the Ohio State University Economics Department for useful comments.

separately, they need two of these rooms. While two can't live as cheaply as one, together they can obtain housing services for less than twice what each could separately. Thus an increase in households, even holding population and income constant, raises the demand for housing. If the formation of one extra household, still holding income and population constant, increases the demand for housing by $5 to $10 thousand, then fifteen million additional households raised the aggregate demand for housing by $75 to $150 billion.

The obvious question is why did the household/population ratio increase so markedly? Part of the increase was due to the movement of the post–World War II baby-boom population into the prime household-forming age group. Even if the rate at which the population in different age groups formed households had remained constant between 1960 and 1980, the household/population ratio would have risen by three percentage points. The remaining four percentage point increase in the ratio reflects an increased demand by Americans for privacy. This increase could reflect rising real incomes, declining real costs of privacy (especially for low-income families with dependent children), improving health of the elderly and/or shifting tastes toward privacy (including a decreased aversion to divorce). This chapter tries to determine the relative importance of these factors in explaining the increase in households. It is divided into three sections. The first develops the household-formation estimation equation, and the second presents and interprets the estimates. A summary concludes the chapter.

THE HOUSEHOLD FORMATION DECISION

From an accounting framework, household formations can be expressed in terms of two factors: the size and age structure of the population, and age-specific headship rates. Age structure is important because persons in different age categories have differing likelihoods of being household heads. An age-specific headship rate refers to the rate at which the population in a specific age category forms itself into households; it is the ratio of the number of household heads in an age category to the number of people in that category. Age-specific headship rates change as the population varies its demand for privacy.

Headship rates for specific age categories are listed in Table 7–1

Table 7–1. Headship Rates.

Age	p_i *(1960)*	*1960*	*1967*	*1974*	*1980*	*1983*	p_i *(1983)*
15–19	0.073	0.017	0.018	0.026	0.032	0.021	0.083
20–24	0.059	0.222	0.242	0.299	0.287	0.251	0.092
25–29	0.060	0.401	0.456	0.478	0.484	0.459	0.090
30–34	0.066	0.459	0.476	0.514	0.533	0.515	0.081
35–44	0.133	0.488	0.504	0.518	0.549	0.542	0.125
45–54	0.115	0.527	0.532	0.548	0.556	0.572	0.097
55–64	0.086	0.559	0.572	0.580	0.583	0.605	0.104
65–74	0.056	0.631	0.639	0.666	0.658	0.662	0.070
75 and over	0.028	0.614	0.628	0.687	0.719	0.728	0.042
All ages		0.295	0.304	0.336	0.363	0.366	
Demographic-adjusted		0.295	0.305	0.321	0.328	0.321	

Source: The appendix.

for March 31 of selected years. Also listed are the shares of the population in each age group (the p_i) in 1960 and 1983. As can be seen, headship rates for all categories rose dramatically between 1960 and 1980. The increases were proportionally greatest for the young (under 35) and old (over 75). For the young, the increase was concentrated in the 1967–74 period. For the elderly, the increase was relatively steady, although the largest increase was again between 1967 and 1974. Between 1980 and 1983, a sharp divergence in headship rates occurred; those for the under 35 age categories fell sharply, while those for the over 44 age groups continued to rise.

The headship rate hh_i for the ith age category is defined as:

$$hh_i = \frac{HH_i}{POP_i}, \tag{7.1}$$

where HH_i is the number of households in the category and POP_i is the population in the category. The aggregate headship rate can be expressed as:

$$hh = \Sigma hh_i p_i,$$

where p_i is share of the population in the ith age category, and the aggregate demographic-adjusted headship rate by:

$$hh^* = \Sigma hh_i p_i^*,$$

where p_i^* is the ith population share in the base period. With 1960 as the base, hh^* rose from 0.295 in 1960 to 0.328 in 1980; with 1980 as the base, the increase was from 0.324 to 0.363. Because the age structure of the population over 14 is relatively exogenous (and there are few household heads under the age of 15), it is useful to partition the growth in households into that due to changes in age-specific headship rates and that due to the exogenous population age structure. The total number of households is:

$$HH = \Sigma HH_i, \tag{7.2}$$

and the change in households between periods o and t is:

$$\Delta HH = HH^t - HH^o. \tag{7.3}$$

Solving equation (4.1) for HH_i and substituting into (4.2) and the result into (4.3) yields:

$$\Delta HH = \sum_i hh_i^t POP_i^t - \sum_i hh_i^o POP_i^o. \qquad (7.3')$$

This formula can be rewritten to reflect two distinct effects:

$$\Delta HH = \sum_i hh_i^o \Delta POP_i + \sum_i POP_i^t \Delta hh_i, \qquad (7.3'')$$

where ΔX is, in general, defined as $X^t - X^o$. The first term indicates the effect of population growth and shifts, and the second term the influence of changes in headship rates.

The effect of population growth and shifts is deduced by computation of the first summation in equation (7.3″). The population has been divided into ten age categories: 0–14 and the nine listed in Table 7–1. The 20–24 and 25–29 age groupings are the prime years during which individuals form new households (see Table 7–1). The computed variable, which indicates the change in households if headship rates remained at the previous year's level, is called exogenous household growth and is denoted by ΔHX.

Income and the Price of Housing

Economic variables appear to explain part of the nondemographic increase in headship rates. Most obvious among these variables are real income and the real price of housing services (Smith et al. 1982). As real incomes rise, potential households are better able to exercise their desire to establish a new household. Similarly, lower real prices of housing services enable groups that otherwise would not have been able or willing to acquire a housing unit to form a household.

The income variable utilized is real disposable income per capita. This variable has increased throughout the period from a level of \$2,697 in 1960 to \$4,545 in 1982. For the real price of housing services for rental housing, we employ the CPI rent component, as adjusted by Lowry (1982) to account adequately for depreciation and to treat utility costs consistently, deflated by the CPI net of shelter. This price series generally declined from 1.017 in the 1962–65 span to 0.947 in the middle to late 1970s and has since risen to near unity. For the real price of housing services from unsubsidized owner-occupied housing, the user cost series for households in the 15 percent tax bracket is approximately that computed by Hendershott and Shilling (1981).[3] The 15 percent tax rate is close to that calculated by Hendershott and Slemrod (1983) as the most relevant to the tenure choice decision in 1977.[4] The user cost declined fairly steadily from 7.8 percent in 1960–63 to 3.9 percent in 1978 and then rose sharply to 12.7 percent in 1982.

Subsidized housing effectively lowers the real price of housing services for households selected to occupy such units. To the extent that subsidies go to groups that would not have been households in the absence of subsidies, household formations and the demand for housing units increases. Over three-quarters of subsidized housing during the 1961–82 period has been rental,[5] and the existence of below-market rents is reflected in the CPI rent index.[6] Because owner subsidies have been small and have not been especially targeted to first-time buyers, no general attempt is made to relate household formations to owner subsidies.[7]

An additional possible determinant of household formations is the real initial mortgage payment burden. With the standard fixed-rate mortgage, nominal mortgage payments are fixed over time, while real mortgage payments decline at the rate of inflation. Moreover, the higher is anticipated inflation and thus the nominal mortgage rate, the larger is the initial mortgage payment. As attractive as expected future inflationary gains may be, young wealth-constrained households may find the initial mortgage payments to be "unaffordable" and thus be compelled to purchase a smaller house than they would if inflation did not tilt the real mortgage payment stream forward in time (Kearl 1979; Follain 1982; Schwab 1983). More important, from our perspective, some persons may not move away from parents, other relatives, or group quarters to form households until they can attain ownership of a "reasonably" sized house. As a result, high initial mortgage payments relative to income could reduce the level of household formations. The real-mortgage-payment-to-income variable is defined as the real net-of-tax mortgage payment on a constant quality house (the average new house constructed in 1974), assuming 75 percent financing at the current mortgage rate or 12 percent, whichever is lower. The truncation of the mortgage rate reflects the widespread use of owner financing and builder buy downs in the 1980s when interest rates exceeded 12 percent. The tax rate employed is the same as that for the real user cost of homeownership. This variable generally increased during the 1960–82 period and increased especially rapidly from 21 percent in1978 to 28 percent in 1981 and 1982.

Summarizing the above, the dependency of the age specific headship rates on economic variables can be expressed as:

$$hh_i = hh_i(\overset{+}{y}, \overset{-}{r}, \overset{-}{o}, \overset{-}{m}), \tag{7.4}$$

where

y = real per capita disposable personal income,
r = real price of rental housing,
o = real price of owner housing, and
m = real mortgage payment burden,

for the particular age category, and the signs above the arguments denote the expected signs of the partial derivatives. From equation (7.3″), the endogenous change in households is the sum of the product of changes in age-specific headship rates and the population in the age groups. The relevant independent variables, based on equation (7.4), are thus changes in the price of housing services (rental and owner), income, and the mortgage-payment burden for each age group times the populations in the groups. We approximate these variables by the products of total population and changes in the economywide variables.

Other Variables

Among social variables, the increase in divorce (the divorce rate per thousand U.S. residents jumped from 2.2 in 1960 to 5.2 in 1980) is sometimes cited as a major factor causing the increase in household formations during the 1960s and 1970s (Rosen and Jaffee 1981:21). The effect of increases in the number of divorces on formations is uncertain, however. While the number of primary individual households will certainly increase (these households increased from under 8 million in 1960 to 20 million in 1980), the impact on total households is ambiguous. If both husband and wife form separate households after a divorce, then one additional household is created. Alternatively, if both husband and wife move back with family or friends, one household is lost. To complicate matters further, the decision the divorcing couple makes will likely be determined in part by the real incomes of the couple, the real price of housing services and, possibly, the form welfare takes (see below).

Nonetheless, four divorce variables are tested in the household-formations equation: the total number of divorces each year, the change during the year in the total number of divorced persons (the first variable less remarriages and deaths of single previously divorced persons), the change in the total number of divorced persons over age 34, and the change in the number of households headed by divorced women with children under age 18. The latter two variables reflect our persumption that older people and those with at least one minor child are less likely to move in with family or friends (Carliner 1975). To put these variables in perspective, the increases in their annual values between the early 1960s and late 1970s were 800,000, 600,000, 300,000, and 50,000.

A likely factor affecting household formations in the late 1960s and early 1970s was the change in the aid for families with dependent children (AFDC). This aid has both income and price dimensions. An increase in real benefits should, like increases in any form of income, raise the demand for privacy and thus increase household formations. However, insofar as the actual benefits received are negatively related to total household income, the effective benefit level can be raised (often from zero) by a single parent establishing a separate household. Thus an increase in scheduled real benefits also lowers the price of establishing a separate household. In fact, the price effect would be expected to far outweigh the income effect.

Between 1960 and 1980, the number of families receiving AFDC rose by 3 million (from 0.8 to 3.8 million). Two-thirds of the increase came in the 1967–74 period. This sharp jump reflected a 30 percent increase in real benefits per recipient (in the 1964–70 period) and a substantial reduction in eligibility requirements. The latter, part of 1967 legislation, required states (after July 1, 1969) to disregard the first $30 of monthly earnings plus one-third of the remainder in computing benefits. The former was largely attributable to the federal government offering in mid-1966 to pay at least one-half of whatever the state paid to AFDC families, provided the state offered Medicaid.[8] Given the substantial increase in incentives to establish a single-parent household, the surge in the divorce rate between 1967 and 1973—60 percent of the increase observed over the entire 1960–80 span occurred in these six years—and the bulge in household formations are hardly surprising. The change in the number of families on AFDC is added to our list of explanatory variables.

The Estimation Equation

The estimation equation is the result of replacing the first sum in equation (7.3″) by $\alpha_1 \Delta HX$ and the second sum by a linear function of total population (*POP*) times the changes in the variables in the functional of equation (7.4), the change in some divorce variable, and the change in families on AFDC. The equation for the change in households is thus:

$$\Delta HH = \alpha_0 + \alpha_1 \Delta HX + \alpha_2 POP\Delta y + \alpha_3 POP\Delta r + \alpha_4 POP\Delta o + \alpha_5 POP\Delta m$$
$$+ \alpha_6 \Delta DIV + \alpha_7 \Delta AFDC, \qquad (7.5)$$

where ΔDIV equals one of the four divorce variables tested. The expected signs, and magnitudes where readily known, of the coefficients are:

$$\alpha_0 = 0 \qquad \alpha_1 = 1.0 \qquad \alpha_2 > 0$$
$$\alpha_3, \alpha_4, \alpha_5 < 0 \quad 0 < \alpha_6, \alpha_7 < 1.0.$$

The means, high and low values, and scaling of each of the series utilized are listed in Table 7–2. Figure 7–1 contains plots of a few of the series, namely endogenous household formations ($\Delta HH - \Delta HX$), the income variable ($POP\Delta y$), the negative of the user cost variable ($-POP\Delta o$) and the change in families on AFDC. The positive correlations between endogenous household formations and the other variables can be discerned by close inspection of the figure.

EXPLANATION OF HOUSEHOLD FORMATIONS

Nine different household equations are presented in Table 7–3. The first equation includes exogenous households and the four basic economic variables: real income, real prices of owner and renter housing, and the real mortgage-payment burden. The exogenous household formations variable, which measures the effect of population growth and changing age structure on household formations, is expected to have a coefficient of one and is about a half standard deviation less than this value. All the other variables are correctly signed,

Table 7-2. Data Summary.

	Mean	*Low*	*High*
y (income – real dollars per capita)	3,739	2,725	4,545
Δ	84	-89	225
r (rent – ratio of indexes (1967 = 100))	98.8	101.7	94.7
Δ*r*	-0.03	-1.50	3.00
o (owner cost – percent per annum)	6.52	3.52	12.75
Δ*o*	0.23	-1.10	3.28
POP (population – millions)	207	181	230
m (mortgage payment to income ratio – percent per annum)	18.58	14.10	28.40
Δ*m*	0.46	-1.10	3.60
Total divorces (thousands)	789	393	1,219
Change in number of divorced (thousands)	411	82	1,066
Change in number of divorced over age 35 (thousands)	256	23	654
Change in number of divorced females with child under age 18 (thousands)	86	9	207
Families on AFDC (thousands)	2,486	853	3,876
Δ*AFDC* (thousands)	125	-315	677
Change in households (Δ*HH* – thousands)	1,401	619	2,051
Exogenous change in households (Δ*HX* – thousands)	1,162	457	1,644

but only the real owner price is significantly different from zero. The adjusted R^2 indicates substantial unexplained variation.

Addition of the AFDC variable improves the relation in numerous respects. Not only does the variable enter appropriately and the explanatory power rise sharply, but the coefficient on endogenous household formations is very close to unity and the constant is much

Figure 7–1. Endogenous Household Formations and Some Key Determinants, 1960–82.

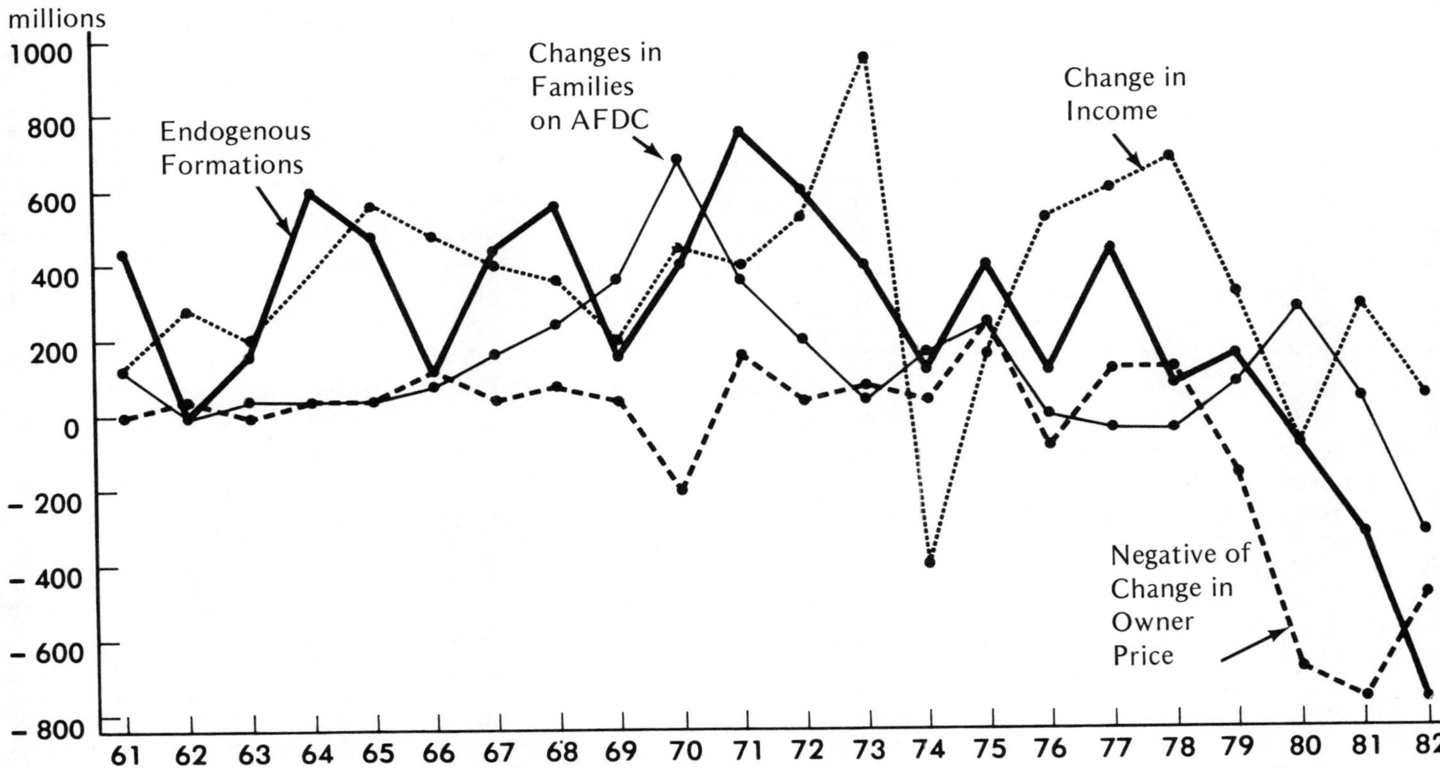

Table 7-3. Household Formations, 1961-82.

Equation No.	*7-3.1*	*7-3.2*	*7-3.3*	*7-3.4*	*7-3.5*	*7-3.6*	*7-3.7*	*7-3.8*	*7-3.9*
Intercept	296.2	103.1	117.7	149.1	108.5	114.3	215.6	133.3	74.7
	(216.2)	(177.9)	(181.3)	(193.1)	(187.8)	(193.1)	(180.0)	(84.0)	(85.1)
ΔHX	0.894	0.973	1.123	0.851	0.948	0.950	0.916	1.0	1.0
	(0.190)	(0.150)	(0.734)	(0.238)	(0.233)	(0.194)	(0.162)		
$POP\,\Delta y$	0.00628	0.00670	0.00671	0.00688	0.00681	0.00672	0.00659	0.00623	0.00661
	(0.00459)	(0.00356)	(0.00371)	(0.00365)	(0.00377)	(0.00370)	(0.00378)	(0.00364)	(0.00343)
$POP\,\Delta r$	-0.155	-0.070	-0.055	-0.031	-0.062	-0.066	-0.092	-0.130	-0.082
	(0.236)	(0.185)	(0.200)	(0.198)	(0.201)	(0.193)	(0.192)	(0.173)	(0.170)
$POP\,\Delta o$	-0.712	-0.664	-0.642	-0.757	-0.695	-0.649	-0.700	-0.722	-0.670
	(0.267)	(0.208)	(0.260)	(0.255)	(0.305)	(0.229)	(0.215)	(0.207)	(0.200)
$POP\,\Delta m$	-0.028	-0.131	-0.070	-0.130	-0.128	-0.131	-0.033	-0.112	-0.154
	(0.283)	(0.223)	(0.240)	(0.227)	(0.232)	(0.231)	(0.248)	(0.192)	(0.178)
$\Delta AFDC$		0.822	0.810	0.841	0.836	0.795	0.400	0.400	0.829
		(0.244)	(0.271)	(0.250)	(0.271)	(0.289)			(0.233)
ΔDIV			-0.242	0.232	0.083	0.193			
			(1.011)	(0.347)	(0.585)	(1.014)			
Specification of Divorce Variable			*Number of Divorces*	*Change in Total Stock*	*Change in over Age 35 Stock*	*With Child under Age 18*			
SEE	260	203	204	206	210	209	212	208	203
$\overline{R}^2$	0.616	0.767	0.763	0.758	0.751	0.751	0.744	0.755	0.781
DW	1.74	2.15	2.31	2.16	2.15	2.16	2.17	2.17	2.13

closer to its expected value of zero. Further, the income coefficient rises slightly and is now statistically greater than zero.

Equations 7–3.1 through 7–3.6 test different divorce variables. The total number of divorces each year has an unexpected negative coefficient in equation 7–3.3, and the annual change in the total number of divorced persons (equation 7–3.4), the change in divorced persons over age 35 (equation 7–3.5), and the change in the total number of divorced females with children under age 18 (equation 7–3.6) all have coefficients smaller than their standard errors. In general, the coefficients on other variables are insensitive to inclusion of the divorce variables.

One might argue that the 0.8 coefficient on the change in AFDC households is too large. First, part of the increase in AFDC families must have been broken families who were separate households prior to going on AFDC. Second, some of the husbands who separated from their families undoubtedly did not establish new households themselves. Moreover, because the change in households on AFDC is part of the independent variable, this coefficient is likely biased toward unity. The AFDC coefficient is arbitrarily constrained to 0.4 in equations 7–3.7 and 7–3.8 to determine the sensitivity of the other coefficients to changes in the AFDC response.[9] As can be seen by comparing equations 7–3.2 and 7–3.7 the decline in explanatory power is small, and the only marked change in coefficients is a doubling of the constant term. In equation 7–3.2 the constant accounts for 2¼ million household formations over the 1961–82 period (103 times 22); in equation 7–3.7 the constant accounts for 4¾ million.

In both equations 7–3.2 and 7–3.7, the coefficient on exogenous household formations is less than the expected unity value. This is not surprising because the variable is obviously measured with error and thus its coefficient will be biased toward zero. To compensate, the unity coefficient has been imposed in equations 7–3.8 and 7–3.9; the 0.4 coefficient on $\Delta AFDC$ is also enforced in equation 7–3.8. The constant terms in the equations decline to compensate for the increased coefficient on exogenous household formations.

Table 7–4 contains elasticities, based on equations 7–3.8 and 7–3.9, of aggregate headship rates with respect to real income, rent, owner price, and the mortgage constraint. The elasticities are evaluated, in turn, at both the sample mean and 1982 value. The income elasticity is 0.075 to 0.08; the "price" elasticities are somewhat smaller, –0.03 for rent (but with a large standard error), –0.015 to –0.025 for the

Table 7-4. Elasticities of Headship Rates.

	Evaluated at	
	Mean	*1982 Value*
Real income	0.075	0.08
Real rent	-0.03	-0.03
Real owner price	-0.015	-0.025
Mortgage payment burden	-0.01	-0.01

Table 7-5. Increase in Households, 1961-82 (millions).

	1961-78	*1979-82*
Total increase	25½	5¼
Due to population growth and age structure changes	17½	6¼
Due to other factors	8	-1
Real income	3	¼
Real cost of housing	¾	-1½
Mortgage payment burden	-¼	-¼
AFDC	1½ to 2½	—
"Trend"	2 to 3	¼ to ½

owner user cost, and -0.01 for the mortgage-payment burden (again with a large standard error).

Table 7-5 details the sources of changes in the number of households for two periods, 1961-78 and 1979-82, based on equations 7-3.8 and 7-3.9.[10] During the 1961-78 period, steady increases in headship rates induced the formation of 8 million households or nearly a third of the total 25½ million households formed. These are attributable to the rise in real income per capita (3 million), to the decline in the real price of owner housing (¾ million, ¼ of which was offset by the increase in the mortgage-payment burden), to the expansion of the AFDC program (1½ to 2½ million), and to the constant term or trend (2 to 3 million). In the 1979-82 period, headship rates fell; the number of households was a million less than that which would have occurred with constant headship rates. The cause was the sharp rise in the owner user cost, which triggered a 1½ million decline in households.

The most perplexing problem is the interpretation of the growth in households "caused" by the constant term. To understand the source of the positive constant term, it is useful to examine the age-specific headship rates more closely. This is accomplished by computations of changes in headship rates by five year intervals (see Table 7-6). Two obvious points stand out. First, the over-75 age category experienced the largest increase in headship rate over the two decades, 0.138, followed by the 25-44 age categories (see the far right column). Second, the changes in the demographic-adjusted headship rate (bottom row of Table 7-6) indicate that headship rates increased far more in the 1967-72 period than in the other five-year spans. Consistent with this, six of the nine age groups experienced their largest five-year increases in the 1967-72 period.

The positive constant term, which accounts for 2 to 3½ million of the increase in households between 1960 and 1982, probably stems in part from the steady increase in household heads over age 75. The increase in this headship rate, along with the growth in population in this age category, accounted for the formation of over a million households. Much of the million is likely attributable to a continuing increase in the health and life span of the elderly. A second factor the constant term may reflect is an apparent increase in the taste for headship by people born after about 1937. These people were age 24 and younger in 1961. Note how their movement into the 25-29 age group in the 1962-67 period sharply raised that headship rate. Later, in 1967-72, they raised the 30-34 headship rate, and again in 1972-82, they continually pushed the 35-44 headship rate upward. People born in even later years maintained this desire for headship (note that the 20-24 rate did not fall in 1962-67, the 25-29 rate did not fall in 1967-72, and the 30-34 rate did not decline in 1972-77). Why people born after 1937 have a greater desire for headship is unclear, but they certainly have it. Possibly they have substantially greater future income prospects owing to greater investment in human capital (Johnson 1985) and our income variable picks this up. But we expect that the positive constant reflects, in part, that people born after 1937 continually constitute a larger proportion of the adult population.

Table 7–6. Changes in Headship Rates.

Age	*1962–67*	*1967–72*	*1972–77*	*1977–82*	*1962–82*
15–19	-0.002	0.006	0.001	-0.001	0.004
20–24	0.001	0.032	0.011	-0.017	0.027
25–29	0.044	0.006	0.018	-0.008	0.060
30–34	-0.001	0.031	0.018	0.005	0.053
35–44	0.013	0.006	0.030	0.019	0.068
45–54	0.009	0.014	0.008	0.006	0.037
55–64	-0.001	0.019	-0.004	0.005	0.019
65–74	0.007	0.017	-0.005	0.010	0.029
75 and over	0.039	0.063	0.013	0.023	0.138
Demographic-adjusted	0.007	0.012	0.008	0.004	0.029

Source: The appendix.

SUMMARY

Between 1961 and 1978, the number of households grew by 25½ million or nearly 50 percent. Of this increase about a third was due to population growth, another third to changes in the age structure of the population (the aging of the postwar baby boom), and the last third to an increase in age-specific headship rates. A doubling of real per capita income and a halving of the real price of owner-occupied housing (the real after-tax mortgage rate) caused headship rates to increase for all age categories. The increases were the greatest for the young (under age 35) and the old (over age 75). The sharply higher headship rates of the young were a response to (1) the abrupt increase in real benefits and lower eligibility standards of the aid to families with dependent children (AFDC) program in the late 1960s and (2) a greater propensity for headship by the population born after 1937. The enormous (over ten percentage point) increase in the over-75 headship rate reflected better health and real incomes that are far greater (due to a 75 percent increase in real social security payments) and more certain (due to indexation) than existed in the early 1960s.

In the early 1980s a sharp divergence in headship rates has occurred; those for population under age 35 have fallen, while those for the population over age 44 have continued to rise. The reduced headship rates for the young reflect both the marked increase in the real price of owner-occupied housing (real after-tax mortgage rate) and the cutback in real benefits and increased eligibility standards for the AFDC program.[11] Each of these tends to fall more heavily on younger households who are more mobile (and thus are more likely to have to pay the market mortgage rate) and are more likely to have dependent children.

Specific numbers of household formations can be attributed to the various factors that have altered headship rates. Increased headship rates between 1960 and 1978 resulted in 8 million additional households, about half of which were induced by rising real incomes (3 million) and falling real prices of owner housing (¾ million). Another 1½ to 2¾ million is attributable to the increased real benefits and lower eligibility standards of the AFDC program. Because actual AFDC benefits received are negatively related to total household income, the effective benefit level can easily be raised by a low-income single parent establishing a separate household. It should not be surprising that a 30 percent increase in real scheduled benefits and significant reduction in eligibility standards in the late 1960s coincided with a jump in the divorce rate, unprecedented increases in families on AFDC, and a surge in household formations. The last 1¾ to 3 million of the 8 million increase is likely explained by both the steadily rising longevity and health of older people and the increasing importance to household formations of those born after the late 1930s.

Between 1979 and 1983, household growth continued at a high level, owing to the further maturation of the baby boom. However, the above-noted sharp rise in real after-tax interest rates, and thus the cost of owner housing, reduced formations (of those under age 34) by1½ million relative to what would have otherwise occurred.

APPENDIX: CONSTRUCTION OF THE HOUSEHOLD SERIES

Data on the number of households and population in the respective age groups are available through two annual U.S. Bureau of the Census, Current Population Survey (CPS) reports: "Household and Family Characteristics" and "Marital Status and Living Arrangements." Numerous adjustments were necessary, however, to develop consistent household and exogenous household series for the 1960–82 period.

For most years the CPS reports contain data on the number of households by age for nine age groups: under 20, 20–24, 25–29, 30–34, 35-44, 45–54, 55–64, 65–74, and 75 and over. In the years 1968–1975, however, the four youngest age groups are combined into two groups: under 25 and 25–34. Because those age groupings comprise the prime household forming years in which large changes in headship rates occur, an attempt was made to divide the number of households in these two broader age groups into the smaller subdivisions. First, the proportion of under-25 households that were under 20 and 20–24 (and the proportion of 25–34 households that were 25–29 and 30–34) were averaged for the three years prior to 1968 and the three years following 1975. The assumed proportions over the 1968–75 period were then obtained by extrapolating linearly between the pre-1968 and post-1975 averages.

A larger problem with the CPS is the reconciliation of the CPS data to the 1970 and 1980 Census counts. When the Census data became available, the CPS population controls were adjusted upward to compensate for the excess of the Census count over the CPS estimates. Thus a large jump in the household data occurs in the year of adjustment. However, various issues of the CPS Series P–25 provide yearly estimates that have been adjusted to correspond to the decennial Census counts. Yearly change in households (and in exogenous households) that are consistent with the decennial data are calculated using the revised population data in equation (7.3″). To apply equation (7.3″), headship rates were first calculated using the unadjusted household and population numbers from the CPS reports, and then these rates and the adjusted population data were employed.

A further problem in this calculation was that prior to 1972, inmates of institutions (which includes, for example, the elderly living in nursing homes) were included in the unadjusted population count; in 1972 and thereafter, they were excluded. All population and thus household data have been converted to a noninstitutionalized basis; that is, inmates of institutions were deleted from the population data prior to 1972. Because the adjusted population series includes inmates of institutions, the sum of the change in household series computed from equation (7.3″) for the 1961–80 period was 800,000 greater than the actual change in households between the 1960 and 1980 decennial counts. The computed change in household series was multiplied by the average ratio of population excluding inmates of institutions to total population in order to make the change series consistent with the decennial counts.

The CPS data are reported for March 31 of each year. To convert the data to an annual basis, we have assumed that households grew linearly between March 31 dates. Thus the calendar year change in households consists of 75 percent of the change in households in one year and 25 percent of the preceding year (for example, the 1964 change would be 75 percent of the change from March 1964 to March 1965 and 25 percent of the change from March 1963 to March 1964).

NOTES

1. See Modigliani and Lessard (1975) and The President's Commission on Housing (1982:73–77).
2. For a simulation analysis of the impact of affordability and the below unity income elasticity on the allocation of capital between residential and industrial uses, see Hendershott and Hu (1983).
3. We thank James Shilling for updating this series for us and for modifying

it to incorporate the changing property tax rate presented in Buckley and Simonson (1984).

4. This tax bracket is roughly appropriate throughout the study period because the effects of bracket creep and increases in mortgage interest deductions have roughly offset each other, leaving the typical new homeowner in approximately the same tax bracket.
5. Owner subsidies were not available until the Section 235 program began in 1969. While owner-subsidized units rose to 41 percent of total subsidized starts in 1972, they averaged only 27 percent of total subsidized starts between 1969 and 1982.
6. The CPI rent component is constructed by asking consumers how much they pay each month for rent. If they are receiving subsidy assistance, they would report only the portion of total rent that they pay. The CPI rental component therefore would reflect the impact of subsidy programs on tenant rental payments.
7. There was significant use of tax-exempt mortgage revenue bonds to assist first-time homebuyers in 1980 and 1982.
8. See Burke (1974) for a fascinating discussion of the politics surrounding the development of the ADFC program (and welfare policy generally).
9. In some preliminary work, household formations have been related directly to changes in real AFDC benefits and the 1969 change in eligibility standards (a dummy variable assuming the value one-third in 1969–71 and zero in all other years). Both variables are marginally significant with the expected sign, and their coefficients suggest that the expansion of the AFDC program increased households by 1½ million. This is the same impact implied by the 0.4 coefficient on ΔAFDC.
10. The calculation of the change in the number of households due to demographic changes holds headship rates for each age group constant at their 1960 and 1978 levels for the respective periods. In the model, however, the exogenous household formations variable is calculated each years based on the preceding years headship rate. Given that headship rates rose (fell) between 1960 and 1978 (1978 and 1982), the sum of the exogenous household formations variable over time would exceed (fall short of) the demographic change in the table. This difference is distributed proportionately across the other variables in Table 7–4.
11. The AFDC changes resulted from passage of the Omnibus Budget Reconciliation Act of 1981, Public Law 97–35.

REFERENCES

Buckley, Robert M., and John C. Simonson. 1984. "Effective Property Tax Rates and Capital Formation Issues: Manvel, Acton and Darby." Washington, D.C.: U.S. Department of Housing and Urban Development. Mimeo.

Burke, Vincent J., and Vee Burke, 1974. *Nixon's Good Deed.* New York: Columbia University Press.

Carliner, Geoffrey. 1975. "Determinants of Household Headship." *Journal of Marriage and the Family* 37, no. 1 (February):28–38.

Follain, James R. 1982. "Does Inflation Affect Real Behavior: The Case of Housing." *Southern Economic Journal* 48 (January):570–82.

Hendershott, Patric H., and Sheng Hu. 1983. "The Allocation of Capital between Residential and Nonresidential Uses: Taxes, Inflation and Capital Market Constraints." *Journal of Finance* 38, no. 3 (June):795–812.

Hendershott, Patric H., and James D. Shilling. 1981. "The Economics of Tenure Choice, 1955–1979." In *Research in Real Estate,* vol. 1, edited by C.F. Sirmans, pp. 105–33. Greenwich, Conn.: JAI Press.

Hendershott, Patric H., and Joel Slemrod. 1983. "Taxes and the User Cost of Capital for Owner-Occupied Housing." *AREUEA Journal* 10, no. 4 (Winter): 375–93.

Johnson, George, 1985. "Investment in and Returns from Education." In *The Level and Composition of Household Saving,* edited by Patric H. Hendershott, pp. 267–295. Cambridge, Mass.: Ballinger Publishing Company.

Kearl, James R. 1979. "Inflation, Mortgages, and Housing." *Journal of Political Economy* 87, no. 5 (October):1115–38.

Lowry, Ira S. 1982. "Inflation Indexes for Rental Housing." Note N–18–32, Santa Monica: The Rand Corporation.

Modigliani, Franco, and Donald Lessard, eds. 1975. *New Mortgage Designs for Stable Housing in an Inflationary Environment.* Boston, Mass.: Federal Reserve Bank of Boston.

President's Commission on Housing. 1982. *The Report of the President's Commission on Housing.* Washington, D.C.

Rosen, Harvey S. 1979. "Housing Decisions and the U.S. Income Tax: An Econometric Analysis." *Journal of Public Economics* 11 (January):1–23.

Rosen, Kenneth T., and Dwight M. Jaffee. 1981. "The Demographic Demand for Housing: An Economic Analysis of the Household Formation Process." Paper presented at the American Economic Association Meetings, Washington, D.C., December 27.

Schwab, Robert M. 1983. "Real and Nominal Interest Rates and the Demand for Housing." *Journal of Urban Economics* 13, no. 2 (March):181–195.

Smith, Lawrence B., Kenneth T. Rosen, Auil Markandya, and Pierre-Antoine Ullmo. 1982. "The Demand for Housing, Household Headship Rates, and Household Formation: An International Analysis." Mimeo.

8 INVESTMENT IN CONSUMER DURABLES

Richard C. Lemmon

In 1982 households held over a trillion dollars of consumer durables, and this constituted over 10 percent of their net worth. However, the greatest interest in demand for consumer durables generally has stemmed from the volatility of purchases of consumer durables. Even though these purchases are important in their own right, comprising about 10 percent of real GNP on average, they are even more important in a business cycle context. Because of the long life of consumer durables (by definition at least three years), purchases are easily postponable in times of economic distress, and swings in these purchases are a major contributor to recessions. For example, during the 1969–70, 1973–75, and 1980 recessions, expenditures for durables accounted, on average for half of the decline in real GNP.[1]

One of the questions addressed in this paper is the sensitivity of investment in consumer durables to macroeconomic policies. The Reagan administration's four major goals included reindustrialization of the United States by boosting investment in plant and equipment. This would tend to increase productivity and alleviate inflationary pressures. Although left unsaid, one method of freeing up personal savings to be used to finance increased business investment is to discourage investment in consumer durables.

Because of their multiyear life (at least three years), purchases of consumer durables logically should be considered as investment. Nevertheless, purchases of consumer durables traditionally are thought of as consumption and are treated as such in the National Income and Product Accounts (NIPA).[2] (In contrast, the Flow of Funds classifies all purchases of consumer durables as investment.) The NIPA data are not sufficient for investment analysis because they do not distinguish between investment that adds to the stock of durables and investment that offsets depreciation of the stock. Fortunately, the Bureau of Economic Analysis has developed the necessary data on the net stocks of consumer durables (Musgrave 1979).

Before examining the particulars of consumer durable demand, it is useful to review how durables have been related historically to disposable personal income. Real disposable personal income per capita has roughly doubled in the last twenty-five years, allowing consumers to spend a larger share of income on luxuries. Because many of these luxury items fall into the durable goods category, one would anticipate that purchases of consumer durables have increased over time as a share of personal disposable income. While this has not been the case with nominal outlays (See Figure 8-1), it is when real magnitudes are considered (as is appropriate).[3] The upward trend is especially apparent after 1960.

Clearly, if the nominal ratio is relatively flat while the real ratio shows an upward trend, prices of consumer durables must have increased less than consumer prices in general over this period. The distinct downward trend in the ratio of the deflator for consumer durables to the deflator for all personal consumption expenditures is shown in Figure 8-2. One might conclude, at least in part, that the increase in the standard of living enjoyed by the U.S. consumer since World War II has been due to the falling real prices of consumer durables.

In order to investigate possible differences in the behavioral relationships, investment in consumer durables is divided into three parts: autos and parts, furniture and household equipment, and other consumer durables (jewelry, boats, and so on). These are the same divisions used in the NIPA. Figure 8-3 shows the net real (1972 dollars) stocks of these three components on a per household basis from 1954 to 1982. All components of consumer durables exhibit the same pattern—low growth through the early 1960s, followed by rapid growth until the late 1970s. (The impact of the 1980 and 1982 reces-

Figure 8–1. Gross Investment in Consumer Durables as a Percentage of Disposable Personal Income.

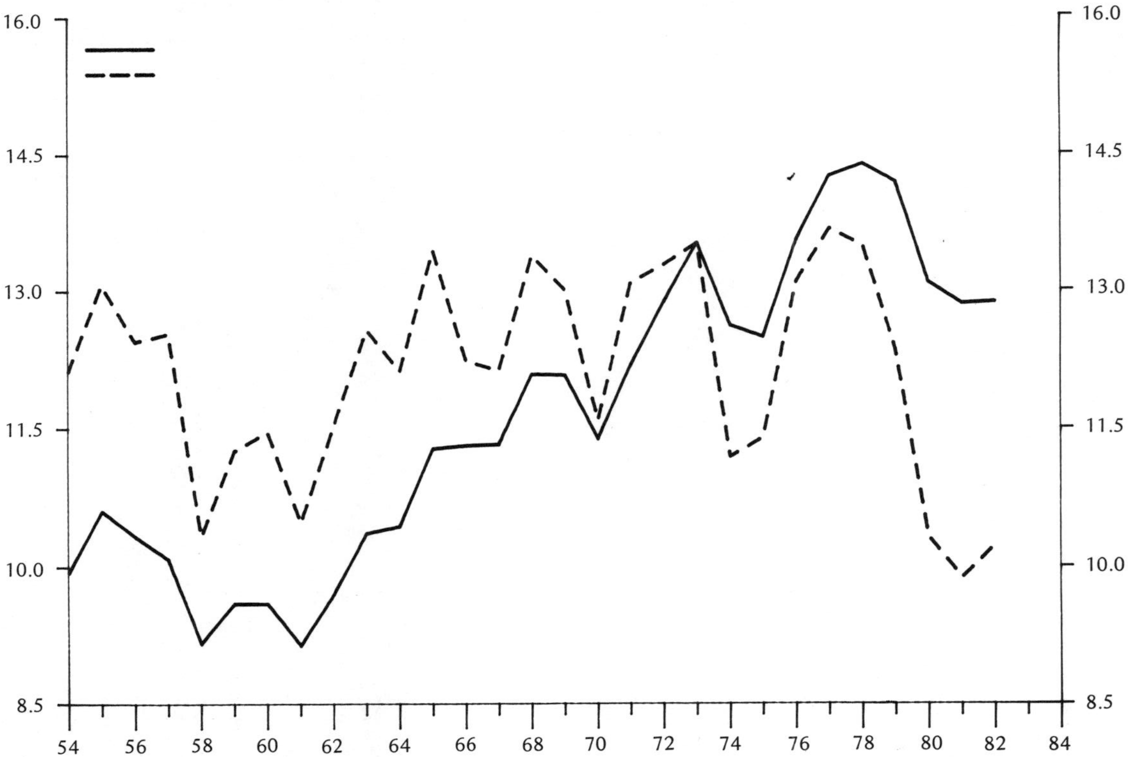

Source: U.S. Department of Commerce, Bureau of Economic Analysis.

Figure 8-2. Ratio of Deflator for Consumer Durables to Deflator for Total Personal Consumption.

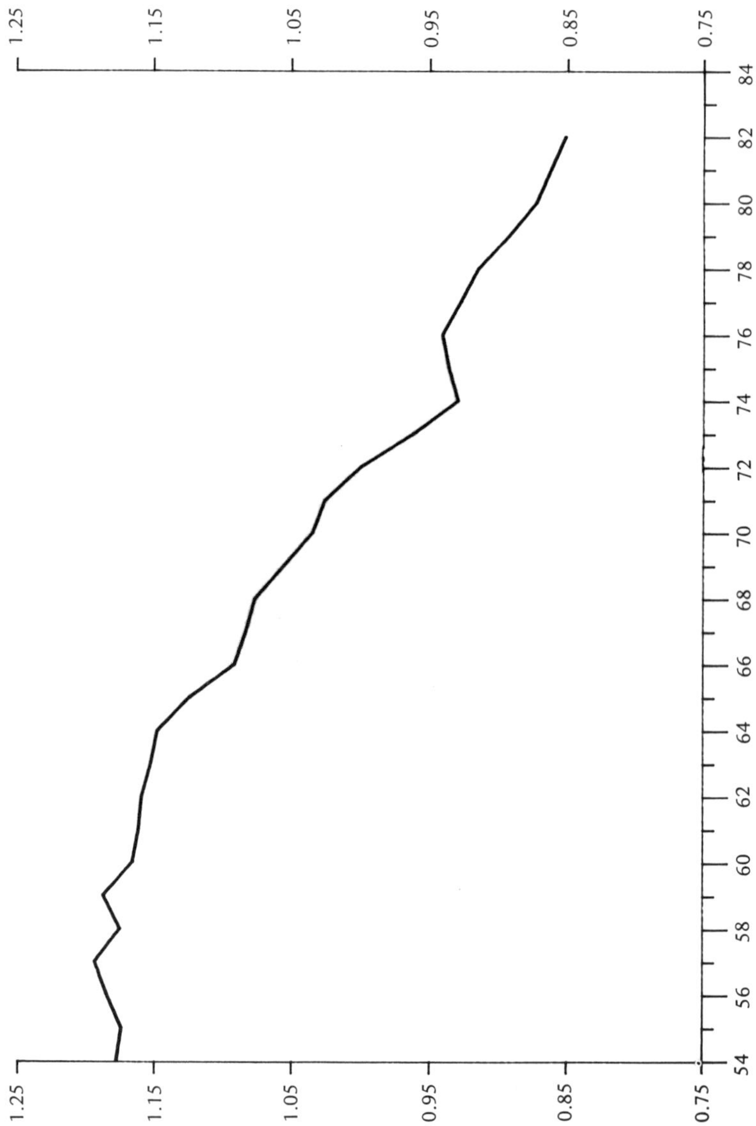

Source: U.S. Department of Commerce, Bureau of Economic Analysis.

Figure 8-3. Net Stock of Consumer Durables Per Household (1972 dollars).

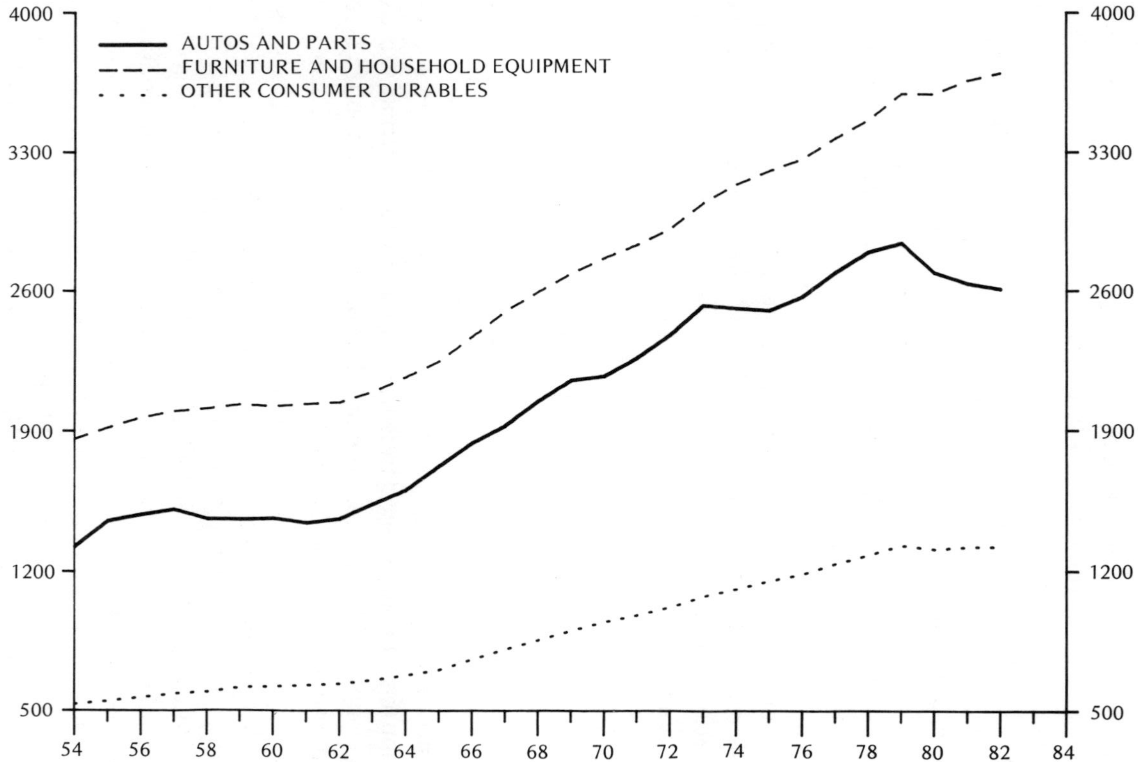

Sources: U.S. Department of Commerce, Bureau of Economic Analysis and Bureau of the Census.

sions is most evident on the autos and parts stock.) The acceleration in the growth of the furniture and household equipment stock in the early 1960s was due to rapid growth in the "radio and television receivers, records and musical instruments" category and corresponds to the period when popular-priced color television receivers were first introduced to the U.S. consumer. Also, high fidelity and stereo equipment met rapidly growing acceptance after 1960. The other consumer goods category, "wheel goods, durable toys, sports equipment, boats, and pleasure aircraft," experienced rapid growth after the early 1960s. Because of the inflection points in the growth rates in the per household stocks of both furniture and other consumer goods, the net investment equations for these two sectors were estimated for the twenty-one-year span from 1962 through 1982. In contrast, the autos and parts equation was estimated for the 1954–82 time frame.

This papter is divided into three major sections. The first presents the model and describes the data, and the second reports the empirical estimates. The final section discusses the results and policy implications and tests the model against 1983 data.

THE MODEL AND THE DATA

The model for investment in consumer durables is developed from the demand side only. The supply response to a change in demand is fairly quick for most consumer durable goods. Increases in production can be accommodated by greater use of overtime, accelerated assembly lines rates, or even by additional production shifts. Decreases in production can be handled just as expediently. Because of the short response time of changes in production to changes in demand, a demand model should adequately capture the dynamics of the sector. This is especially so when annual data are employed.

In the model, the household is assumed to be the primary decision-making unit. This seems logical because many consumer durables are associated with the household unit itself, rather than any one person in it. For example, one thinks of a household having one washer and dryer, no matter how many people (within reason) reside in the household unit. Obviously, this is in contrast to the case of some consumer nondurables, such as clothing, where aggregate demand would be a function of total population, not the number of households.[4]

Households do not demand consumer durables directly. Rather, they demand the services provided by the durables. However, if the services equal a constant fraction of the real net stock of consumer durables, then demand relationships can be developed based on the stock of consumer durables. The per household demand for consumer durables takes the same form as the demand for any investment good. That is, it depends positively on real income per household and negatively on the real service price (the cost of capital or user cost) and on income uncertainty. One would also think that demand would depend positively on the real price of close substitutes (the price of substitutes generally is included via the use of the real service price) and negatively on the real price of complements. Symbolically, the desired real durable stock per household (S^*) can be expressed as:

$$S^* = S^* (\overset{+}{y}, Pd\overset{+}{u}r, \overset{-}{\sigma y}, Ps\overset{-}{u}b, Pc\overset{+}{o}m), \qquad (8.1)$$

where

y = real disposable personal income per household,
$Pdur$ = the real service price (user cost) of durables,
σy = income uncertainty,
$Psub$ = the real price of close substitutes, and
$Pcom$ = the real price of complements.

If there were no transactions costs or friction in the system, one would expect the actual stock of consumer durables to always equal the desired stock. Because of costs of adjustment, lack of perfect knowledge, and so on, we expect households to adjust only gradually to changes in the desired stock.[5] Thus:

$$\Delta S_t = k(S_t^* - S_{t-1}), \qquad (8.2)$$

where

ΔS_t = *net* purchases of durables divided by households, and
S_{t-1} = the actual stock per household at the beginning of the period.

Turning to the user cost variable, from the Jorgenson (1963) framework the cost of capital is:[6]

$$Pdur = Pd/P \quad [(1 - \lambda) \; i - p^e + \delta] \,, \qquad (8.3)$$

where

Pd = the relevant consumer durable deflator,
P = the personal consumption deflator,
λ = the marginal personal income tax rate,
i = the nominal financing rate,
p^e = the expected inflation rate, and
δ = the depreciation rate.

In the estimation of the relationships, the cost of capital is entered in two parts, $Pd/P\ [(1 - \lambda)\ i - p^e]$ and $(Pd/P)\ \delta$.[7] As such, the value of δ is embedded in the coefficient on the relative price term. The expected inflation rate is assumed to be the actual increase in the appropriate deflator over the prior year. The interest rate is somewhat of a problem, as no consumer durable loan rate series covering the entire postwar period is available from the Federal Reserve or other sources. Car loan rate series are available, but only for the period after 1971. In order to investigate a longer time period, the rate on three-year Treasury securities is used as a proxy for the consumer durable loan rate. We test alternative marginal tax rates, namely 0, 15, and 30 percent.[8] Also, the prime rate is tested as a substitute for the three-year Treasury rate.

Two proxies are used for income uncertainty. The first is the unemployment rate. A decline in this rate tells consumers that the economic climate is improving—that the probability of being laid off has fallen—while a rise means the reverse. We expect that the unemployment rate will enter the relationship negatively. The second income uncertainty variable is an index of consumer confidence.[9] The confidence variable in these relationships is the index of attitudes about current personal finances. It is published by the Survey Research Center of the University of Michigan and is one of five components that comprise the Center's familiar Index of Consumer Sentiment. The actual question asked by the Center is, "We are interested in how people are getting along financially these days. Would you say that you (and your family living there) are better off or worse off financially than you were a year ago?" The Index is calculated as the percentage of those who respond that they are better off less the percentage of those who respond that they are worse off, plus 100. Because of its construction, the consumer confidence variable is expected to enter the relationships positively.

Energy is the complement whose real price is tested. The argument underlying this variable is that there is a significant cost of operation for many consumer durables—electricity to run an air conditioner or gasoline to operate a car or truck, for example. As these costs of operation rise relative to other costs, one would expect a smaller share of income to be devoted to purchases of consumer durables. Durables become more expensive not only when their own price increases but also when the cost of operating them increases.

Although theory indicates that the price of close substitutes should be relevant, most obviously that of used cars in the autos and parts relationship, efforts to include them were unsuccessful. In the case of autos and parts, the reason for the lack of success is clear; the used car market exactly parallels the new car market. That is, strong demand in one market is always accompanied by strong demand in the other. As such, used car prices are not independent of the variables already included in the relationship to determine overall net investment in autos and parts. The low and high values, together with the mean, for the various series employed in the analysis are listed in Table 8-1.

THE ESTIMATED EQUATIONS

The equations were estimated by ordinary least squares methods, and many combinations of variables were tested in order to investigate various possible behavioral relationships. Estimates for autos and parts, furniture and household equipment, and other durables are presented in turn.

Net Investment in Autos and Parts

The results of equations explaining net investment in autos and parts per household are shown in Table 8-2, with *t* ratios shown below the coefficients. The estimated coefficients all have the expected signs and all are statistically significant.

One method of evaluating the coefficients on income and relative price is to calculate their respective elasticities relative to the stock of durables per household. Calculated in this manner, the income elasticity is 1.34 and the price elasticity is -1.70. These magnitudes seem

Table 8-1. Data Summary for Consumer Durables.

	Minimum	*Maximum*	*Mean*
YD72HH: Real income per household	8586	13134	11094
Real deflators			
DEFAP: Autos and parts	0.921	1.149	1.037
DEFFH: Furniture and household equipment	0.762	1.210	0.994
DEFOTH: Other consumer durables	0.883	1.103	0.992
Real after-tax interest rate for autos and parts X *DEFAP*			
RATIAP(0): Assuming 0 percent marginal tax rate	-0.0219	0.0598	0.0249
RATIAP(15)	-0.0317	0.0506	0.0158
RATIAP(30)	-0.0414	0.0421	0.0066
RATIAPRIME(0)	-0.0212	0.0937	0.0351
Real after-tax interest rate for furniture and household equipment X *DEFFH*			
RATIFH(0): Assuming 0 percent marginal tax rate	-0.0017	0.0723	0.0429
RATIFH(15)	-0.0121	0.0575	0.0328
RATIFH(30)	-0.0226	0.0428	0.0227
Real after-tax interest rate for other consumer durables X *DEFOTH*			
RATIOH(0): Assuming 0 percent marginal tax rate	-0.0196	0.0849	0.0305
RATIOH(15)	-0.0356	0.0678	0.0202
RATIOH(30)	-0.0517	0.0507	0.0098
UN: Unemployment rate	3.49	9.72	5.82
ICPF: Index of attitudes about personal finances	84.3	124.8	105.5
AUTOSTKHH: Stock of autos and parts per household	1325	2840	2037
FURNSTKHH	1990	3694	2770
OTHERSTKHH	610	1320	960

Sources: U.S. Department of Commerce, Bureau of Economic Analysis and Bureau of the Census; Federal Reserve Board; U.S. Department of Labor, Bureau of Labor Statistics; Survey Research Center, University of Michigan.

Table 8-2. Net Investment in Autos and Parts Per Household, 1954–82.

	A1	*A2*	*A3*	*A4*
Constant	825 (3.17)	859 (3.22)	893 (3.25)	848 (3.40)
YD72HH	0.101 (4.07)	0.101 (3.99)	0.101 (3.88)	0.088 (3.99)
DEFAP	-1345 (6.48)	-1386 (6.43)	-1426 (6.31)	-1302 (6.71)
RATIAP(0)	- 970 (3.43)	—	—	—
RATIAP(15)	—	-1017 (3.29)	—	—
RATIAP(30)	—	—	-1015 (3.10)	—
RATIAPRIME(0)	—	—	—	- 768 (3.86)
ΔUN	-21.1 (3.89)	-21.1 (3.83)	-21.1 (3.76)	-21.2 (4.08)
$(ICPF + ICPF(T-1))/2$	3.484 (2.35)	3.658 (2.43)	3.851 (2.52)	3.349 (2.35)
$AUTOSTKHH(T-1)$	- 0.410 (4.34)	- 0.421 (4.30)	- 0.430 (4.21)	- 0.365 (4.30)
Adjusted R^2	0.83	0.83	0.82	0.85
Standard error of residuals	27.5	27.8	28.4	26.3
Durbin–Watson statistic	1.82	1.82	1.80	1.82

quite reasonable; that is, the income elasticity of the demand for consumer durables is normally estimated in the 1.0 to 2.0 range. Relative price elasticities have been estimated over a very large range, but an elasticity in magnitude greater than 1.0 is intuitively appealing for any "luxury" good.

The unemployment rate term by itself is not significant in the estimated equation. However, when the *change* in the unemployment rate was tested, it was found to be highly significant ($t = 3.89$). Given the high degree of volatility of net investment in autos and parts per household, this is not surprising. The consumer confidence term is also significant ($t = 2.35$), suggesting that consumer confidence is a factor in the purchases of durables over and above the various direct economic factors. In fact, both the current year and previous year's confidence index are significant.[10] Finally, the -0.41 coefficient on the auto stock implies that over 40 percent of the gap between current and desired stock levels is closed in one year.

Because a major channel of economic policy is changes in interest rates, the real after-tax interest rate variable received particular attention. The difficulty in obtaining an appropriate consumer durable loan rate has already been discussed. Another issue is the sensitivity of the marginal tax rate assumed. In Table 8–2's equation (A1), a zero marginal tax rate was assumed. Equations (A2) and (A3) show the same regression with the rate variable based on 15 and 30 percent marginal tax rate. The results are largely the same, although, using the zero marginal tax rate provides a slightly higher explanatory power. As such, the remainder of the results concentrate on the zero marginal tax rate, although results assuming other marginal rates will be shown for reference purposes. An additional test on the interest rate term was the substitution of the highly publicized prime rate for the three-year Treasury rate, assuming a marginal tax rate of zero. Therefore, equation (A4) should be compared with (A1). The equations are quite similar. The conclusion, at least in this time series framework, is that the actual selection of which interest rate variable to use in these relationships is not crucial. Therefore, the apparent shortcoming of not having a consumer durable loan rate in these investment equations is of minor concern.

One variable that was not significant in the auto and parts or the other two consumer durables sectors' equations is relative price of energy. The absence of the relative energy variable in the autos and parts equation may seem surprising because the U.S. auto industry was clearly decimated in the wake of the increases in world oil prices in 1973–74 and again in 1979. The answer to this apparent dilemma is that the coefficient in a regression equation estimates the impact of a change in relative energy prices with all else constant. In actuality, the major impact of the increases in world oil prices was a sharp reduction in real income. This is the avenue that led to greatly reduced car and truck sales in 1974–75 and again following 1979. On further reflection, it seems reasonable that the major impact of a change in relative energy prices on car sales, assuming that real incomes were held constant, would not be a reduction in the total number of cars sold but rather a change in the mix of product sold. Of course, the mix of car sales did change rapidly toward smaller, more fuel-efficient products following the 1974 and 1979 oil price shocks.

Figure 8–4 shows actual and fitted equation (A1) net investment in autos and parts per household. As can be seen, the equation picks up all of the major swings in this highly volatile series.

Net Investment in Furniture and Household Equipment

The estimated equations using the three different assumptions about marginal tax rates are shown in Table 8–3. As can be seen from Figure 8–5, the equation (F1) tracks net investment in furniture and household equipment per household closely over the twenty-one year period. Moreover, the estimated coefficients all have the expected signs and are of reasonable magnitude. The calculated long-run income elasticity is 0.95, well below the 1.34 of autos and parts. The lower income elasticity is consistent with estimated income elasticities of housing demand that are less than unity (Rosen 1979). The relative price elasticity for furniture, -1.55, is also somewhat lower in magnitude than that for autos and parts. As is the case in the autos and parts equation, the estimated relationships assuming a zero marginal tax rate have a slightly higher degree of explanatory power than do those that assume higher marginal tax rates.

One change from the auto and parts equation is that the level of the unemployment rate is significant, whereas the change in the unemployment rate is not. The lower degree of volatility in net investment in furniture and household equipment per household is consistent

Figure 8–4. Net Investment in Autos and Parts Per Household (1972 dollars).

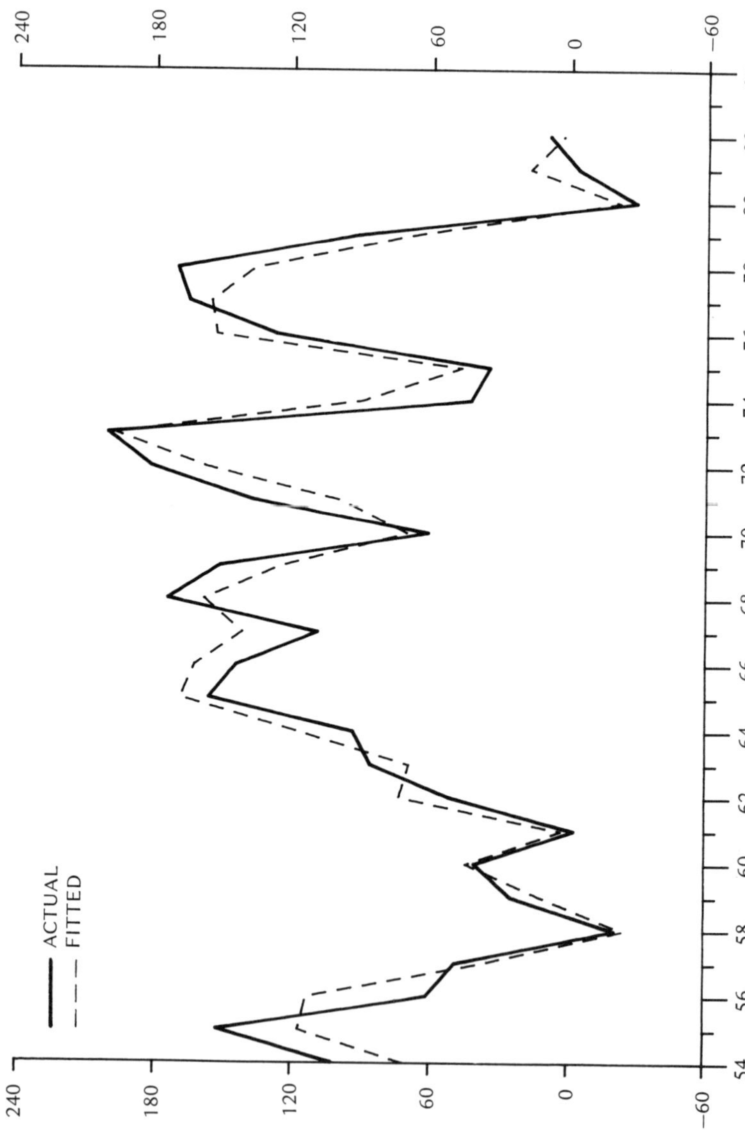

Sources: U.S. Department of Commerce, Bureau of Economic Analysis and Bureau of the Census.

Table 8-3. Net Investment in Furniture and Household Equipment Per Household, 1962-82.

	F1	*F2*	*F3*
Constant	848 (4.13)	826 (3.88)	795 (3.58)
YD72HH	0.035 (5.06)	0.036 (5.06)	0.037 (5.05)
DEFFH	-646 (5.47)	-641 (5.22)	-631 (4.89)
RATIFH(0)	-623 (5.24)	–	–
RATIFH(15)	–	-642 (4.93)	–
RATIFH(30)	–	–	-652 (4.54)
UN	-16.51 (7.83)	-15.99 (7.39)	-15.40 (6.85)
ICPF	0.767 (2.59)	0.819 (2.60)	0.861 (2.54)
FURNSTKHH(*T* - 1)	- 0.156 (4.43)	- 0.160 (4.34)	- 0.163 (4.20)
Adjusted R^2	0.97	0.96	0.96
Standard error of residuals	6.88	7.16	7.53
Durbin-Watson statistic	2.41	2.24	2.03

with this result. The confidence variable also is significant in this relationship, although the coefficient is far smaller. Finally, the coefficient on the lagged stock term is lower than in the autos and parts equation (-0.156 versus -0.410), indicating a slower speed of adjustment. Again, this seems consistent with the lower volatility of net investment in furniture and household equipment than in autos and parts.

Figure 8-5. Net Investment in Furniture and Household Equipment Per Household (1972 dollars).

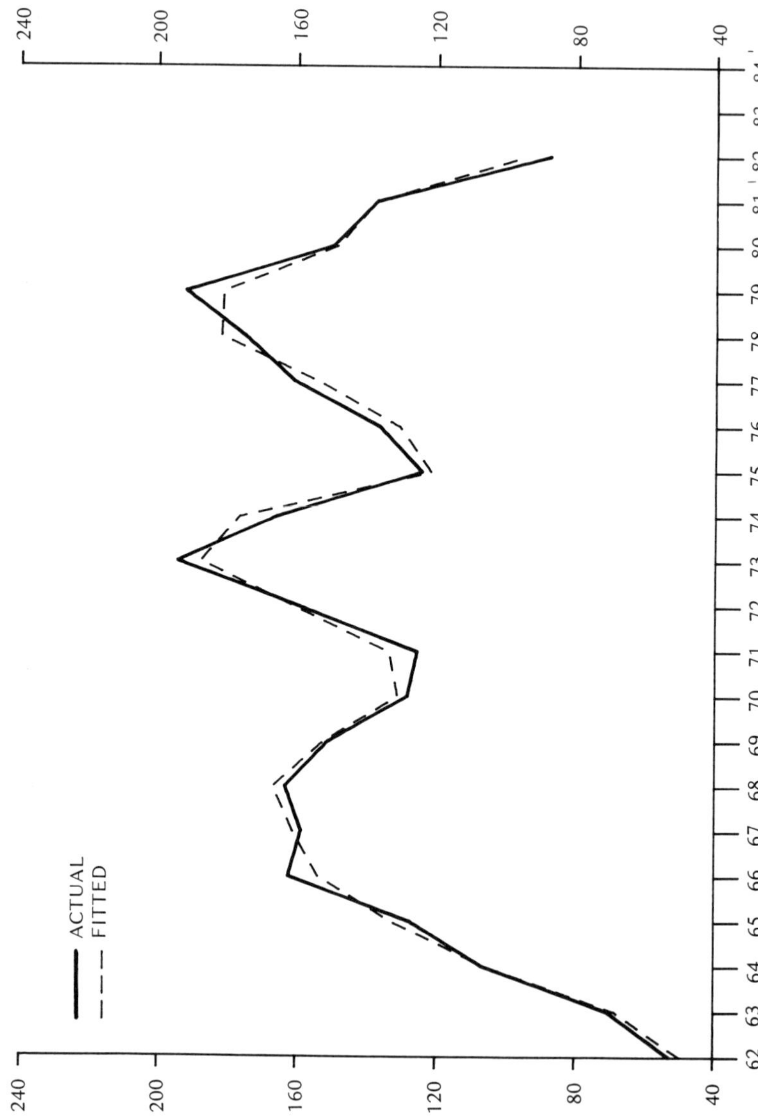

Sources: U.S. Department of Commerce, Bureau of Economic Analysis and Bureau of the Census.

Net Investment in Other Consumer Durables

This category of durables contains a wide assortment of items, all the way from jewelry and toys to boats and airplanes. However, the items have the common dimension of being luxury goods. Thus we expect an income elasticity significantly above unity. The regression results using the different marginal tax rates are shown in Table 8-4. In this series of relationships, the equation assuming a 15 percent

Table 8-4. Net Investment in Other Durables Per Household.

	O1	*O2*	*O3*
Constant	406 (2.14)	444 (2.30)	485 (2.46)
YD72HH	0.0352 (9.54)	0.0350 (9.50)	0.0349 (9.42)
DEFOTH	-551 (3.80)	-584 (3.96)	-621 (4.09)
RATIOTH(0)	-253 (3.94)	–	–
RATIOTH(15)	–	-272 (3.95)	–
RATIOTH(30)	–	–	291 (3.94)
ICPF	0.425 (1.77)	0.474 (1.94)	0.527 (2.11)
OTHERSTKHH(*T* - 1)	-0.271 (6.37)	-0.281 (6.53)	-0.294 (6.66)
Adjusted R^2	0.89	0.89	0.89
Standard error of residuals	6.07	6.06	6.07
Durbin-Watson statistic	1.90	1.87	1.81

marginal tax rate is slightly superior to the other two. However, for consistency with the other two durable sectors, the equation assuming a zero marginal tax rate is used for computing elasticities. The income elasticity relative to the stock of other consumer durables per household is 1.60, while the price elasticity is -2.13. As expected, this is the highest estimated income elasticity. Neither the level nor the change in the unemployment rate proved significant in this relationship. However, the other income uncertainty variable, the index of personal financial attitudes, was marginally significant ($t = 1.77$). The speed of adjustment coefficient of 0.271 falls between that of autos and parts (0.410) and furniture and household equipment (0.156). The estimated and actual series are shown in Figure 8-6.

Summary

The three components of consumer durables show a certain commonality in their elasticities relative to income, prices, real interest rates and consumer confidence (see Table 8-5). However, there are sufficient differences to justify the analysis of three separate components. One major difference relates to the income elasticities. Both the autos and parts and other durables categories have elasticities well above one, while the furniture and household goods sector exhibits slight income inelasticity. One interpretation is that the other goods category is the most luxury oriented, while the furniture and household equipment sector is the least.

Table 8-5. Long-Run Elasticities Evaluated at Mean.

	Autos and Parts	*Furniture and Household Equipment*	*Other Consumer Durables*
Income	1.34	0.95	1.60
Real asset price	-1.70	-1.55	-2.13
Real interest rate	-0.03	-0.06	-0.03
Consumer confidence	0.44	0.18	0.17
Speed of adjustment	0.41	0.16	0.27

Figure 8-6. Net Investment in Other Consumer Durables Per Household (1972 dollars).

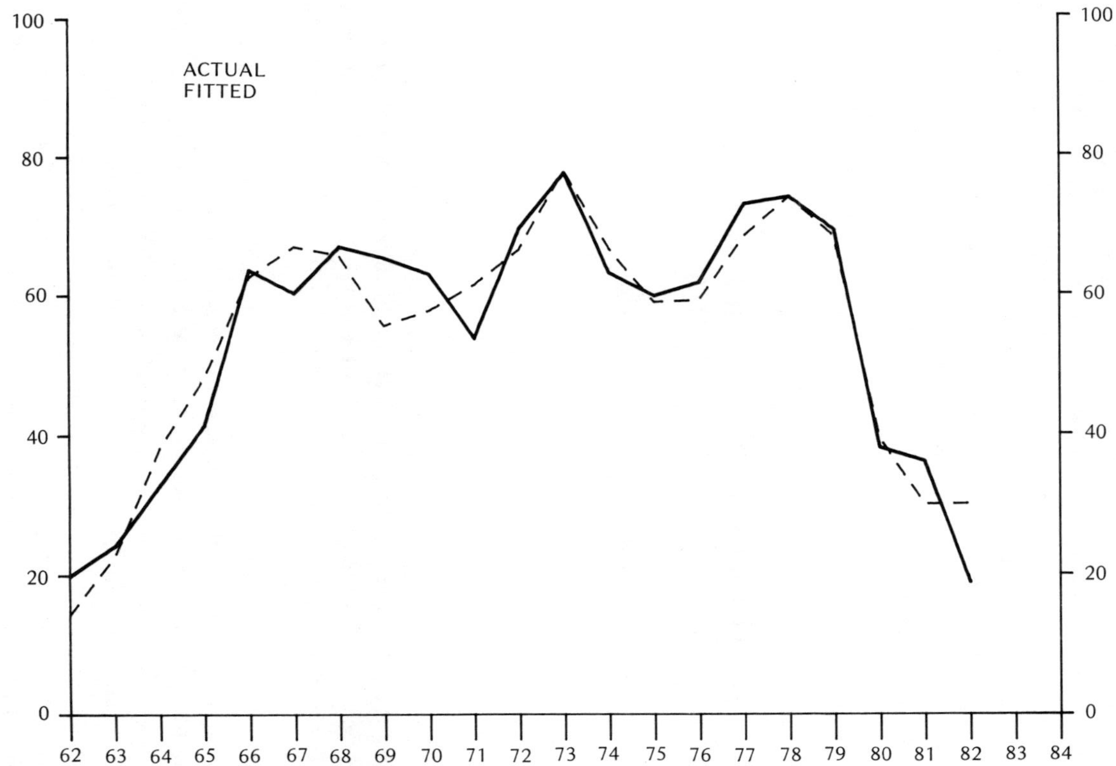

Sources: U.S. Department of Commerce, Bureau of Economic Analysis and Bureau of the Census.

All three sectors have price elasticities greater than 1.0 in absolute magnitude, with the other consumer durable goods sector again having the elasticity with the highest value. Elasticities with regard to real interest rates are very modest for all three sectors, which suggest that real income and relative prices are a much more important determinant of the stocks of consumer durables than are real interest rates. Stocks of durables are somewhat more sensitive to consumer confidence. However, elasticities relative to consumer confidence all are well less than 1.0, with autos and parts having the highest value at 0.41. This is not surprising, given the greater degree of volatility of autos and parts investment than the other two sectors of consumer durables. Much of that volatility can be traced to changes in consumer confidence.

THE SENSITIVITY OF DURABLE DEMAND TO MACROECONOMIC POLICIES

Interest Sensitivity

One way of interpreting the size of the coefficients on real interest rates and consumer confidence is to examine the impact of a change in each variable across its entire range on the various stocks of consumer durables. Over the 1954–82 period, the range of the consumer confidence variable was 40.5 points, while that for real interest rates was 0.09. Table 8–6 presents the results of increases in real rates and decreases in consumer confidence of this magnitude. For the autos and parts sector, the drop in consumer confidence has a slightly larger impact than does the increase in real interest rates. For the other two sectors, the situation is reversed. For all three sectors, the impacts are roughly equal. Either of these changes will eventually depress the stock of consumer durables by roughly $600 per household or $50 billion (1972 dollars) in the economy as a whole, based on the 1982 number of households. Even such enormous changes, considered individually, would alter demand by less than 10 percent.

Changes in consumer confidence could well reflect changes in interest rates, real or nominal. To test for this relation, the index of personal finances is regressed on the level of the unemployment rate, the change in the unemployment rate from a year earlier, the year-over-year change in the NIPA consumption deflator (our expected

Table 8-6. Impact of a 9 Percentage Point Increase in the Real Interest Rate and a 40 Percent Decline in Consumer Confidence.

	Autos and Parts	*Furniture and Household Equipment*	*Other Consumer Durables*	*Total*
1982 actual stock per household	2607	3694	1320	7622
9 percentage point increase in real intérest rate	-189.3	-295.6	-97.5	-582.4
40 point drop in consumer confidence	-344.2	-199.0	-63.5	-606.7

inflation series), and various nominal interest rates. The latter were found not to be significant. The relationship estimated over the period 1954–82 is:

$$ICPF = \underset{(37.4)}{126.9} - \underset{(2.82)}{1.825}\, UN - \underset{(3.53)}{2.641}\Delta UN - \underset{(7.98)}{2.427}\, PC\%$$

$$R^2 = 0.85$$
$$SE = 4.12$$
$$DW = 1.41$$

Both the inflation ($PC\%$) and unemployment (UN) rates are measured in percentage points. It is relatively clear from Figure 8–7 that this equation picks up the major movements in consumer confidence. Changes in inflation account for 65 percent of the movement in consumer financial attitudes, with the remainder attributable to the level and change in the unemployment rate. Changes in inflation, holding nominal interest rates constant, are, of course, changes in real interest rates.

Although no one knows for certain what the real interest rate should be, there is no doubt that for much of 1982 and 1983 the real rate was well above its historical norm, probably by about three percentage points. Table 8–7 summarizes what the impact of a return to the historical level of real interest—a one-time three percentage point decline—would have on the real net stock of durables per household.

Figure 8-7. Index of Attitudes about Current Personal Finances.

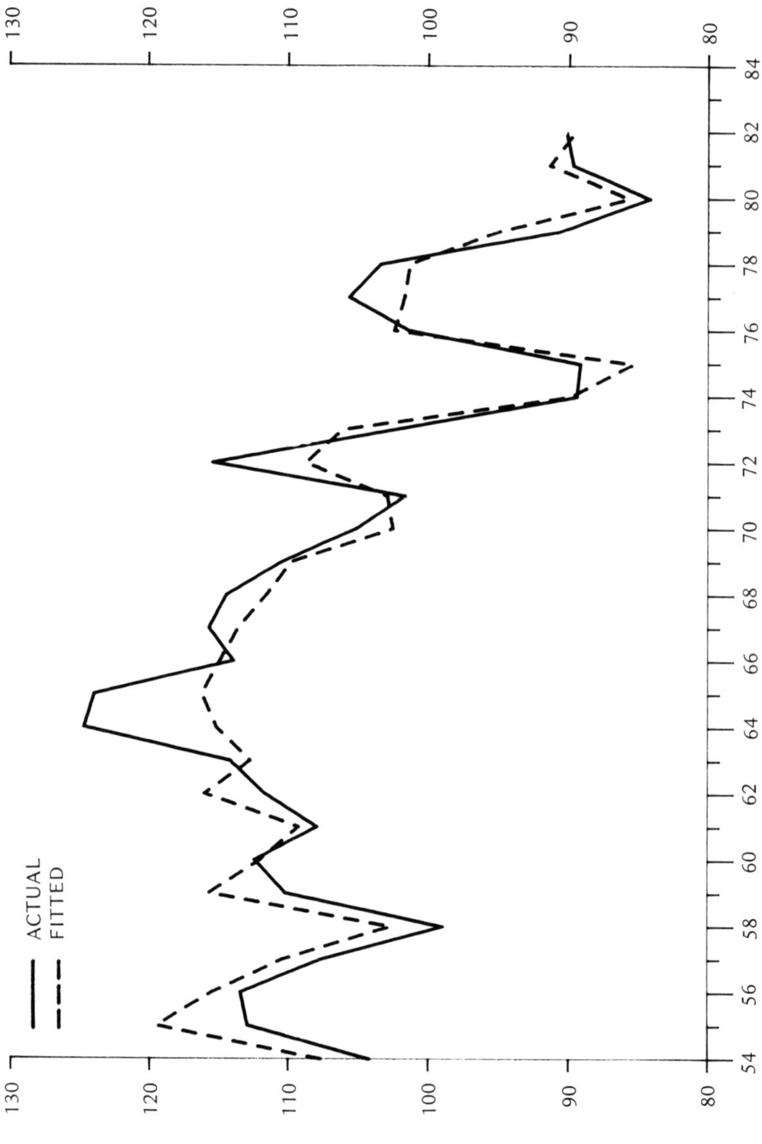

Source: Survey Research Center, University of Michigan.

Table 8-7. Impact of Changes in Real Interest Rates on Net Durable Stocks Per Household (in 1972 dollars).

	Autos and Parts	*Furniture and Household Equipment*	*Other Consumer Durables*	*Total*
1982 actual	2608	3694	1320	7622
Increase due to 3 percentage point decrease in nominal interest rates	66	91	25	182
Percentage change	2.53	2.46	1.89	2.39
Increase due to 3 percentage point increase in inflation rate	4	55	14	73
Percentage change	0.15	1.47	1.06	0.95

End-of-year stocks for 1982 are used as the starting point. The second row is the response if the lower real rate were achieved by a lower nominal rate; the fourth row is the response if the lower real rate were caused by an increase in inflation. An increase in the rate of inflation is not as expansionary as a reduction in nominal interest rates because higher inflation lowers consumer confidence, tending to offset the impact of lower real interest rates on consumer durable demand.

A three-point decrease in the nominal rate of interest, holding inflation constant, would eventually increase the net stock of autos and parts per household by 66 1972 dollars or 2.53 percent. The long-term impact of a one-time three percentage point decrease in nominal rates for the furniture and household equipment per household would be an increase in net stock of $91 per household, a rise of 2.46 percent. The other durable goods category would eventually show a $25 or a 1.89 percent increase in the net stock per household. Another way of gauging the impact of a decrease in nominal rates is to examine the effect in terms of aggregate GNP data. Given the 83.5 million households in the United States in 1982, a three-point decrease in nominal rates would translate eventually into an increase of $15.2 billion (1972 dollars) of net investment in consumer durables, or about 1.5 percent of real disposable personal income if the change occurred all in one year.

With an increase in the rate of inflation, the positive impact of a drop in real interest rates is significantly offset by a decline in consumer confidence. For autos and parts, the effects almost cancel; for consumer durables in total, an increase in inflation has only 40 percent of the impact of the reduction in nominal rates.

Taxes

Fiscal policy can also be used to alter the course of investment in consumer durables. Table 8-8 shows the results of two fiscal actions that generate approximately the same federal revenue. The first policy is an increase in personal income taxes of 5 percent. Using 1982 as a base, this action would generate about $15 billion dollars. An alternative action that would generate the same federal revenue (in this static analysis) would be an imposition of a sales or an excise tax on consumer durables of 6.2 percent.

Table 8-8. Impact of Tax Increases on Net Durable Stocks Per Household (in 1972 dollars).

	Autos and Parts	*Furniture and Household Equipment*	*Other Consumer Durables*	*Total*
1982 actual	2608	3694	1320	7622
Decrease due to a 5 percent increase in federal personal income taxes	22	20	12	54
Percentage decrease	0.84	0.54	0.91	0.71
Decrease due to a 6.2 percent increase in the relative price of durables	197	213	116	526
Percentage decrease	7.55	5.77	8.79	6.90

Table 8–9. Estimates of Net Investment in Consumer Durables for 1983 (in 1972 dollars).

	Billions				
	Gross Investment from NIPA	*Less Estimated Depreciation*	*Less Adjustment*	*Equals Net Investment*	*Net Investment Per Household*
Autos and parts	68.0	56.6	3.0	8.4	100.1
Furniture and household equipment	64.7	54.4	—	10.3	122.7
Other consumer durables	23.7	21.5	—	2.2	26.2

Table 8-10. Forecast Evaluation: Net Investment in Durables Per Household (in 1972 dollars).

	Consumer Confidence	*Autos and Parts*	*Furniture and Household Equipment*	*Other Consumer Durables*	*Total Consumer Durables*
1982 actual	90.2	-3.06	88.00	18.82	103.76
1983 forecast	100.2	96.30	122.45	33.84	252.59
1983 from NIPA	104.7	100.10	122.70	26.20	249.00
Error	4.5	3.80	0.25	-7.64	-3.59
Percentage error	4.3	3.80	0.20	-29.20	-1.40

An increase in federal personal income tax receipts of 5 percent in 1982 would translate into a reduction in real disposable personal income per household of only 0.7 percent. As such, the impact on net durable stocks per household is not dramatic. In fact, the stocks would decline by less than 1 percent. An increase of 6.2 percent in the relative price of durables, on the other hand, has a large impact. Using 1982 as a base, net durable stocks per household would be reduced by $526 or 7 percent by this action. That is, a targeted $15 billion increase in taxes would have three times as large an impact as a three percentage point increase in real interest rates. The results of these two fiscal policy actions are in line with what one would expect: a targeted excise tax has a much larger impact than does a broad-based increase in personal income taxes.

FORECASTS FOR 1983

One of the best methods of evaluating estimated equations is to see how well they predict beyond the sample period. Unfortunately, the net investment data for 1983 are not available until August 1984. However, an approximation of the net investment data can be derived from the gross investment data already available and estimates of depreciation obtained from equations that relate current depreciation to lagged values of gross investment. The underlying data are shown in Table 8–9; the $3 billion adjustment for the autos and parts equation is due to different NIPA treatment accorded that sector compared to the net stock of consumer durables data (see note 2). To fully test the model, we first forecast consumer confidence and then use this value in forecasting durable investment. The results are shown in Table 8–10.

Net auto investment per household in 1983 is forecast at $96.30, very close to the NIPA data estimate of $100.10. For the furniture and household equipment sector, net investment per household is $122.45 projected by the estimated equation and $122.70 from the NIPA. Finally, the other durables sector shows a net investment of $33.84 per household from the estimated realtionship, and $26.20 per household from the NIPA data. For total consumer durables, the estimated relationship projects $252.59 per household while the NIPA data show $249.00 per household.

The year 1983 witnessed an enormous surge in net investment per household in all consumer goods categories. While a substantial increase is expected in the first year of an economic recovery, the 160 percent increase is the largest in the last thirty years. Nonetheless, our equations explain a full 97 percent of this increase.

CONCLUSION

The principal conclusion that we can draw from all these results is that investment in consumer durables is not very sensitive to changes in real interest rates. We saw that a three percentage point decrease in real rates would eventually increase the stock of durables by only $15.2 billion (1972 dollars) over the course of many years. The first year's impact would be only $4 billion. Thus, it seems clear that changes in real interest rates by themselves have a fairly small direct impact on investment in consumer durables. It is true that investment in consumer durables is volatile. However, that volatility stems primarily from changes in real after-tax income, not from changes in real interest rates.

While monetary policy is not an effective means of controlling investment in consumer durables, the imposition of an excise or sales tax on durables would be effective because of the high sensitivity of investment in consumer durables to relative prices. In fact, a 6.2 percent excise tax, which would generate $15 billion in tax revenues at 1982 levels of activity, would have three times as large an impact on durable demand as would a three percentage point increase in real interest rates.

NOTES

1. The unusually modest decline in consumer durable purchases during the 1982 recession is a result of durable purchases not having recovered fully from the impact of the 1980 recession. In addition, rebates and other incentives distorted the normal pattern of durable purchases during 1981–82. Real durable purchases did decline by $10.6 billion between the first and fourth quarters of 1981.
2. However, purchases of cars and light-duty trucks for business use are treated as investment.
3. The data used in Figure 8–1 are for gross investment or the consumer durable consumption data from the NIPA. Gross investment data are plotted

instead of net investment data because of the negative net real investment in the auto and parts sector in several years.

4. Unpublished research by the author indicates that the demand for cars is more strongly related to the number of households than to total population.
5. The stock-adjustment model was pioneered by Chow (1957, 1960) and Nerlove (1957).
6. See also Hendershott and Hu (1981) for an application involving producers' durable equipment. Hamburger (1967) was one of the first to include an interest rate term in his demand for consumer durables model.
7. Besides the normal user cost connotation for interest rates, real interest rates can also be given a psychological interpretation. That is, when interest rates are high, consumers tend to believe that "bad times" lie ahead, while low interest rates denote "good times." Thus, in a period of high real interest rates, consumers are less confident about their financial future and would tend to be less likely to commit themselves for a multiyear installment contract. Note that the interest rate effects are unambiguous. In both the cost of capital and the consumer confidence concepts, lower interest rates imply higher purchases of consumer durables.
8. Mankiw (1983) states that the appropriate marginal tax rate should be 0.3.
9. Hymans (1970), Juster and Wachtel (1972), and Mishkin (1976, 1977) have all investigated the relationship between consumer confidence and demand for consumer durables.
10. Somewhat surprisingly, our variable based on current personal financial attitudes is significant, but confidence variables relating to expected personal financial position are not. It was anticipated that expectations about future personal finances would be more important, considering that many durable purchases can involve a financing commitment over a multiyear period. It may be that the expectations component of confidence is fully captured by the economic variables already included in the regression.

REFERENCES

Chow, G.C. 1957. *Demand for Automobiles in the United States:* Amsterdam: North-Holland.

———. 1960. "Statistical Demand Functions for Automobiles and Their Use for Forecasting." In *The Demand for Durable Goods,* edited by Arnold C. Harberger, pp. 149–78. Chicago: University of Chicago Press.

Hamburger, M.J. 1967. "Interest Rates and the Demand for Consumer Durable Goods." *American Economic Review* 57 (December): 1131–53.

Hendershott, P.H., and Sheng Hu. 1981. "Investment in Producers' Equipment." In *How Taxes Affect Economic Behavior,* edited by Henry Aaron and Joseph Pechman, pp. 85–126, Washington, D.C.: Brookings Institution.

Hymans, S. 1970. "Consumer Durable Spending: Explanation and Prediction." In *Brookings Papers on Economic Activity*, vol. 2, edited by A.M. Okum and G.L. Perry, pp. 173–206. Washington: Brookings Institution.

Jorgenson, D.W. 1963. "Capital Theory and Investment Behavior." *American Economic Review* 53 (May):247–59.

Juster, F.T., and P. Wachtel. 1972. "Anticipatory and Objective Methods of Durable Goods Demand." *American Economic Review* 62 (September):564–79.

Mankiw, N.G. 1983. "Consumer Durables and the Real Interest Rate." Working Paper no. 1148. Cambridge, Mass.: National Bureau of Economic Research.

Mishkin, F. 1976. "Illiquidity, Consumer Durable Expenditure, and Monetary Policy." *American Economic Review* 66 (September):642–54.

———. 1977. "What Depressed the Consumer? The Household Balance Sheet and the 1973–1975 Recession." *Brookings Papers on Economic Activity* 1:123–64.

Musgrave, J.C. 1979. "Durable Goods Owned by Consumers in the United States 1925–1977." *Survey of Current Business* (March):17–25.

Nerlove, M. 1957. "A Note on Long-Run Automobile Demand." *Journal of Marketing* 22 (July):57–64.

Rosen, H.S. 1979. "Housing Decisions and the U.S. Income Tax: An Econometric Analysis." *Journal of Public Economics* (January):1–23.

9 THE GROWTH IN PENSION SAVING

*Sheng-Cheng Hu**

The past three decades have seen a tremendous increase in pension saving relative to other forms of household saving. Contributions to private pensions net of benefit payments in 1980 amounted to $33 billion or about 30 percent of personal saving. The real value of pension assets accumulated by private pension plans rose at an annual rate of more than 10 percent from $24 billion (1980 dollars) in 1950 to $452 billion in 1980. Half of all full-time private employees and three-fourths of government civilian personnel are now covered by pension plans other than social security.

Several studies have considered the effects of private pensions on aggregate saving. Munnell (1976) used the National Longitudinal Survey (1966, 1969, and 1971 waves) to analyze the impact of pension coverage on the saving behavior of men in their preretirement years. She concluded that the evidence is consistent with the hypothesis that pension coverage discourages other forms of savings. However, the substitution of pensions for other forms of private savings is not complete, probably owing to the lack of vesting and other uncertainties. Consequently, private pension plans appear to increase aggregate

*I wish to thank Dan Black and especially Patric Hendershott for helpful comments and criticisms on earlier versions of this paper.

saving. Her estimates suggest that each dollar of increase in pension saving leads to an increase in aggregate saving by roughly $0.38.

Higher estimates have been obtained by Blinder, Gordon, and Wise (1978) and Kurz (1981). The former, based on the Retirement History Survey, found that each dollar of vested pension wealth increased total wealth by $0.84. The Kurz study used the data file compiled from a random sample of U.S. families taken in 1979 by the President's Commission on Pension Policy (1981). He found that for historically reasonable values of population growth and interest rates, a one-dollar expansion of private pension wealth may expand aggregate capital stock by as much as $0.70–$0.80.[1]

Using time-series data for 1930–74, Feldstein (1978) estimated that pension saving resulted in a slight but not significant increase in total saving. In an earlier paper (1974), he provided evidence that unfunded social security greatly reduced the nation's total capital formation.[2] Like social security, some pensions are unfunded. The question that arises is whether this portion of pension saving has the same consequence for the nation's total savings as has social security. Feldstein and Seligman (1981) argued that this need not be the case if the unfunded pension liability of a firm reduces the equity value of the firm and thereby provides its shareholders with an incentive to save more for themselves. Therefore, unfunded private pensions are different from unfunded social security and other governmental civilian and military pensions in that the former do not necessarily entail a decline in total private savings. Feldstein and Seligman's interpretation of the evidence from a sample of 200 manufacturing firms was consistent with shareholders accepting the conventional measure as the best available information and reducing the share price of a firm by the corresponding amount of its unfunded pension liability.

In this regard, it should be noted that the relationship between share prices and unfunded pensions may have been altered by the enactment of the 1974 Employee Retirement Income Security Act (ERISA), which included the following major provisions:

1. It established the Pension Benefit Guaranty Corporation (PBGC) within the Department of Labor to insure and regulate pension plans.
2. It imposed a limited legal responsibility on the part of firms for their unfunded pension liabilities. An employer becomes liable

for the minimum of its total unfunded vested pension benefits or 30 percent of its net worth. This lien is senior to all unsecured liabilities except for wages.

3. It established some minimum funding standard by requiring that pension liabilities due to past services be amortized over a period not exceeding forty years for existing plans and thirty years for new plans. In addition, any increased liabilities that arose from a liberalization of pension benefits must be amortized over thirty years.

Gersovitz (1982) argued that the limitation of unfunded pension liabilities to 30 percent of the firm's net worth without providing for alternative funding implicitly transfers part of the firm's liability to the PBGC, thereby opening up the possibility that the firm's share value will not be depressed by the full extent of unfunded vested benefits. Therefore, shareholders will have less incentive to increase their own savings. On the other hand, by imposing some funding standard, ERISA helps reduce the risks of pension saving and thereby leads to possible increases in the demand for pensions by workers. Whether the net effect of ERISA on total private saving is positive or negative depends on the relative strength of these two effects.[3]

The relative growth of pensions also has significant implications for the structure of financial markets. Tepper (1981) has shown that because of tax policy, it is optimal for pension funds to invest totally in bonds. To the extent that bonds tend to be less risky than equities, a relative increase in pension saving would shift portfolio composition in favor of less risky assets. However, Chen (1983) argued that by imposing a limited legal responsibility on the part of firms ERISA created an insurance effect that reduced the risk in equity investment and shifted the portfolio composition in favor of these instruments. Thus the impact of pension growth on the structure of financial markets depends on whether the insurance effect dominates the tax effect. Indeed, the insurance effect may have been the stronger one. Corporate shares have been the most important part of the portfolios of private pension plans and their importance has been increasing steadily. By 1980 equities constituted nearly 60 percent of the portfolios of private pension plans. In contrast, the proportion of corporate bonds in these portfolios declined from nearly 40 percent in the early 1960s to slightly more than 20 percent in 1980.[4]

The purpose of this paper is to explain the factors contributing to the rapid growth of pension saving. In addition to ERISA, we are particularly interested in how income and social security taxation and inflation affect the demand for pensions by individual workers. Current tax law accords favorable treatment of pensions relative to other forms of compensation: Employers' contributions to pensions are deductible as business expenses but are not considered as taxable income to employees until they are received in the form of pension benefits. The earnings of pension funds are also exempt from income taxation. As recent inflation pushed individuals into higher tax brackets, this tax advantage became even more important. On other hand, most pensions are defined benefit plans in which retirement benefits are determined by a fixed formula usually based on past earnings and service years. As such, inflation is not fully indexed in pension benefits and therefore tends to have a negative effect on the rate of return on pension saving. The implications of these tax advantages and inflation for the relative demand for pensions are the main focus on this paper.

The remainder of this paper is divided into four sections. The following section derives the demand for pension saving in an inflationary environment within the life-cycle model of individual behavior, taking into account the favorable tax treatment of pensions and the substitutability between pension annuities and social security. The next section describes the time-series behavior of pension saving and other explanatory variables. The final section reports some regression results and considers the implications of the estimated results.

THE MODEL

Individual Lifetime Allocation Problem

The theoretical framework for the present analysis is the N-period life-cycle model of individual behavior, in which retirement consumption is provided by pension saving, nonpension saving, and social security benefits. The difference between pension and nonpension assets is that the former usually cannot be withdrawn before retirement without severe penalty and frequently their withdrawals must take the form of annuity payments. Thus, pension saving is long-term saving and cannot be used as a provision of preretirement consumption.[5] As mentioned earlier, pension saving is treated more favorably by tax law. Social security has the same properties as pensions except that it is compulsory.

The problem for the individual is to choose a path of consumption and an allocation of wealth between pension and nonpension assets so as to maximize his expected life-time utility.[6] Let the current age of the individual be 0 and the conditional probability that he survives until age N be $f(N)$. Following Yaari (1965), we write the individual's expected life-time utility function as:

$$EU(N) = \Sigma f(N) \Sigma u[c(t)] \delta^t, \tag{9.1}$$

where

$$U(N) = \Sigma u[c(t)] \delta^t \tag{9.2}$$

is his life-time utility given that he survives until N, δ is the constant discount rate ($\delta < 1$), and $u(c)$ is the utility of consumption at age t, which is assumed to be increasing and concave with respect to the level of consumption in that period, labelled $c(t)$. The concavity assumption on the utility function implies that the individual is averse to uncertainty in consumption. As such, pension annuities allow the individual to reduce the uncertainty in retirement consumption owing to uncertain mortality.

Suppose the individual works full time until age R, earning a wage compensation of $W(t)$ each period t, then retires for the rest of his life. Assume that compensation is subject to an income tax at the rate of x. The portion of compensation that takes the form of contributions to pensions either by the worker himself or by his employer in his behalf is, however, tax deferred until retirement, when it is received in the form of retirement benefits. His wage income net of pension contributions is also subject to the payroll tax for social security at the rate of z. Moreover, this portion of tax payment is not deductible from taxable income. Thus, assuming that he contributes a fraction v of his compensation to pensions, his real after-tax disposable labor income each working year is $(1 - x - z)(1 - v)w(t)$, where $w(t) = W(t)/P(t)$, and $P(t)$ is the price level expected to prevail at t.

Assume that returns from pension assets are tax exempt but those from nonpension assets are subject to taxation at the rate specified below. Let $i_p = e_p + g_p$ be the expected nominal after-tax (zero) rate of return on pensions, including both earnings (e_p) and expected capital gains (g_p). Then, the nominal market value of pension wealth expected by the individual at the end of each working period is:

$$A_p(t) = (1 + i_p)A_p(t - 1) + vW(t), \qquad t \leqslant R. \tag{9.3}$$

Dividing both sides by $P(t)$ gives:

$$a_p(t) = (1 + r_p)a_p(t - 1) + vw(t), \tag{9.4}$$

where $a_p(t) = A_p(t)/P(t)$ is real pension wealth, $r_p = i_p - \pi$ is the real after-tax (zero) rate of return on pensions, and π represents the expected inflation rate. Let $a_p^*(t)$ be the desired terminal level of pensions. Real desired gross pension saving each period is equal to:

$$s_{pg}^*(t) = a_p^*(t) - a_p(t - 1)(1 - \pi + g_p). \tag{9.5}$$

In this definition, pension saving includes both the net accumulation of real pension wealth and the replacement saving that arises from the depreciation of pension wealth owing to expected inflation and capital loss, represented in the above equation by $(\pi - g_p)a_p(t - 1)$. Real desired net pension saving is equal to gross pension saving less depreciation:

$$s_{pn}^*(t) = a_p^*(t) - a_p(t - 1). \tag{9.6}$$

Let $A_z(t)$ be the level of nominal social security wealth and i_z be the rate at which the accumulation of A_z is computed. The terminal level of real social security wealth in period t accumulated by the individual is:

$$a_z(t) = (1 + r_z)a_z(t - 1) + (1 - v)zw(t), \qquad t \leqslant R, \tag{9.7}$$

where $r_z = i_z - \pi$, and $a_z(t) = A_z(t)/P(t)$.

Each period after retirement, the individual receives a pension benefit of $b(i_p)$ per unit of pension wealth and a social security benefit of e per unit of social security wealth, accumulated at retirement. Assume that private pension benefits are taxable at x but social security benefits are exempt (as they were prior to 1984). Then his real after-tax retirement income each year is:

$$[(1 - x)bA_p(R) + eA_z(R)]/P(t) = [(1 - x)ba_p(R) + ea_z(R)][P(R)/P(t)]. \tag{9.8}$$

During his working years, after-tax income is $(1 - x - z)(1 - v)w$ per year. Given that his real desired consumption is $c^*(t)$, his real desired nonpension wealth at the end of each period is:

$$a_n^*(t) = a_n(t - 1)(1 + r_n) + y(t) - c^*(t), \tag{9.9}$$

where $r_n = i_n - \pi$, i_n is the nominal after-tax rate of return on nonpension saving (including both earnings and capital gains), and $y(t)$ is given by:

$$y(t) = \begin{cases} (1 - x - z)(1 - v)w & \text{if } t \leqslant R \\ [(1 - x)ba_p(R) + ea_z(R)][P(R)/P(t)] & \text{if } t \geqslant R + 1. \end{cases} \tag{9.10}$$

From equation (9.9), real nonpension saving can be derived:

$$s_n^*(t) = a_n^*(t) - a_n(t - 1)(1 - \pi + g_n), \tag{9.11}$$

where g_n is the capital gains on nonpension assets. This, as gross pension saving, includes both the net accumulation in nonpension wealth and the amount of saving required to replace the depreciation of nonpension assets owing to inflation and capital loss, $(\pi - g_n)a_n$.

Because employers frequently impose vesting requirements and some pension plans are not funded, it is difficult for lenders to determine the true collateral value of pensions. Furthermore, pensions in general cannot be withdrawn before retirement without substantial penalty. As a result, it seems reasonable to assume that the individual cannot borrow against his future pension. These considerations imply an additional constraint on the above life-time allocation problem that nonpension wealth cannot be negative, that is:

$$a_n^*(t) \geqslant 0. \tag{9.12}$$

After-Tax Rates of Return and Inflation

The real rates of return on the two assets depend critically on the degrees to which the returns on these assets are indexed. Assume that pension benefits are γ indexed, where $\gamma \leqslant 1$. Thus:

$$i_p = r_{pb} + \gamma\pi, \tag{9.13}$$

and

$$r_p = r_{pb} - (1 - \gamma)\pi, \tag{9.14}$$

where r_{pb} is the rate of return paid by pension plans in the absence of inflation.

Assume that the nominal nonpension rate of return is ϕ indexed with inflation. Although the inflation component of earnings is taxed as ordinary income, nominal capital gains on housing and equities are not taxed until the assets are sold, at which time they are taxed at the lower capital gains tax rate. For this reason, it will be assumed that the real component of earnings from nonpension assets is taxed at x, while the inflation component of income from such assets is taxed at $x_i \leqslant x$. Thus,

$$i_n = (1 - x)r_{nb} + (1 - x_i)\phi\pi, \tag{9.15}$$

$$r_n = (1 - x)r_{nb} - [1 - (1 - x_i)\phi]\pi, \tag{9.16}$$

where r_{nb} is the before-tax rate of return on nonpension saving in the absence of inflation.

As can be seen from equations (9.14) and (9.16), inflation may either increase or decrease the real rate of return on pension saving relative to that on nonpension saving, depending on whether γ is higher or lower than $(1 - x_i)\phi$. Acceleration of inflation is more likely to raise the relative rate of return on pensions the higher the degree of indexation of pension benefits and the tax rate on the inflation component of income from nonpension assets.

The Pension Saving Function

As shown in the appendix to this chapter, when the utility function is of the Cobb–Douglas form [i.e., $u(c) = \log(c)$] and constraint [equation (9.12)] is not binding, the optimal level c^* of current consumption that solves the problem of maximizing equation (9.1) subject to equations (9.4), (9.7), and (9.9) is given by:

$$c^* = Y/\Sigma\left[[1/[g(t)(1 + r_n)t]\right] = \alpha(r_n)Y, \tag{9.17}$$

$$Y = a_n + \Sigma y(t)/(1 + r_n)^t, \tag{9.18}$$

where $g(t) = f(t)\delta^t$. This represents the well-known life-cycle theory that current consumption depends on the present value of life-time income (Y). Here, Y is the sum of the present value of life-time wage compensation net of income tax liabilities (YW), the present value of expected after-tax pension benefits net of expected pension contribution (YP), and the present value of social security benefits net of expected social security tax payments (YS). That is:

$$Y = YW + YP + YS, \tag{9.19}$$

where

$$YW = a_n + \Sigma(1 - x)w/(1 + r_n)^t,$$
$$YP = \Sigma(1 - x)ba_p(R)/(1 + r_n)^t - \Sigma(1 - x)vw/(1 + r_n)^t,$$
$$YS = \Sigma ea_z(R)/(1 + r_n)^t - \Sigma(1 - v)zw/(1 + r_n)^t.$$

In the absence of uncertainty in mortality, the portfolio equilibrium condition is given by:[7]

$$i_p = \theta i_n + (1 - \theta)i_z, \tag{9.20}$$

$$r_p = \theta r_n + (1 - \theta)r_z, \tag{9.21}$$

where $\theta = (1 - x - z)/(1 - x)$. The right-hand side is the hurdle rate of return that the individual would insist upon receiving from pensions. In the absence of social security, it is the after-tax rate of return on nonpension saving. The effect of social security is to decrease this hurdle rate if the expected rate of return on social security is lower than the nonpension rate of return. In this case, social security represents a life-time burden to the individual. A higher tax rate gives rise to a greater incentive for him to shelter from the tax. This, in turn, lowers the hurdle rate of return on pensions. The converse holds if $r_z > r_n$.

By the concavity assumption on the utility function, the individual is averse to uncertain consumption. He is willing to forgo a risk premium in order to have pensions so he can reduce or even eliminate the uncertainty in retirement consumption that arises from the uncertainty in lifespan. Letting q be the risk premium, the portfolio equilibrium condition now becomes:

$$r_p = \theta[r_n - q(a_T, b, a_z)] + (1 - \theta)r_z, \tag{9.22}$$

where $a_T = a_n + a_p$ and $b = a_p/a_T$. The risk premium depends on a number of factors. First, if the individual displays increasing relative risk aversion, the risk premium that he is willing to pay for pensions increases with his total current pension and nonpension wealth. Second, as the fraction of pension in total wealth increases, the uncertainty in retirement consumption owing to uncertain mortality decreases. Moreover, the chance increases that the constraint on non-pension assets [equation (9.12)] will be binding in the future. There fore, the risk premium that he is willing to pay for pensions decreases. Third, an increase in social security wealth reduces the uncertainty in retirement consumption and therefore the risk premium that the individual is willing to pay.

Solving equation (9.22) to obtain the desired level of pensions:

$$a_p^* = a_p^*(a_T, a_z, r_p, r_n, r_z). \tag{9.23}$$

Upon substituting this relationship in equations (9.5) and (9.6), we obtain the pension saving function as:

$$s_p^* = a_p^*(a_T, a_z, r_p, r_n, r_z) - a_p(-1)(1 - \eta\pi), \tag{9.24}$$

where $\eta = 1$ for gross pension saving and $\eta = 0$ for net pension saving. Because $a_T = a_T(-1) + y - c^*$, the above equation can be reduced to:

$$s_p^* = a_p^*[Y, y, a_T(-1), a_z, r_p, r_n, r_z] - a_p(-1)(1 - \eta\pi). \tag{9.25}$$

We have assumed here that full adjustment to the desired level of pensions takes place each period. However, because of institutional inertia it is possible that full adjustment is not realized within the period. If this is the case, the above equation becomes:

$$s_p = \Gamma\Big[[a_p^*(Y, y, a_T(-1), a_z, r_p, r_n, r_z) - a_p(-1)(1 - \eta\pi)]\Big], \tag{9.26}$$

where $\Gamma \leqslant 1$ is the adjustment coefficient.

In this model, an increase in the income tax rate affects the relative allocation of savings to pensions by causing a reduction not only in after-tax life-time income but also in the after-tax rate of return on nonpension saving. The former (income) effect causes a reduction in total saving and thereby in both pension and nonpension saving. The latter (substitution) effect, on the contrary, causes a portfolio shift in favor of pension saving. If the substitution effect dominates, the total effect of a higher income tax rate is to increase pension saving.

The effect of expected inflation on pension saving is threefold. First, as noted above, unless pension benefits are fully indexed and there is no tax on earnings from pension saving, a rise in expected inflation will cause a change in the real rates of return on pension and nonpension saving. Second, it causes a rise in nominal income and thus pushes the individual into a higher tax bracket; unless there is a corresponding tax cut, the increased tax advantage raises pension saving. Third, it leads to a larger depreciation of pension assets and therefore increases the need for maintaining the desired level of real pension wealth. This may be called the Mundell effect (1963). The first two effects are embodied in the r_n and r_p terms in equation (9.25) while the last effect is represented by the π term.

In equation (9.25), the effect of an increase in a_T is twofold. First, under increasing risk aversion, an increase in a_T raises s_p. Second, the wealth effect on consumption is to reduce total and thereby pension saving. Whether its net effect on pension saving is positive depends on the relative strength of these two effects. Other things (such as a_T and π) being equal, a larger a_p implies a smaller requirement for net accumulation to achieve a given desired level of terminal pension wealth.

The Regression Equation

Aggregating individual pension saving functions over the entire population and following the standard procedure by approximating the present value of lifetime income by weighted sum of current and past disposable income, the total pension function can be written in linear form as:

$$s_p = b_0 + b_1 y + b_2 y(-1) + b_3 a_T(-1) + b_4 a_z + b_5 r_p a_p(-1) + b_6 r_n a_p(-1) + b_7 a_p(-1) - b_8 \pi a_p(-1). \tag{9.27}$$

Here, the r_p and r_n terms are multiplied by pension wealth because the magnitudes of their effects on pension saving are greater the larger the amount of pension wealth. One would expect b_1 and b_5 to be positive, and b_2, b_4, and b_6 to be negative. The term b_3 can be positive or negative depending on the relative strengths of the risk aversion and wealth effects on consumption. Equation (9.25) suggests that b_7 equals -1 if there is instantaneous intraperiod adjustment toward the desired level of pension saving. However, slower adjustment is possible. For net pension saving, b_8 equals 0. For gross pension saving function, b_8 is expected to equal b_7 if instantaneous adjustment occurs in pension saving. But given uncertainty about capital gains, risk-averse individuals may adjust slowly. This implies that $b_8 < 1$. While theory suggests that the rate of return on social security is an argument in the pension saving function, it is not included in (9.27) because it is implicitly taken into account in the social security variable used in the following section.

DATA

Pension Wealth and Saving

Pension wealth is taken to be the total reserves and assets of insured and noninsured private pension plans,[8] excluding the government-administered Raiload Retirement, Federal Civilian Employees, and State and Local Employees plans. The reserves of insured pension plans are based on the series compiled by the American Council of Life Insurance (See Pension Facts). The assets of noninsured pension plans, measured at current cost, are taken from the Federal Reserve Flow-of-Funds Accounts. Data for personal savings and household net worth are also taken from the Flow-of-Funds Accounts.

Because pension benefits are taxed, the appropriate measure of pension wealth must be net of the expected accrual tax liabilities in order that it yields the same flow of consumption as does nonpension wealth of equal amount. To illustrate, consider a person who has just retired and has a certain lifespan of T years after retirement. Assume that he holds \$1 of each type of assets. Then his nonpension wealth yields a stream of consumption of:

$$r_n(1 + r_n)^T/[(1 + r_n)^T - 1]. \tag{9.28}$$

The stream of consumption provided by his pension wealth, on the other hand, is equal to:

$$(1 - x)r_p(1 + r_p)^T/[(1 + r_p)^T - 1]. \tag{9.29}$$

A comparison of the above two expressions shows that when $r_p = r_n$ each dollar of pension wealth is worth only $(1 - x)$ dollars of nonpension wealth in terms of its ability to provide for retirement consumption. That is, the net value of pension wealth, in terms of its ability to provide for retirement consumption, is $(1 - x)$.

To deduct the expected tax liabilities, the above pension wealth measure is multiplied by $(1 - x)$. Likewise, household net worth is obtained by deducting the expected tax liability on pension wealth (xa_p) from the Flow-of-Funds series. The term x is taken to be the marginal income tax rate paid by retirees computed from the U.S. Internal Revenue Service, *Statistics of Income.* However, the tax data for retirees are not available prior to 1961. Therefore, between 1950 and 1968, x is approximated by the average effective tax rate for all returns[9] adjusted for the difference in the tax rate paid by the two groups.

While one would expect tax rates paid by retirees to be lower than the average rate, the Statistics of Income suggests otherwise. For example, between 1974 and 1978, the effective income tax rate averaged 23.5 percent for taxpayers age 65 and over in contrast to 19.48 percent for all returns. Likewise, the income tax as a percentage of adjusted gross income was 15.3 percent for taxpayers age 65 and over, compared with 13.5 percent for all returns. The difference in the tax rates paid by all returns and by taxpayers age 65 and over averaged 5 percent in the 1960s. This is assumed to be true also for the 1950s.

The first two columns of Table 9-1 show the year-end outstandings of per capita before-tax and after-tax pension wealth, divided by

Table 9-1. Pension Saving and Wealth (per capita, in 1972 dollars).

	Pension Wealth[a]		*Pension Saving*		*Percentage of Net Pension to*
Year	*Before-Tax*	*After-Tax*	*Gross*	*Net*	*Total Saving*
1950	115.6	86.1	16.7	13.0	10.6
1955	237.4	170.7	53.5	20.9	14.2
1960	376.5	271.1	25.2	25.1	17.1
1965	598.7	450.0	50.7	39.5	18.4
1970	773.1	577.2	42.4	37.3	12.9
1975	865.9	645.2	124.9	67.3	16.2
1980	1273.9	975.6	186.3	129.5	27.6

Source: Board of Governers of the Federal Reserve System, *Flow of Funds Accounts* (1950–80); U.S. Internal Revenue Service, Statistics of Income, various issues.

a. Year-end outstandings.

the price deflator for personal consumption expenditures in the National Income and Product Accounts. Per capita real pension wealth before deducting expected tax liabilities on pension benefits rose at an annual rate of 8.3 percent from $115 to $1,274 in 1972 dollars between 1950 and 1980. After deducting expected tax liabilities, real pension wealth per capita rose from $86 to $976 (in 1972 dollars) during the same period. In contrast, household net worth rose at a much slower rate of 3.5 percent from $855 in 1972 dollars in 1950 to $2,400 in 1980. As a result, the ratio of pension to total household net worth rose from 1.0 percent in 1950 to 3.8 percent in 1980. The relative expansion in pension wealth has been rather steady, the only exception being in 1973–74 when pension plans were hurt by the decline in stock prices.

Gross and net pension savings are defined in equations (9.5) and (9.6), respectively. Upon substituting equation (9.4) into (9.5), gross pension saving is equal to the sum of net pension contributions, earnings of pension plans, and real capital gains on pension assets, while net pension saving equals net contributions plus investment earnings by pension plans. The latter is taken to be the sum of net acquisitions of both insured and noninsured pension plans as reported in the Flow-of-Funds Accounts, divided by the deflator for consumer expenditures in the National Income and Product Accounts. The former also includes revaluations of pension assets as reported in the Flow-of-Funds Accounts.

Revaluations of pension assets include both expected and unexpected nominal capital gains on equities held by the pension plans. Unexpected capital gains result in unintended saving. However, it is intended saving that we are interested in explaining. For this purpose, expected capital gains are important. To derive the latter, we assume that the nominal value of pension assets rose at the rate of αg_a where α represents the fraction of pension assets that are held in the form of equities and g_a denotes the actual rate of increase in the Standard and Poor Index of 500 stocks. The expected increase in pension assets, on the other hand, is taken to be αg_e where g_e denotes the expected twelve-month increase in the Standard and Poor Index as reported in the Livingston Survey. The ratio between these two values determines the fraction of actual nominal capital gains on pension assets that are expected. The rest is assumed to be unexpected.

Expected real capital gains equal expected nominal gains less the expected depreciation of pension assets owing to inflation, the latter being the expected rate of inflation multiplied by the stock of pension assets at the beginning of the year. The expected rate of inflation is taken to be the expected twelve-month increase in the Consumer Price Index (CPI) reported in the Livingston Survey.

The third and fourth columns in Table 9–1 report per capita gross and net pension savings. Per capita net pension saving in 1972 dollars rose from $13, or 10.6 percent of Flow-of-Funds personal saving (adjusted for expected accrual tax liabilities on pension income), in 1950 to $12.9, or 30.9 percent of Flow-of-Funds personal saving, in 1980. This increase was due to an increase in both the number of workers covered by pension plans and the total employer and employee contributions per covered worker. In 1950 only 9.9 million workers, or 16.6 percent of civilian employment, were covered. By 1960 the number of workers covered had doubled; by 1980 it was nearly 36 million, or 36 percent of civilian employment. Contributions per covered worker likewise rose from $293 (in 1972 dollars) in 1952 to $1,235 in 1980.

Gross pension saving per capita in 1972 dollars was $16.7 in 1950. It rose at the annual rate of 3.6 percent to $186 in 1980. Because of the fluctuations in stock prices, gross saving tends to be more volatile than net pension saving. As can be seen from Figure 9–1, these fluctuations are particularly important in the 1970s. For example, gross pension saving was $120.6 or twice the amount of net pension saving ($61.5) in 1972. But it fell to –$72 in 1973 and –$45 in 1974 and then jumped back to $125, or twice the amount of net pension saving, in 1975.

Rates of Return on Pension and Nonpension Saving

The pension rate of return is derived from the following equation representing pension wealth dynamics:

$$A_p(t) = A_p(t-1)(1+i_p) + C_p(t) - B_p(t),$$

or

$$i_p(t) = [A_p(t) - A_p(t-1) - C_p(t) + B_p(t)] / A_p(t-1), \tag{9.30}$$

where i_p is the nominal rate of return on combined pension and nonpension plans, $C_p(t)$ is the total contributions to, and $B_p(t)$ is the

Figure 9-1. Net and Gross Pension Saving.

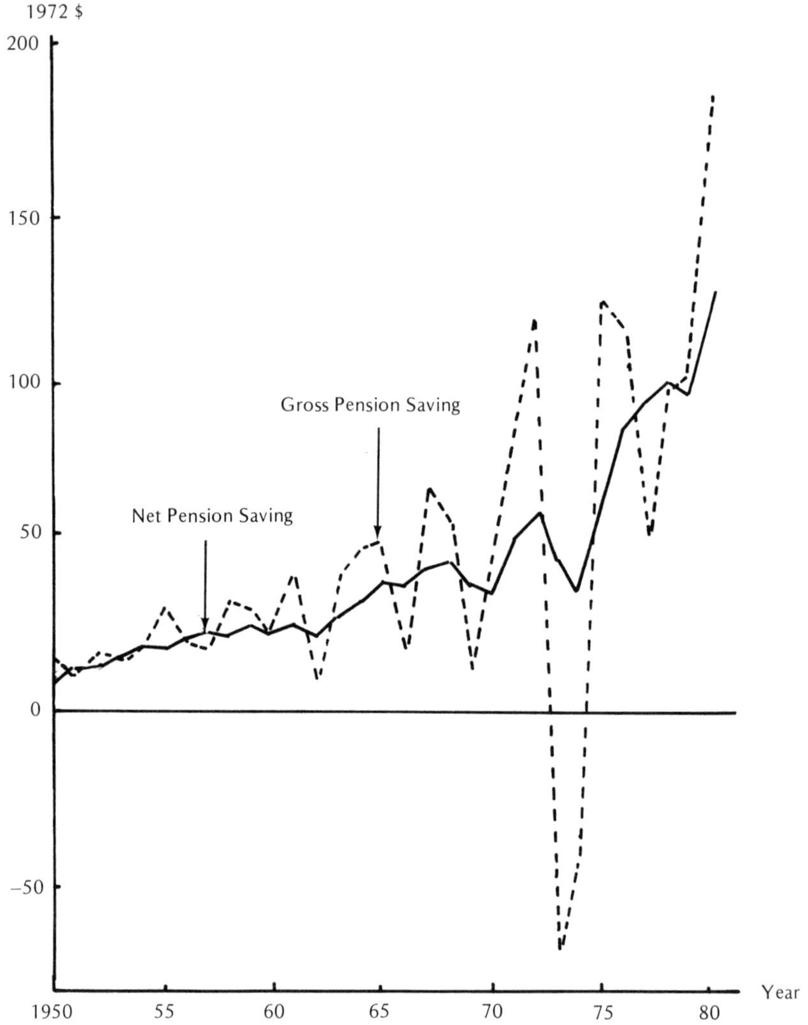

Sources: Calculations based on Board of Governors of the Federal Reserve System, *Flow of Funds Accounts* (1948–78, 3rd quarter 1983).

benefits paid by pension plans (insured and noninsured) in current dollars. A three-year average is used as a proxy for the expected rate. The expected nominal rate of return on nonpension assets is approximated by Moody's Aaa bond rate adjusted for the average marginal tax rate on capital income (based on Estrella and Fuhrer 1983).

Both nominal rates of return on pension and nonpension savings are adjusted for expected inflation to yield their respective real rates. The expected twelve-month increase in the CPI as reported in the Livingston Survey is utilized.

The estimated real rate of return on pensions averaged 1.44 percent between 1950 and 1980. It tended to move inversely with the inflation rate. For example, it rose steadily from 1.68 percent in 1952 to 4.9 percent in 1960 as the expected rate of inflation fell from 2.0 percent to 0.65 percent. During 1965–70 it fell by 7 percent as the expected rate of inflation rose from 1.6 percent to 3.8 percent. During the 1970s the real pension rate of return fluctuated more widely, as did the inflation rate, and was generally negative. The rate of return on insured plans was lower but more stable than that on noninsured plans.

The estimated real after-tax rate of return on nonpension saving averaged 1.96 percent for 1950–80, compared with the average real pension rate of return of 1.74 percent over the same period. As can be seen from Figure 9–2, both rates of return follow a similar cyclical pattern, but the nonpension rate of return tends to be less volatile than the pension rate return. The volatility of the latter is, of course, due to the volatility of stock prices.

The more volatile movement in the real pension rate of return indicates that the nominal rate of return to pensions tends to adjust more slowly to changes in the expected rate of inflation. As a result, the cyclical pattern of $(r_n - r_p)$ follows closely the expected rate of inflation, although the fluctuations in the differential were much larger than those in the expected inflation rate in the 1970s. A simple regression between the rates of return on the two types of assets and inflation shows that while the real pension rate of return moves inversely one to one with inflation, the real after-tax nonpension rate falls by 0.5 percentage points for each percentage point of increase in inflation.

Social Security Wealth

The revised social security wealth series constructed by Feldstein (1982) is used. In the Feldstein algorithm, social security wealth is defined as the present actuarial value of the social security benefits that individuals could anticipate being eligible to receive at age 65.

In his 1974 paper, Feldstein estimated a substantial negative effect

Figure 9-2. Inflation and the Rates of Return on Pension and Nonpension Saving.

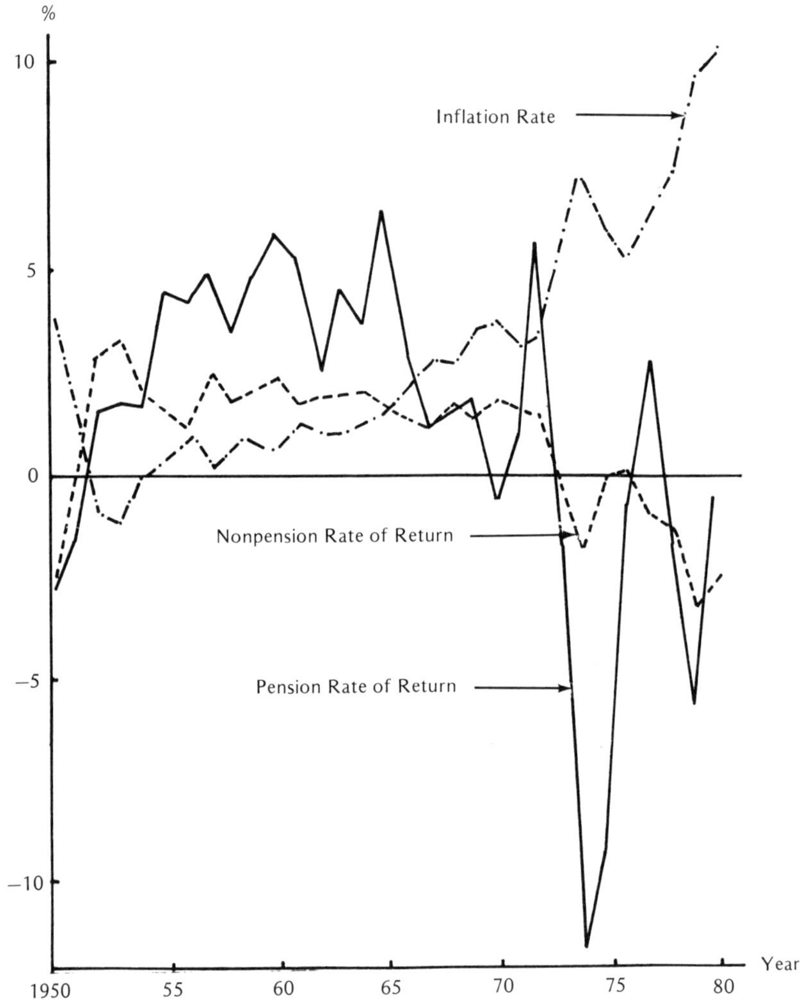

Sources: Calculations based on Board of Governors of the Federal Reserve System, *Flow of Funds Accounts* (1948–78 and 3rd quarter 1983); American Council of Life Insurance *Pension Facts* (1981, 1982); and *Economic Report of the President* (1984).

of social security on the incentive to save: It reduced the nation's total capital stock by as much as one-third. The algorithm he used in calculating social security wealth, however, contained a programming error that treated a one-time increase in benefits for widows enacted in 1956 as a repeated increase for each succeeding year. As a result of this error, social security wealth was overestimated. The revised series corrects this error and takes into account the jump in social security benefits beginning in 1972, which resulted in a rise in the replacement ratio from an average of 40 percent before 1972 to an average of 48 percent after 1972.

The revised Feldstein series is available only through 1976. For 1977–79, the series is extrapolated using the average growth rate between 1973 and 1976. This growth rate reflects the post-1972 trend of social security.

REGRESSION RESULTS

Estimated Coefficients

The first three equations of Table 9–2 are ordinary least-square estimates of the pension-saving function for the period 1950 through 1976, corrected for autocorrelation with the Cochrane-Orcutt iterative method. The figures inside the parentheses are standard deviations. The revised Feldstein series of social security wealth is used in all equations. Current and lagged income are based on the National Income and Product Accounts series of wage income multiplied by 1 minus the effective income tax rate. Because, as illustrated in Figure 9–1, gross pension saving is volatile and is easily susceptible to fluctuations in stock prices, we choose to concentrate on explaining net pension saving.

Equation (9.2.1) in Table 9–2 is a straightforward estimation of the net pension saving function as specified in equation (9.27), with b_8 set equal to zero. With the possible exception of lagged income, all coefficients have the signs predicted by the theory. In particular, the coefficient of the real pension rate of return is significantly positive and the coefficient of the real after-tax nonpension rate of return is significantly negative.

The coefficient of current income is 2 percent and is insignificantly different from zero, but the coefficient of lagged income is 4 percent and is significant. The positive coefficient of lagged income suggests that, because of the long-term nature of pension saving, saving from transitory income is put in nonpension assets. As a result, the marginal propensity of pension saving is lower in the short run [represented

Table 9-2. Pension Saving Function, Labor Income.

Equation No.	*9–2.1*	*9–2.2*	*9–2.3*	*9–2.4*
Sample Period	1950–76	1950–76	1950–76	1950–79
Constant	-0.0743 (0.0177)	-0.0129 (0.0101)	-0.0133 (0.0101)	0.0151 (0.0168)
Income (y)	0.0206 (0.0246)	0.0101 (0.0112)	0.0144 (0.0119)	0.0059 (0.0186)
Lagged Income [$y(-1)$]	0.0422 (0.0161)	0.0394 (0.0130)	0.0289 (0.0164)	0.0441 (0.0191)
Total Wealth [$a_T(-1)$]	0.0037 (0.0032)	-0.0024 (0.0014)	-0.0017 (0.0016)	-0.0013 (0.0023)
Social Security Wealth (a_z)	-0.0014 (0.0041)	-0.0023 (0.0022)	-0.0020 (0.0021)	-0.0041 (0.0015)
Pension Returns [$a_p(-1)r_p$]	0.5710 (0.1360)	0.6972 (0.0888)	0.6315 (0.1081)	0.5644 (0.0600)
Nonpension Returns [$a_p(-1)r_n$]	-0.5339 (0.6186)	-0.3423 (0.4131)	-0.5645 (0.4660)	-0.5056 (0.2320)
Pension Wealth [$a_p(-1)$]	-0.1271 (0.0350)	-0.0086 (0.0202)	-0.0020 (0.0211)	-0.0027 (0.0357)
Real Capital Gains			0.0436 (0.0416)	
ERISA		0.0020 (0.0002)	0.0017 (0.0003)	0.0014 (0.0004)
R-square	0.9146	0.9697	0.9699	0.9660
DWS	1.9785	1.8979	1.9000	2.3416
Rho	0.3967	-0.7266	-0.7207	-0.4127

Source: Author's estimations. Standard errors in parentheses.

by b_1 in equation (9.27)] than in the intermediate run [represented by $b_1 + b_2$ in equation (9.27)].

The discussions in the previous sections suggest that pension saving may have been affected by the enactment of ERISA. The effect of ERISA is two-fold. First, by imposing certain funding restrictions, it makes pension saving less risky to the worker and therefore reduces the hurdle rate of return that he would insist upon receiving from pensions, which in turn increases his demand for pension saving. On the other hand, as argued in Gersovitz (1982), limitation of unfunded pension liabilities to 30 percent of the firms' net worth may have reduced shareholders' incentives to save for themselves. The net effect of ERISA is therefore expected to raise pension saving but to cause either an increase or a decrease in total saving depending on whether the increased incentive to save on the part of workers exceeds the disincentive to save on the part of shareholders. To capture this impact on pension saving, a dummy variable, denoted by ERISA, is added to the regression equation. The dummy assumes the value for 0 for 1950–73 and takes the value of total wealth for the post-1973 period.

As reported in equation (9–2.2), the coefficient of the ERISA dummy is significantly positive. Moreover, the addition of this variable lowers the unexplained variance by 35 percent. Income and the interest rates retain their expected signs and roughly the same levels of significance. Unfortunately, the coefficient of lagged pension wealth becomes near zero, implying an incredibly slow rate of adjustment of pension wealth to changes in its determinants.

The above estimations have constrained b_8 in equation (9.27) to zero. To test the robustness of this assumption, equation (9.27) is reestimated without this constraint. As reported in equation (9–2.3), the coefficient of this variable is positive but is insignificantly different from zero. Thus we cannot reject the hypothesis that $b_8 = 0$.

The coefficient of social security has the expected negative sign, but is insignificant, for all equations for the 1950–76 period. This result is consistent with those obtained by Turner (1980) for 1951–74 and Munnell (1982) for 1930–40 and 1947–77.

In view of the substantial impact of ERISA estimated in equations (9–2.2) and (9–2.3), it is desirable to see whether this result still holds when the sample period extends beyond 1976. Equation (9–2.4) shows that the extension of the sample period to 1979 leaves the earlier results regarding the interest and income sensitivity (and regrettably the speed of adjustment) unchanged. However, the social security coefficient doubles in absolute magnitude and the ERISA coefficient falls by 30 percent.

The near zero estimated speed of adjustment is, of course, very troubling. This has led us to test alternative specifications. In particular, we follow Feldstein (1978) in approximating permanent income by current and lagged disposable income and the unemployment rate, rather than just current and lagged labor income. As can be seen from Table 9-3, the adjustment coefficient does rise modestly; in equation (9-3.2) it is within a standard error of 8 percent. Current, rather than lagged, income is now important, and the social security variable is even more sensitive to the estimation period. Also the

Table 9-3. Pension Saving Function, Disposable Income.

Equation No.	*9-3.1*	*9-3.2*
Sample Period	1950-76	1950-79
Constant	-0.0793 (0.0161)	-0.1156 (0.0252)
Income (y)	0.0284 (0.0123)	0.0809 (0.0183)
Lagged Income [$y(-1)$]	0.0225 (0.0139)	-0.0164 (0.0185)
Unemployment (u)	0.0005 (0.0005)	0.0019 (0.0007)
Total Wealth [$a_T(-1)$]	-0.0030 (0.0013)	-0.0008 (0.0022)
Social Security Wealth (a_z)	-0.0006 (0.0017)	-0.0052 (0.0015)
Pension Returns [$a_p(-1)r_p$]	0.5791 (0.0738)	0.4203 (0.0565)
Nonpension Returns [$a_p(-1)r_n$]	-0.0552 (0.3509)	-0.5828 (0.2173)
Pension Wealth [$a_p(-1)$]	-0.0258 (0.0178)	-0.0474 (0.0347)
ERISA	0.0020 (0.0002)	0.0011 (0.0004)
R-square	0.9771	0.9768
DWS	2.2840	2.1355
Rho	-0.7605	0.0791

Source: Author's estimations. Standard errors in parentheses.

interest rate responses are slightly lower, especially those for nonpension returns for the 1950–76 period.

Elasticity Estimates

Before computing the estimated elasticities of pension wealth with respect to its determinants, it is useful to provide benchmarks for the estimated coefficients. In Tables 9–2 and 9–3, the range of estimates of the coefficient of pension returns goes from 0.42 to 0.70 but centers around 0.55. Thus, the value of 0.55 will be used as a benchmark for the coefficient of pension returns. The benchmark for the coefficient of nonpension returns is taken to be 0.45 because the estimated values of this coefficient are in the average lower than those of the coefficient of pension returns by 0.1. The range of estimates of the sum of the coefficients of current and lagged income is between 0.043 and 0.065, but clusters at 0.060, which will serve as the benchmark for the marginal propensity of pension saving with respect to income. The estimated coefficient of social security wealth is between -0.0006 and -0.0052. A reasonable benchmark for this coefficient seems to be -0.003. A reasonable estimate of the adjustment coefficient is more difficult to arrive at because of the wide range of estimates obtained in different equations. We take it to be 6 percent. This is the average of the values estimated by equations (9–2.1) and (9–2.2) and is within one standard error of the coefficient estimated in equation (9–3.2).

Let $e(r_p)$ be the elasticity of pension demand with respect to pension returns:

$$e(r_p) = (\partial a_p/\partial r_p)(r_p/a_p). \tag{9.31}$$

From equations (9.26) and (9.27),

$$\partial a_p/\partial r_p = (1/\Gamma)(\partial s_p/\partial r_p) = (b_5/\Gamma)a_p. \tag{9.32}$$

Thus,

$$e(r_p) = (b_5/\Gamma)r_p \approx (0.55/0.06)r_p = 9.2r_p. \tag{9.33}$$

The pension rate of return in 1972 was 5.5 percent. Using this as a reference, the elasticity of pension wealth with respect to pension returns is 0.51. This estimate is roughly the preferred estimate of the interest elasticity of private saving (0.4) obtained by Boskin (1978).

Replacing r_p by r_n in the above two equations gives the elasticity of pension wealth with respect to nonpension returns. Taking the nonpension rate of return also to be 5.5 percent, the elasticity pension wealth is -0.41.

The income elasticity of pension demand is

$$\begin{aligned} e(y) &= (\partial a_p/\partial y)(y/a_p) = [(b_2 + b_3)/\Gamma](y/a_p) \\ &\approx (0.06/0.06)(y/a_p). \end{aligned} \tag{9.34}$$

which is 4.4, assuming the ratio of income to pension wealth to be at its 1972 level (4.4).

The elasticity of pension wealth with respect to social security wealth is

$$\begin{aligned} e(a_z) &= (\partial a_p/\partial a_z)(a_z/a_p) = (b_4/\Gamma)(a_z/a_p) \\ &\approx -(0.003/0.06)\,a_z/a_p) \end{aligned} \tag{9.35}$$

or -0.81, given that the ratio of social security to pension wealth was 16.23 for 1972.

It should be noted that these estimates can only be considered tentative because of the large variation in the coefficients estimated by different equations.

The Effect of Income Taxation

The significance of the coefficient of pension returns in Tables 9-2 and 9-3 suggests that tax exemption of pension earnings has a positive effect on the growth of pension saving. To illustrate, in 1972 the nominal rate of return on pension savings was 9.22 percent, and the expected inflation rate was 3.47 percent. Thus the real rate of return on pension saving was 5.74 percent. If pension earnings were subject to the capital-income tax, which was 31 percent in 1972, the real after-tax rate of pension returns would have been reduced by one half to 2.86 percent. Given the elasticity of pension wealth with respect to pension returns of 0.51, the taxation of pension returns would have reduced pension demand by 25 percent.

The Effect of ERISA

As can be seen from Figure 9–1, pension saving grew much faster during the 1970s than in the previous two decades. Per-capita pension saving in 1972 dollars averaged \$87.9 per annum for 1974–80, compared with the average level of \$42.4 for the preceding seven years. The high income elasticity of the demand for pension wealth suggests that income growth was an important factor contributing to the rapid expansion of pension saving. Another contributing factor was the enactment of ERISA.

The range of estimates of the ERISA coefficient, denoted by b_9 below, is between 0.001 and 0.002, and all estimates are significantly different from zero. The percentage increase in the demand for pension wealth brought about by ERISA equals

$$\Delta a_p / a_p = (b_9 a_T / \Gamma) / a_p . \quad (9.36)$$

With the ratio of total wealth to pension wealth being about 25 in the 1970s, the effect of ERISA was to raise the demand for pension wealth by between 42 percent ($b_9 = 0.001$) and 83 percent ($b_9 = 0.002$).

The 1972 Social Security Amendment

In contrast to ERISA, the 1972 amendment of social security had a negative effect on pension demand. The amendment resulted in a rise in the replacement ratio from an average of 40 percent before 1972 to an average of 48 percent after 1972. The effect of this amendment on social security wealth can be approximated by the increase in the revised Feldstein series on social security wealth between 1971 and 1973. The increase of 3500 (1982) dollars per capita would, in the long run, lower pension wealth by 20 to 40 percent.

Inflation and Pension Demand

The acceleration of inflation in the 1970s also had a negative effect on pension demand because of the negative impact of inflation on stock prices. To assess the effect of inflation on pension saving, a simple regression is first run to determine the impact of inflation on the proxies for the rates of return on pension and nonpension assets. It is found that each percentage point increase in inflation reduced the real pension rate of return by a full percentage point and the real after-tax rate of return on nonpension saving by one half of a percentage point. Thus, the rise in inflation from an average of 3.2 percent for 1966–72 to an average of 6.7 percent for 1973–79 reduced the pension rate of return by 3.5 percentage points and the after-tax rate of nonpension returns by 1.75 percentage points. Using the benchmark values of asset returns (5.5 percentage points), pension wealth would eventually be reduced by 21 percent.

CONCLUDING REMARKS

The above analysis has provided evidence that the demand for pension wealth is positively related to the real pension rate of return and negatively related to the real after-tax nonpension rate of return. This suggests that tax exemption of pension saving has a positive effect on pension demand. If pension returns were subject to the capital-income tax, the demand for pension wealth could decline by 25 percent. In contrast, if the President's Commission on Pension Policy's (1981) recommendation that favorable tax treatment be extended to employee contributions to pension plans, including a refundable tax credit for people with low and moderate income, were adopted, pension saving would increase. Assuming that the after-tax return on pension assets would rise by 2 percentage points, the demand for pension saving might increase by 15 percent.

Our analysis suggests that the passage of ERISA played an important role in the growth of pensions in the 1970s. More specifically, ERISA is expected eventually to raise the demand for pension wealth by between 45 and 85 percent. On the other hand, both the acceleration of inflation in the 1970s and passage of the 1972 social security amendment reduced the demand for wealth. The estimated effect of the 3.5 percentage point rise in the inflation rate between 1966–72 and 1973–79 was a 20 percent reduction in pension demand. The social security amendment likely reduced demand by another 30 percent.

It should be emphasized that the results obtained here are highly tentative for two reasons. First, as noted in Feldstein (1982), expectations about future income and social security benefits cannot be fully captured in time-series studies by current income and social security wealth. Demographic structure and expected asset returns are necessary inputs, and they are notoriously difficult to measure. Second, because of the long-term nature of pension saving and transactions cost involved in pension adjustments, responses to deviations of actual from desired pension wealth are likely to be stepwise and thus not accurately represented by a linear stock-adjustment model (which is used because of limited data availability). Possibly owing to these problems, the estimated regression equations are not as stable as we have hoped for.

APPENDIX

This appendix derives the first-order conditions for the lifetime maximization problem described in the second section, in which v and c are chosen so as to maximize equation (9.1) subject to (9.4), (9.7), (9.9), and (9.12). With the exception of the introduction of social security, this is the discrete-time version of the Yaari (1965) problem, and his method can be applied. Write the Lagrange function:

$$\begin{aligned} L = \Sigma\Big[& u[c(t)]\,g(t) + \lambda(t)[(1 + r_n)a_n(t-1) + y(t) - c(t) - a_n(t)] \\ & + \phi(t)[(1 + r_p)a_p(t-1) + vw - a_p(t)] \\ & + \psi(t)[(1 + r_z)a_z(t-1) + (1 - v)w - a_z(t)] \\ & + \mu(t)a_n(t)\Big], \end{aligned}$$

where $g(t) = f(t)\delta^t$, while $\lambda(t)$, $\phi(t)$, $\psi(t)$, and $\mu(t)$ are the Lagrange multipliers for constraints (6.9), (6.4), (6.7), and (6.12), respectively.

The first-order conditions are now given by

$$u'[c(t)]g(t) = \lambda(t) \qquad \text{for all } t, \tag{9A.1}$$

$$(1 + r_n)\lambda(t+1) = \lambda(t) - \mu(t) \qquad \text{for all } t, \tag{9A.2}$$

$$(1 + r_p)\phi(t+1) = \phi(t) \qquad \text{for } t \langle R, \tag{9A.3}$$

$$\phi(R) = (1 - x)b\Sigma\lambda(\tau). \tag{9A.4}$$

$$(1 + r_z)\psi(t+1) = \psi(t) \qquad \text{for } t \langle R, \tag{9A.5}$$

$$\psi(R) = e\Sigma\lambda(\tau), \tag{9A.6}$$

$$\phi(t) = (1 - x - z)\lambda(t) + z\psi(t) \qquad \text{if } 0 < v < 1, \tag{9A.7}$$

$$\mu(t) \geqslant 0,\ \mu(t)a_n(t) = 0. \tag{9A.8}$$

If the constraint on nonpension wealth is not binding, then, by equation (9A.8) $\mu(t) = 0$. Condition (9A.2) now reduces to

$$\lambda(t) = \lambda(0)(1 + r_n) - t. \tag{9A.2$'$}$$

Assuming that the utility function is of the Cobb–Douglas form [i.e., $u(c) = \log(c)$], equation (A1) reduces to:

$$g(t)/c(t) = \lambda(t) \tag{9A.1$'$}$$

Substituting this equation into (9A.2′), we further obtain:

$$c(t) = c(0)[g(t)(1 + r_n)^t]. \tag{9A.9}$$

Substituting this equation into equation (9.9) in the second section and then integrating yields:

$$c^* = c(0) = Y/\Sigma\left[1/[g(t)(1 + r_n)^t]\right] = \alpha(r_n)Y, \tag{9A.10}$$

where

$$Y = a_n(0) + \Sigma y(t)/(1 + r_n)^t.$$

This represents the well-known life-cycle theory that current consumption depends on lifetime income, Y.

Upon combining equations (9A.2) through (9A.7), it can be shown that if $\mu(t) = 0$ for all t, then the condition for portfolio equilibrium at $t = 0$ becomes:

$$\Sigma(1 + r_n)^{-T}[(1 - x)B - zE] = 1 - x - z, \tag{9A.11}$$

where

$$B = b(1 + r_p)^R [P(R)/P(\tau)], \qquad \text{and}$$

$$E = e(1 + r_z)^R [P(R)/P(\tau)].$$

B is the annual retirement benefits expected per dollar of current pension contribution, and E is the annual social security benefit expected per dollar of current contribution to social security. The right-hand side of equation (9A.11) represents the cost per dollar of current contribution to pensions. It is less than one dollar because of the sheltering from current income and social security taxes that pension saving accords. The left-hand side is the present value of after-tax pension benefit net of reduced social security benefits (because of reduced contribution to social security resulted from the pension contribution). By definition:

$$\Sigma bf(t)/(1 + i_p)^t = 1, \qquad (9A.12)$$

$$\Sigma ef(t)/(1 + i_z)^t = 1. \qquad (9A.13)$$

Suppose first that there is no uncertainty concerning the life span. That is, there is a T such that $f(t) = 1$ for $t \leqslant T$ and $f(t) = 0$ for $t > T$. Upon substituting from equations (9A.12) and (9A.13), it can be shown that for T sufficiently large, (A11) reduces to:

$$(1 - x)r_p - zr_z = (1 - x - z)r_n. \qquad (9A.14)$$

If, however, $f(t) < 1$ and decreasing for $t \leqslant T$, then (9A.11) implies that:

$$(1 - x)r_p - zr_z \leqslant (1 - x - z)r_n.$$

In other words, there is a q such that:

$$(1 - x)r_p - zr_z = (1 - x - z)(r_n - q). \qquad (9A.15)$$

Term q may be called the risk premium that the individual is willing to pay for pensions.

NOTES

1. The data file of the President's Commission contains direct measures of economic variables such as income, wages, and especially private pension assets and entitlements and social security wealth and entitlement. The Retirement History Survey also provides information on expected (actual) benefits in total, from the previous job and the longest job. In contrast, the National Longitudinal Survey does not provide direct measure of pension wealth. Thus, Munnell (1976) had to rely on the coverage data to infer the wealth figure. She practically assumed that all individuals having the same level of income also have the same pension wealth and entitlement. For a review of these data sets, see Packard (1980).
2. The 1974 study by Feldstein contained a programming error that resulted in overestimation of social security wealth. Upon correcting for this error, he (1982) found that his conclusion regarding the effect of social security on capital accumulation is not significantly affected. See discussions below.

3. For discussions of other effects of ERISA, see J. Bulow (1979).
4. Cash and deposits, U.S. Government securities, mortgages, and others constitute the remaining 20 percent of pension assets. Interestingly, mortgages play only a minor role in pension portfolio (less than 2 percent in 1980).
5. For an interesting discussion of the unique properties of pension saving as opposed to nonpension saving, see Blinder (1982).
6. The question is of course whether the pension contribution rate is a choice variable for the individual. Both Feldstein (1978) andMunnell (1976) assumed the level of pension saving to be exogenous, thus implying that the pension contribution rate is a variable determined exclusively by the firms. On the other hand, it may be argued that unlike social security, private pensions are voluntary arrangements between workers and firms. Thus the pension contribution rate must be a choice variable to individual workers, although because of the high transactions cost involved in their set-up, pension plans are tailor-made to suit the average worker and not the needs of each individual. Even in this case, workers seem at least to some extent to self-select into jobs which provide pension plans most desirable to them (see Blinder 1982, and Taubman 1981). Recent extension of Individual Retirement Accounts to all employed persons further increases such flexibility. Therefore it seems reasonable to assume v to be a choice variable in the lifetime maximization problem.
7. In deriving this condition, it is assumed that the remaining lifespan is sufficiently long for the representative individual.
8. An insured pension plan is one administered by a life insurance company, while a noninsured plan is one that is self-administered or placed with a bank or trust company. Insured plans account for about one-third of total pension assets.
9. The effective rate is the ratio of income tax payments after credit to taxable income.

REFERENCES

American Council of Life Insurance. Various editions. *Pension Facts.* Washington, D.C.

Blinder, A.S. 1982. "Private Pensions and Public Pensions: Theory and Fact." Working Paper No. 902. Cambridge, Mass.: National Bureau of Economic Research.

Blinder, A.S.; R.H. Gordon; and D. Wise. 1978. "An Empirical Study of the Effects of Pensions on the Saving and Labor Supply Decisions of Older Men." Working paper. Princeton: Mathtech.

Board of Governors of the Federal Reserve System. Various editions. *Flow of Funds Accounts.*

Boskin, M. 1978. "Taxation, Saving, and the Rate of Interest." *Journal of Political Economy* 86, no. 2 (April): S3–S26.

Bulow, J. 1979. "Analysis of Funding under ERISA." Working Paper No. 402. Cambridge, Mass.: National Bureau of Economic Research.

Chen, A. 1983. "Taxes, Inflation, and Corporate Pension Policy." Southern Methodist University. Mimeo.

Economic Report of the President. Statistical Appendix. 1984.

Estrella, A., and J.C. Fuhrer. 1983. "Average Marginal Tax Rates for the U.S. Household Interest and Dividend Income, 1954–80." Working Paper No. 1201. Cambridge, Mass.: National Bureau of Economic Research.

Feldstein, M.S. 1974. "Social Security, Induced Retirement, and Aggregate Capital Accumulation." *Journal of Political Economy* 82, no. 5, pt. 2 (September/October): 905–26.

———. 1978. "Do Private Pensions Increase National Savings?" *Journal of Public Economics* 10, no. 3 (December): 277–82.

———. 1982. "Social Security and Private Saving: A Reply." *Journal of Political Economy* 90, no. 3 (June): 630–43.

Feldstein, M.S., and S. Seligman. 1981. "Pension Funding, Share Prices and National Saving." *Journal of Finance* 36, no. 4 (September): 801–24.

Gersovitz, M. 1982. "Economic Consequences of Unfunded Vested Pension Benefits." *Journal of Public Economics* 19, no. 2 (November): 171–86.

Kurz, M. 1981. "The Life Cycle Hypothesis and the Effects of Social Security and Private Pensions on Family Savings." Technical Report No. 335. Palo Alto: Stanford University, Institute of Mathematical Studies in Social Sciences.

Mundell, R. 1963. "Inflation and Real Interest Rate." *Journal of Political Economy* 71, no. 3 (June): 280–83.

Munnell, A. 1976. "Private Pensions and Saving: New Evidence." *Journal of Political Economy* 84, no. 5 (October): 1013–32.

———. 1982. *The Economics of Private Pensions.* App. A. Washington, D.C.: Brookings Institution.

Packard, M. 1980. "A Review of Data Source for Use in Microeconomic Studies of Life Cycle Consumption, Saving and Labor Supply." Washington, D.C.: Office of Research and Statistics, Social Security Administration.

President's Commission on Pension Policy. 1981. "Report of the President's Commission on Pension Policy: Executive Summary." *Social Security Bulletin* 44, no. 5 (May): 14–17.

Taubman, P. 1981. "Pensions Mortality." Working Paper no. 811, Cambridge, Mass.: National Bureau of Economic Research.

Tepper, I. 1981. "Taxation and Corporate Pension Policy." *Journal of Finance* 34, no. 1 (January): 1–13.

Turner, J. 1980. "Inflation and the Accumulation of Assets in Private Pension Funds." ORS Working Paper No. 14. Washington, D.C.: Social Security Administration.

U.S. Internal Revenue Service. Various issues. *Statistics of Income.*

U.S. Social Security Administration. 1973. *Retirement History Survey.*

Yaari, M. 1965. "Uncertain Lifetime, Life Insurance and the Theory of the Consumer." *Review of Economic Studies* 32, no. 1 (April):137–50.

10 INVESTMENT IN AND RETURNS FROM EDUCATION

George E. Johnson

INVESTMENT IN SCHOOLING IN THE UNITED STATES

The "theory of human capital" has now been a part of the apparatus of economics for a quarter of a century (back to Shultz 1961). This theory focuses on the process of investment in people (their initial education or schooling, subsequent on-the-job training, location, health, and so forth). This chapter examines selected questions concerning the economic role of investment in education in the United States. As in many topics of economics, there was a flurry of activity immediately following the birth of the topic. Then in the early 1970s interest in the economics ineducation waned somewhat—even though there were several important but difficult questions that were only partially resolved. Some good work has been done on these questions over the past ten years, however, and it seems a useful exercise to summarize what we have learned about the efficacy of investment in schooling.

The scale of the cost of schooling in the United States is, as is clear from examination of Table 10–1, enormous. In addition to these direct costs, which exceed 7 percent of GNP, education also involves an indirect cost in terms of the partial or complete withdrawal from

Table 10-1. GNP, Direct Schooling Costs, and Gross Private Nonresidential Investment, 1929–79.

	Billions of Current Dollars			Percentage of GNP		Percentage of Population Age 5–17[b]
Year	GNP[a]	Schooling[b]	Investment[a]	Schooling	Investment	
1929	103.4	3.2	10.6	3.1	10.3	25.8
1939	90.9	3.2	5.9	3.5	6.5	23.0
1949	258.3	8.8	24.4	3.4	9.4	20.3
1959	487.9	24.7	45.9	5.1	9.4	24.5
1969	944.0	70.4	101.3	7.5	10.7	25.8
1979	2417.8	169.2	290.2	7.0	12.0	20.9

a. *Economic Report of the President* (1983: Table B-1).
b. Office of Education (1982: Table 16).

the labor force of full time students. Even if one ignores the opportunity cost of the 31.8 million "K through 8" students (as of the fall of 1980), the aggregate opportunity cost of more advanced students is very large. Assume that each high school student was worth, in 1979 terms, $2.50 per hour and would have worked 1,500 hours per year; that each college student was worth $4.00; and that each full-time student would have supplied an additional 1,700 hours and each part-time student an additional 500 hours. Because there were 14.8 million high school students and 7.1 and 5.0 million college students in full and part-time status, respectively, in 1980, an indirect opportunity cost of $105.4 billion must be added to the $169.2 billion direct cost figure for 1979. This sum implies that education costs society approximately as much as investment in nonresidential physical capital.

The resources devoted to education doubled as a fraction of GNP between the end of World War II and the late 1960s. As a result, the educational attainment of the labor force increased markedly (see Table 10-2). For the aggregate labor force, the proportion of students who have attended or graduated from college doubled between 1952 and 1979 and the proportion of students who have not graduated from high school halved. This trend is especially strong for blacks, as the black distribution of educational attainment moved toward equality with the white distribution.

Table 10-2. Distribution of Labor Force by Educational Attainment, Selected Years 1952–79.

		Completed Schooling					
	Year	*<5*	*5–8*	*9–11*	*12*	*13–15*	*16+*
Entire labor force	1952	7.5	30.4	18.7	26.8	8.5	8.1
	1959	5.2	25.0	19.6	31.3	9.3	9.6
	1964	3.2	20.9	19.2	34.5	10.6	11.2
	1969	2.7	15.9	17.8	38.4	12.6	12.6
	1974	1.8	10.9	18.1	39.2	15.1	15.0
	1979	1.4	7.5	15.9	40.0	17.5	17.6
White Males	1959	4.4	26.1	20.2	28.6	9.6	11.2
	1969	2.4	16.9	17.4	35.4	13.1	14.7
	1979	1.3	8.3	15.3	36.8	17.7	20.6
Black Males	1959	17.8	35.5	21.1	16.5	4.9	4.1
	1969	10.9	24.2	24.7	25.6	8.1	6.5
	1979	3.4	11.6	23.0	37.5	15.5	9.0

Source: U.S. Department of Labor, Bureau of Labor Statistics (1975: Table 12, 1980: Table 68).

The huge scale of the annual cost of education raises the obvious question of whether we are spending too much on this activity. This is also very much a public policy issue because 81 percent of aggregate direct costs in 1979–80 are accounted for by public educational institutions. A nontrivial proportion of the operating expenses of private colleges and universities are derived from government, both directly and through tax expenditure. Are the future benefits to society worth the present costs? Could some portion of current educational expenditures be profitably reallocated to investment in physical capital (either private or public), or vice versa? These questions of the *impact evaluation* of education as a global program should be based on evidence on the issues with which human capital specialists were very much concerned just when interest in the topic waned ten years ago. Specifically, how does the social return to resources invested in schooling compare with the returns to alternative uses of these resources? If careful empirical analysis shows that, for example, the social return to schooling is less than the return to physical capital in the private sector or in social infrastructure, the policy implication is rather clear, as is the policy implication of the opposite finding.

There is overwhelming evidence that persons with higher levels of schooling have, on average, higher earnings throughout their work lives than do persons with lower levels of schooling. Calculated internal social rates of return to educational investment based on these estimates range from 6 to 8 percent, much higher than the 3 to 4 percent figure usually assumed to be the real social discount rate (Gramlich 1981:108). However, the conventional estimates are widely recognized as overstating the impact of schooling because they fail to adjust earnings for innate ability and motivation or to correct for selection bias (those who can benefit most from schooling tend to undertake it). Most of the empirical studies specific to human capital issues of the past decade have centered on the magnitude of this overstatement. Typically, these studies conclude that the estimated rate of return should be adjusted down by no more than 10 percent, which still leaves the rate of return to schooling in a range well above the real social discount rate.

An equally important question concerns the effect of the upward shift in the distribution of educational attainment on the rate of return to schooling. To the extent that labor groups with different schooling levels are not perfect substitutes in production, this upward shift should have lowered returns from their 1960 values. There is some evidence that there has been a slight decline, but not enough to alter the fundamental conclusion that benefits exceed costs.

In addition to the interrelations among schooling, ability, and earnings, several other important questions can be addressed in this framework. First there is some initial evidence that the social rate of return to "quality" of schooling, i.e., an additional *X* dollars spent on direct costs, holding time in school constant, yields a higher return than increasing time in school at a cost of *X* dollars. If this is correct, a misallocation of expenditure between the intensive and extensive forms of schooling is implied—although the returns to both are still above the social discount rate.

Second, there is a strong negative association between lifetime unemployment and education. This implies that calculated rates of return to schooling based on annual earnings are larger than those based on hourly earnings. Which basis is more appropriate depends on *why* there is this association. If the difference in unemployment rates between more- and less-educated persons reflects differential involuntary unemployment, and if an upward shift in the distribution of educational attainment will reduce aggregate unemployment by an amount consistent with the cross-sectional estimates, then part of the reduction in unemployment should be included as a benefit to schooling.

The second section of the paper sets out the simple analytics of the procedure for estimating the economic returns to schooling, and the third section contains a survey of the major empirical evidence. A summary of the major results is given in the final section.

CONCEPTUAL ISSUES

The Simple Human Capital Model

The early development of the theory of optimal investment in human capital (see Becker 1964) stressed that a particular functional form is implied by the model. Assume that an individual is considering investing in the Sth year of schooling. Future annual earnings will be W_S or W_{S-1} depending on whether or not the investment is undertaken. The present values associated with the two options are:

$$V_S = -C_S + \sum_{t=0}^{N} W_S(1 + r)^{-t}$$

and

$$V_{S-1} = W_{S-1} + \sum_{t=0}^{N} W_{S-1}(1 + r)^{-t},$$

where C_S is the direct cost of the Sth year of schooling, N is one less than the number of years to retirement, and r is the discount rate. The internal rate of return (RR_S) associated with the investment is the value of r that makes these the present values equal. Assuming that N is sufficiently large so that $(1 + r)^{-N} \simeq 0$, the rate of return is:

$$RR_S = \frac{W_S - W_{S-1}}{C_S + W_{S-1}} = \frac{W_S - W_{S-1}}{W_{S-1}} \Big/ \left(1 + \frac{C_S}{W_{S-1}}\right). \qquad (10.1)$$

In words, the rate of return to the Sth year of schooling is the proportionate increase in annual earnings due to their investment divided by one plus the ratio of its direct cost to its opportunity cost.

The first implication of equation (10.1) concerns the functional form of a multiple regression that explains cross-sectional variation in earnings levels across individuals. The rate of return to schooling without adjustment for the direct costs of schooling (i.e., assuming $C_S = 0$) is $(W_S - W_{S-1})/W_{S-1}$. Thus, if this rate of return is constant over all relevant schooling levels (i.e., $RR_S = RR'$ for all S), the earnings level of a person with S years of schooling is:

$$W_S = (1 + RR')^S W_0, \tag{10.2}$$

where Y_0 is the earning level of a person with zero years of schooling. Taking logarithms, the log of the earnings of the ith person with S years of schooling is:

$$\begin{aligned} \log W_i &= S_i \log(1 + RR') + \log W_0 + \ldots \\ &\cong RR'S_i + \log W_0 + \ldots, \end{aligned} \tag{10.3}$$

where the dots reflect individual specific variables. This means that the coefficient on schooling in an earnings equation—with log earnings as the dependent variable—is the rate of return to schooling without allowance for direct educational costs. Although this is obviously an approximation, it is very useful for subsequent purposes.

A second implication of equation (10.1) concerns the distinction between the private and the social rate of return to investment in schooling. If the real marginal product of labor with the Sth schooling level equals gross before-tax earnings, W_S and C_S is the real resource cost of the Sth year of schooling, the *social* rate of return associated with the Sth year of schooling is given by (10.1). From the perspective of aggregate social welfare, society should set the distribution of education attainment such that RR_S equals the social discount rate. Within the Golden Rule framework, of course, the social discount rate should equal the rate of economic growth, so if investment in physical capital is optimal in an intergenerational sense, RR_S "should" equal about 3.5 percent (the average rate of economic growth in the United States from 1947 to 1979).

The private rate of return to schooling is calculated from equation (10.1) on the basis of net earnings and private schooling costs. Thus, most taxes and any government subsidization of schooling cost will in general cause social and private returns to diverge. For example, suppose that there is only a progressive income tax on labor earnings with annual proceeds $\Theta(W_i - X)$, where Θ is the fixed marginal tax rate and X is a constant tax exemption. In addition, γ of the resource costs of schooling are paid by government, so private tuition cost is $C_S^{priv} = (1 - \gamma)C_S$. While the social rate of return is given by:

$$RR_S = \frac{\dfrac{W_S - W_{S-1}}{W_{S-1}}}{1 + \dfrac{C_S}{W_{S-1}}}, \tag{10.4}$$

the private rate of return to this investment is:

$$RR_S^{priv} = \frac{(1 - \theta)[W_S - W_{S-1}]}{(1 - \theta)C_S + W_{S-1} - \theta(W_{S-1} - X)}. \tag{10.5}$$

In principle, social and private rates of return should be the same (and equal to the social discount rate). If there were no tax system, Θ would equal zero, and equations (10.4) and (10.5) would be equal so long as students paid the full cost of their schooling ($\gamma = 0$). For a positive income tax rate, however, the "optimal" subsidy rate is in general not equal to zero. The subsidy rate that equates private and social rates of return is found by setting equation (10.4) equal to (10.5) and solving the result for γ. This value is easily shown to be:

$$\gamma^* = \Theta\left(1 + \frac{X}{C_S}\right). \tag{10.6}$$

The optimal subsidy rate is larger the greater the value of the flat income tax rate and given $\Theta > 0$, the higher is X (which is to say, the more progressive is the income tax system). Notice that the optimal subsidy rate could exceed unity. For example, plausible values of the relevant parameters in the high school to college zone are $\Theta = 0.35$, X=10,000, and C_S=5,000, which implies a subsidy rate necessary to equate RR_S and RR_S^{priv} of 105 percent of resource cost. Because of the progressivity of the tax system, private decision makers will overvalue opportunity cost (the lost W_{S-1}) relative to future income gains due to schooling. The high subsidy rate on the resource cost of schooling compensates for this distortion.

Interestingly, the *average* subsidy rate in higher education in the United States in 1978 was approximately 0.75 (see Johnson 1984). In the United Kingdom, on the other hand, university students receive full tuition plus a small living allowance, which is a subsidy rate in excess of unity. There are no doubt more straightforward reasons for the existence of high subsidy rates than the adjustment of relative prices to offset distortions due to the tax system. Whatever their legislative intent, however, these subsidies may be socially efficient.

The implications for optional subsidy rates of other forms of taxation can be worked out in an analogous manner. For example, a proportionate tax on payrolls (such as the employer side of FICA) raises the marginal product of labor relative to the wage. Ignoring the upper limit on taxable earnings per employee, $(W_S - W_{S-1})/W_{S-1}$ is still equal to the proportionate difference in marginal products, but W_{S-1} is less than the social opportunity cost of labor with $S - 1$ years of schooling. This implies that individuals will undervalue the opportunity cost of schooling and that the subsidy rate should be lower. A consumption tax would, of course, require no educational subsidy because it does not distort the choice between present and future income.

A Behavioral Model

The preceding specification of the relation between earnings and schooling level is useful for measurement purposes, but it does not address the question of the *behavior* of investors in human capital. Becker (1967) modified the simple model in this regard. He posited that the demand for human capital is a downward-sloping function of its rate of return and of the innate ability of the individual and that the supply of human capital is an upward-sloping function of the rate of return and of the financial resources of the individual (or his/her family). Variations in the level of investment in schooling may arise from differences in either innate ability (what Becker termed the "elite approach" to the question) or financial resources (the "egalitarian approach"). The demand curve for more able persons will be to the right of that for less able persons, similarly for supply curves of richer as compared to poorer persons.

Although it is not possible to derive Becker's supply curve of human capital from any utility-based model with an imperfect capital market (Gustman and Stafford 1972), his framework suggests that the task of estimating RR_S is not simple. The observed earnings of individuals are a positively-sloped function of their schooling level and innate ability (A, which includes special skills, motivation, and the like):

$$W = \Phi(S,A). \tag{10.7}$$

The level of investment in schooling will then depend positively, in general, on the person's ability level and on family financial resources available during the period of investment (Z), or:

$$S = \Psi(A,Z). \tag{10.8}$$

The egalitarian approach specifies that $\Psi_Z > 0$; with a perfect capital market $\Psi_Z = 0$.

Equations (10.7) and (10.8) can be linearized, with error terms (reflecting luck, accidents, and the like), so that the model becomes:

$$\log W = \alpha_1 S + \alpha_2 A + \epsilon_1 \tag{10.9}$$

and

$$S = \beta_1 A + \beta_2 Z + \epsilon_2. \tag{10.10}$$

(Other influences on log W, such as current location and the constant term, are ignored, although they would obviously be included in any empirical equations.) An alternative to equation (10.9), more in the spirit of Becker's original model, would be to include an interaction term, $\alpha_3 AS$, in the equation explaining log W, but the fundamental point concerning the estimation of α_1 is little changed. In a regression of log W on S, with no information on A, the statistical expectation of α_1 is:

$$E(\alpha_1) = \alpha_1 + \alpha_2 b_{AS}, \tag{10.11}$$

where b_{AS} is the slope coefficient of a regression of innate ability on schooling. To the extent that $\beta_1 > 0$, b_{AS} tends to be positive and α_1 to be upward-biased (α_2 is positive). The bias is reduced to the extent that partial measures of A (such as current IQ) are included in the regression.

Intensive versus Extensive Investment in Education

To this point it has been assumed that the process of investment of schooling is described by a fixed coefficients production function: The direct cost of the Sth unit of schooling is simply C_S. Intuitively, this is implausible. We all know that each year of schooling could be gotten through with higher or lower quality teachers, larger or smaller class sizes, more or less equipment, and so forth. From both a private and a social point of view—especially since the direct costs of education are such a large component of GNP and of aggregate investment—it is useful to compare the returns from making schooling more extensive (more years)—with those from increasing its intensity (more real dollars efficiently spent per year).

To generalize the model, assume that future earnings of a typical student depend on expenditure per year of schooling (C) as well as years of schooling and ability:

$$W = \Gamma(S,C,A). \tag{10.12}$$

For expositional purposes, C is taken to be constant over the entire schooling period (although, in fact, higher levels of schooling are inherently more expensive). It is also easier to set out the model in continuous rather than discrete time. The net present value as of the time of school entry of the cost/earnings stream of the typical student is:

$$V = -\int_0^S Ce^{-rt}dt + \int_S^N \Gamma(S,C,A)e^{-rt}dt. \tag{10.13}$$

The first-order conditions for maximization of V with respect to S and C are:

$$\frac{\partial V}{\partial S} = (C + W)e^{-rS} + \int_S^N \Gamma_S e^{-rt}dt = 0 \tag{10.14}$$

and

$$\frac{\partial V}{\partial C} = -\int_0^S e^{-rt}dt + \int_S^N \Gamma_C e^{-rt}dt = 0. \tag{10.15}$$

Assuming that Γ_S and Γ_C are independent of t and $e^{-rN} \simeq 0$, these conditions reduce to:

$$r = \frac{\Gamma_S}{C + W} = \frac{\Gamma_S/W}{1 + C/W} \tag{10.16}$$

and

$$\Gamma_C + 1 = e^{rS} \quad \text{or} \quad r = \frac{1}{S}\log(\Gamma_C + 1). \tag{10.17}$$

The first of these is, of course, the continuous analogue of equation (10.1), and the second says that C should be increased to the point where its "marginal product" equals $e^{rS} - 1$, or, approximately, $\Gamma_C = rS$.

If one has estimates of C (at the time of schooling) for a cross-section of the labor force, the rates of return to both the extensiveness and intensity of investment in schooling, RR_S and RR_C respectively, can be estimated by solving discrete versions of both equations (10.14) and (10.15). If, for example, the estimated value of RR_C exceeds RR_S, a reallocation of educational resources from time spent in school to expenditure per unit of schooling would increase total effective aggregate labor input for the same cost. An interesting question concerns the effect of increasing C on RR_S. If C is increased, does the optimal time spent in schooling increase or decrease? The answer, it turns out, depends on the functional form of the Γ function. Another set of interesting questions concerns the optimal allocation of educational resources between bright and dull students (high and low values of A). The answer to this also depends on the functional form of Γ (especially on Γ_{SA} and Γ_{CA}). Because A is inherently unobservable, this issue if very difficult to resolve. It is, however, at the heart of questions concerning the desirability of "compensatory education."

Education in Production

One of the major policy issues concerning education in the United States is the extent to which rates of return to schooling have fallen. One argument is that the dramatic increase in the average level of attainment must have lowered the relative earnings of more educated labor. This would lower α_1 in equation (10.1), reducing the rate of return to schooling. To address this issue, it is necessary to set out the role of education in the production process.

Assume that the role of education is to prepare individuals for different skill levels or "occupations." Let E_i be the level of employment for skill level i, and these levels are ordered from low, 1 (very little schooling), to high, M (college plus professional degree). Aggregate output (Y) is then a function of the different types of labor and of capital (K), say:

$$Y = F(E_1, \ldots, E_M, K). \tag{10.18}$$

Now suppose that investment in physical capital is such that the marginal product of capital always equals the interest rate (either because of a world capital market constraint or fiscal policies designed to satisfy the Golden Rule), $F_K = r$. Output net of capital costs is:

$$Y_N = Y - rK = G(E_1, \ldots, E_M), \tag{10.19}$$

which depends only on the skill distribution of employment, for $\partial Y_N / \partial K = 0$. Further, if F is linear homogenous, G is also linear homogeneous. That is, increasing all labor inputs by X percent increases Y and Y_N (as well as K) by X percent.

The relative wage of one education level labor group relative to another, say W_M / W_{M-1}, is (ignoring payroll taxes) given by:

$$\frac{W_M}{W_{M-1}} = \frac{F_M(E_1, \ldots, E_M, K)}{F_{M-1}(E_1, \ldots, E_M, K)}. \tag{10.20}$$

Now consider changing one person with skill level $M-1$ into a person with skill level M, so $-dE_{M-1} = dE_M = 1$. What will happen to log (W_M / W_{M-1}), that is, to the rate of return on the schooling associated with the schooling necessary to attain skill level M? It can be shown that the proportionate change in E_M is:

$$\frac{d[\log(W_M/W_{M-1})]}{d(\log E_M)} = \frac{E_M}{Y}\Bigg[[W_{M-1}C_{M-1,M-1} + W_M C_{MM} - (W_M + W_{M-1})C_{M,M-1}] + \frac{\alpha_k(C_{Mk} - C_{M-1,k})}{1 - a_k C_{kk}}(W_M C_{Mk} - W_{M-1}C_{M-1,k})\Bigg], \tag{10.21}$$

where C_{ij} is the partial elasticity of complementarity between factor i and j and $\alpha_k = rK/Y$ is the share of output going to capital. The first expression within brackets in equations (10.21) reflects substitution between labor inputs, and it is negative unless E_M and E_{M-1} are perfect substitutes in production. The second expression represents the effect of a change in capital stock on relative labor demand. If the two types of labor are equally complementary with capital ($C_{Mk} = C_{M-1,k}$), this term is zero. If, however, more skilled labor is more complementary with capital than is less skilled labor, $C_{Mk} > C_{M-1,k}$ and, since $W_M > W_{M-1}$, the second expression is positive.

In the case of a C.E.S. production function, $C_{ij} = -(1 - \alpha_i)/\sigma\alpha_i$ for i=j and $= 1/\sigma$ for $i \neq j$, where σ is the single elasticity of factor substitution. Then equation (10.21) reduces to:

$$\frac{d[\log(W_M/W_{M-1})]}{d(\log E_M)} = \frac{E_M}{\sigma Y}\left[\frac{W_{M-1}}{\alpha_{M-1}} + \frac{W_M}{\alpha_M}\right]$$

$$= \frac{1}{\sigma}\frac{E_M}{E_M + E_{M-1}}. \qquad (10.22)$$

W_M/W_{M-1} is unaffected by the skill distribution of the labor force if the two labor groups are perfect substitutes ($\sigma = \infty$), but the effect of E_M on W_M/W_{M-1} gets larger as σ gets smaller.

There are remarkably few estimates of the parameters of labor demand functions where the inputs are delineated by educational category. Welch (1970), Johnson (1970), and Dougherty (1972) report estimates of a single σ parameter of, respectively, 1.4, 1.3, and 3.3. Hamermesh and Grant (1979) discuss some work (by Grant) in which partial elasticities of substitution among different educational categories and capital are derived, and the implied value of σ is somewhat smaller than in the earlier estimates. Given that the rate of return to schooling has not fallen significantly as the educational distribution has shifted to the right, the larger estimates of σ are probably more accurate. On the other hand, it is possible that the relative demand function for more educated labor shifted to the right due to technological change.

EMPIRICAL EVIDENCE ON THE RETURNS TO SCHOOLING

Earnings Functions

One of the stylized facts of labor economics is that the estimated coefficient on years of schooling (S) in a cross-sectional earnings function (1) is extremely significant and (2) has a remarkably consistent value. The earnings function relates the earnings of individuals to a set of explanatory variables. These variables can be classified into eight types:

1. *Human capital:* including S, potential experience, and, in principle, ability and motivation;
2. *Nonpecuniary:* variables reflecting the relative desirability of the individual's job—its safety, social prestige, onerousness, flexibility, and so forth;
3. *Locational:* dummy variables for region of job, reflecting differences in costs-of-living and amenities among areas;
4. *Disequilibrium:* variables indicating temporary shortages or gluts of particular skills;
5. *Monopoly:* variables reflecting a possible departure from competitive wage levels, such as unionism or public employment; and
6. *Discrimination:* variables representing identifiable subgroups in the population, such as women, blacks, and hispanics.

The logarithmic functional form that was suggested for schooling (see equation (10.3)) is also convenient in the interpretation of the coefficients on all dummy variables. For example, in an equation with schooling, union membership (U = 1 or 0), and other variables:

$$\log W = \alpha_0 + \alpha_1 S + \alpha_2 U + \ldots, \tag{10.23}$$

the value of α_2 is interpreted as the logarithm of the union/nonunion wage differential, log (W_U / W_N). Thus, the union/nonunion wage gap (the proportionate wage advantage union members, other influences held constant) is:

$$\text{gap} = \frac{W_U - W_N}{W_N} = \exp(\alpha_2) - 1. \tag{10.24}$$

The estimated slope coefficients on dummy variables on sex and race may be similarly interpreted as estimates of the extent of discrimination in the labor market; estimates of coefficients on dummy variables by region provide estimates of relative wage levels by region; and so forth.

One important possibility is that with respect to some variables the earnings function may not take the semilogarithmic form. Of particular interest for present purposes, suppose that one wants to test the hypothesis that the returns to schooling differ for blacks and whites. This can be done by specifying an interactive earnings function:

$$\log W = \alpha_0 + \alpha_1 S + \alpha_2 B + \alpha_3 SB + \ldots, \quad (10.25)$$

where B is a dummy variable for blacks. The estimated value of $\partial(\log W)/\partial S$ is α_1 for whites and $\alpha_1 + \alpha_3$ for blacks. A test of the hypothesis that $\partial(\log W)/\partial S$ differs for blacks and whites is simply the standard significance test for α_3.

Estimates of the Effect of Schooling on Earnings

The early estimates of the internal rate of return to schooling (Becker 1964) were very large. Hansen (1963) obtained a rate of return for four years of high school (going from grades 8 through 12) of 11.4 percent, and for four years of college of 10.2 percent. These and similar estimates were calculated from aggregate Census data. To make these results analogous to the more recent estimates using microdata, a simple earnings function based on Hansen's data has been estimated. Column (1) of Table 10–3 contains the result of the regression. The logarithm of median annual earnings for each age/education cell on S and potential experience (X = age − S −6.5) and its square. In column (2) S^2 is added. The estimated coefficient on S in column (1) is 0.092, which is very similar to the values estimated with similar equations on different microdata sets in the 1960s, 1970s, and 1980s that are cited below. The coefficient on S^2 is positive in column (2), which means that the derivative of log earnings with respect to S rises with schooling. Average earnings of a high school graduate are $\exp(4 \times 0.079 + (12^2 - 8^2).0014) = 1.47$ times those of an elementary school graduate; earnings of a college graduate 1.54 those of a high school graduate. The ratio of direct to opportunity costs rises as S increases, so RR_S tends to fall as S rises.

More recent estimates have been obtained from microeconomic data—samples with individual observations on wage rates, education, and a variety of socioeconomic information. A *sample* of the results (there are perhaps 400 published studies reporting the estimated coefficients of earnings functions) is given in Table 10–4. The first five of these report estimates of $\partial(\log W)/\partial S$ that are between 0.05

Table 10-3. Estimates of Determinants of Logarithm of Earnings Level from Aggregate Data, 1949.

	(1)	*(2)*
S	0.092 (0.004)	0.069 (0.014)
S^2	–	0.0014 (0.0008)
X	0.054 (0.005)	0.055 (0.005)
X^2	-0.000683 (0.000106)	-0.000734 (0.000703)
Constant	6.364 (0.808)	6.403 (0.816)
R^2	0.938	0.943
S.E.E.	0.130	0.126

Source: 1950 U.S. Census data reported in Hansen (1963). Data restricted to all age/education cells above age 21 and below age 65. Estimated standard errors in parentheses.

and 0.08, which is a sufficiently high range to guarantee an internal rate of return in excess of four percent. All of these estimates adjust for hours of work, and because (as will be shown later in this section) involuntary unemployment depends negatively on *S*, they may understate the true contribution of education to GNP.

The different studies do point to an interesting diversity of estimated values of $\partial(\log W)/\partial S$. Corcoran and Duncan (1979), for example, report higher estimates for women than for men. Smith's (1976) estimates, on the other hand, are at $S = 13$ (roughly the average schooling level), $S = 0.071$ for men, and $S = 0.062$ for women. Chiswick's (1983) finding that Jewish males benefit from schooling more than their non-Jewish counterparts is extremely interesting. The sixth study reported in Table 10-4, by Podgursky (1983), is restricted to production workers (the occupational categories craftsmen, operatives, and laborers) and is not a representative sample of the entire population (i.e., part of the reason why $\partial(\log W)/\partial S$ is so high is that schooling qualifies persons for higher-level occupations). It shows, however, that institutional features of the work place—in this case,

Table 10-4. Selected Estimates of the Impact of Schooling on the Logarithm of Hourly Earnings.[a]

Study	Group		
Johnson and Stafford (1973)	White Males		0.076
(1) Productive Americans			(0.005)
(2) Employed white males, 1965			
(3) Experience, schooling expenditure, urban, grew up urban			
Corcoran and Duncan (1979)	White Males		0.059
(1) Panel Study on Income Dynamics			(0.004)
(2) Employed persons, 1975	Black Males		0.061
(3) Detailed work history, labor force attachment, locational			(0.006)
	White Females		0.077
			(0.006)
	Black Females		0.076
			(0.008)
		S	S^2
Smith (1976)	Males	0.037	0.0013
(1) Current Population Survey		(0.007)	(0.0003)
(2) Employed persons, 1973			
(3) Experience, race, locational, type of employer	Females	0.021	0.0016
		(0.010)	(0.0004)
Rizzuto and Wachtel (1980)		*1959*	*1969*
(1) U.S. Census, earnings dependent variable	Whites	0.070	0.077
		(0.001)	(0.001)
(2) Employed males, 1959 and 1969			
(3) Experience, locational, weeks worked	Blacks	0.058	0.065
		(0.004)	(0.005)
Chiswick (1983)			
(1) U.S. Census	Jews		0.080
(2) Native-born males of foreign-born parents, 1970	Non-Jews		0.068
Podgursky (1983)			
(1) Current Population Survey	Non-union		0.036
(2) Production workers, 1971			(0.002)
	Union		0.015
			(0.002)

a. (1) = Study/data set
(2) = Sample
(3) = Control variables

whether or not wages are determined by collective bargaining—have a large impact on the relation between earnings and schooling. Unions apparently attempt to minimize differences in earnings due to differences in labor quality (see Johnson and Youmans (1971) for an extensive discussion of this).

Most of the estimated earnings functions that are reported in the literature are based on calculations of the gross wage net of fringe and nonpecuniary benefits. If fringe benefits are proportional to wage rates, they can be ignored in the estimation of $\partial(\log W)/\partial S$. However, Duncan (1976) finds that the estimated effect of schooling on wages increases from 0.054 to 0.058 when the monetary value of fringes is included on the left-hand side of the earnings function. Further, Duncan also finds a positive association between nonpecuniary benefits and schooling, which implies that conventional estimates of returns to schooling are biased downward for this reason. The relevant data sets, however, are not sufficiently rich to put precise numerical values on these nonpecuniary benefits.

Bias in α_1 Due to Exclusion of Ability

As pointed out earlier, estimates of the rate of return to schooling may be biased upward given that the true ability variable (A) is not observed. Most of the research in the economic impact of education during the past ten years has dealt with the task of adjusting for this bias. We *know* that workers with more schooling earn more than those with less schooling; the question is *why* they do. Some of the more important studies in this vein are Gintis (1971), Grilliches and Mason (1972), Taubman (1976), and Willis and Rosen (1979). The basic finding is that the inclusion of measures of cognitive ability and adjustment for selection bias do not seem to lower the estimated rate of return by as much as ten percent.

An interesting recent study of this problem is Filer (1981). His sample is taken from the files of a personnel consulting firm and includes results of extensive testing for cognitive ability (verbal and quantitative) and affective (personality) traits. The latter includes scores concerning general activity ("drive"), ascendancy, sociability and friendliness, masculinity, objectivity, and restraint. Characteristics that did not appear to influence wages were emotional stability, thoughtfulness, and personal relations. What is interesting for present purposes is the effect of including all these variables on the estimated impact of schooling on earnings. A sample of Filer's result are shown in Table 10–5 (he rejected the semilogarithmic form as inappropriate for his A variables). The "% Reduction" figures refer to the adjustment in the estimated impact of each marginal schooling increment on earnings. This is roughly the percentage by which α_1 should be lowered.

It is obvious, however, that the adjustments are small. Indeed, they are sufficiently small that, particularly in light of the bias introduced by excluding fringes, they can be ignored. Whether this means that the *true* A is orthogonal to S or that psychologists' measures are too primitive, one cannot say. What one *can* say is that thus far no one has blown the estimated value of $\partial(\log W)/\partial S$ out of the water.

Changes in the Returns to Schooling over Time

What impact has the dramatic upward shift in the distribution of educational attainment had on the rate of return to schooling? As pointed out in the second section, this should depend on the degree to which different groups are substitutable for each other in production. If, for example, a college graduate can do *any* job $(1 + x)^4$ as efficiently as a high school graduate, $\partial(\log W)/\partial S$ will equal x regard-

Table 10–5. Estimated Impact of Schooling on Monthly Earnings with Adjustments for Cognitive and Affective Ability Traits.

	No Adjustments	*Cognitive Only*	*Cognitive and Affective*
High School to associate degree	73.86	66.22	67.86
(percent reduction)		10.3	8.1
High School to college	128.98	115.78	119.55
(percent reduction)		10.2	7.3
College to masters	68.42	67.98	64.21
(percent reduction)		0.6	5.5
College to doctorate	276.13	270.84	266.56
(percent reduction)		1.9	3.5

Source: Filer (1981: Table 5).

Table 10-6. Ashenfelter-Ham Estimates of the Effect of Schooling on Earnings and Wages for White Males.

				Percentage of Unemployment	
Year	*Earnings*	*Wages*	*Difference*	*Sample*[a]	*Economy*[b]
1967	0.091	0.089	0.002	1.1	2.1
1968	0.094	0.089	0.005	1.1	2.0
1969	0.095	0.088	0.007	0.9	1.9
1970	0.096	0.092	0.004	1.9	3.2
1971	0.096	0.090	0.006	1.9	4.0
1972	0.092	0.083	0.009	1.2	3.6
1973	0.092	0.084	0.008	1.3	3.0
1974	0.099	0.088	0.011	2.2	3.5
Average	0.094	0.088	0.006	1.2	2.9

a. Estimated unemployment rates in PSID sample, reported in Ashenfelter and Ham (1979: S99–S116).

b. Unemployment for white males ⩾ years of age, from *Economic Report of the President* (1983: Table B-33).

less of the distribution of educational attainment. If, on the other hand, the proportionate productivity advantage of more educated labor differs across tasks, the equilibrium wage differential across educational categories falls as the distribution shifts to the right.

The existence of a finite elasticity of substitution between labor with different levels of educational attainment implies that the coefficient on S in earnings functions should have fallen to some extent over most of the postwar period. The evidence on this is somewhat mixed. For example, the Ashenfelter-Ham (1979) estimates of $\partial(\log W)/\partial S$ in Table 10-6 exhibit no secular pattern whatsoever. On the other hand, Freeman (1977) argues, based on aggregate data, that the social rate of return to the four-year college degree fell from 11.5 percent to 9.0 percent from 1968 to 1973 (see also Freeman 1975, 1980).

Tables 10-7 and 10-8 report estimated coefficients for spline functions of log earnings on schooling. (School 1 equals the number of years of schooling up to 12; school 2 the number of years of schooling beyond 12.) The study by Becketti et al. (1983), which concerned the reliability over time of the Panel Study on Income Dynamics,

Table 10-7. Estimated Coefficients on Logarithm of Annual Labor Earnings from the Current Population Survey (CPS) and from the Panel Study on Income Dynamics (PSID), 1968 and 1981.

	1968		*1981*	
	CPS	*PSID*	*CPS*	*PSID*
School 1[a]	0.072	0.067	0.095	0.075
School 2[a]	0.078	0.089	0.078	0.091
BLK	-0.327	-0.297	-0.293	-0.250
X	0.033	0.040	0.048	0.054
X^2	-0.00056	-0.00013	-0.00076	-0.00086
Constant	7.712	7.797	8.049	8.279

Source: Becketti, Gould, Lilland, and Welch (1983).

Table 10-8. Estimated Coefficients on Schooling for White and Black Males Age 21-35, 1972 and 1978.

	Whites		*Blacks*	
	72	*78*	*72*	*78*
School 1 (years to 12)	0.046	0.075	0.031	0.020
School 2 (years above 12)	0.080	0.059	0.063	0.136

Source: Hoffman (1983: 311-18).

shows that the estimated impact of schooling on the logarithm of annual earnings increased in both samples from 1968 to 1981 but the returns to post-high school education were remarkably stable. To a large extent, however, these results must reflect the increase in the unemployment rate (from 2.0 to 5.6 percent for adult white males and from 3.9 to 12.1 percent for males). To the extent that the increase in overall unemployment influenced less-educated workers relatively more than more-educated workers, the coefficients for 1981 would have to be adjusted downward.

Hoffman (1983) obtains results, reproduced in Table 10-8, that are much more dramatic. Using the Panel Study for Income Dynamics, he finds that estimated value of $\partial(\log W)/\partial S$ for college education for white males between ages 21 and 35 declines by two percentage points from 1972 to 1978. In contrast, the coefficient on the first twelve years of schooling rises by three percentage points. That is, for the younger cohort that incurred the most dramatic increase in educational attainment, the returns to finishing high school increased but the returns to college fell by a quarter. The most startling result is the increase in the estimated return to higher levels of schooling for blacks, a more than doubling of $\partial(\log W)/\partial S$. Taken at face value, this suggests that affirmative action programs aimed at getting blacks into the higher strata of occupations were *enormously* successful. The decline in the estimated coefficient on school 1, however, suggests that these programs did not focus on the "lower" 60 percent of the black population.

The diversity of results with respect to the trend in the rate of return to schooling clearly implies that we simply do not yet know the extent to which RR_S has changed over the last decade. It is, however, interesting to ask by roughly how much the rate of return to schooling *should* have changed over the past two decades given the upward shift in the distribution of educational attainment. Assume that the appropriate aggregation of labor inputs is such that individuals with some college (thirteen or more years of schooling) and individuals with no college (twelve years or less) are the two relevant types of labor. Between 1952 and 1979, as derived from Table 10–2, this ratio of more- to less-educated labor, which I shall call L, increased from 0.198 to 0.541. Let the ratio of wages for individuals with sixteen years of schooling to those with twelve years of schooling be given by P. The relative demand for the two types of labor is determined according to:

$$L = AP^{-\sigma}, \tag{10.26}$$

where σ is the elasticity of substitution between the two types of labor. A is a relative demand shift parameter; an increase in A would reflect technological change that increases the relative demand for educated labor. Taking logarithms of both sides of equation (10.26), the proportionate change in the relative wage between one period and another is:

$$\Delta(\log P) = -\frac{1}{\sigma}[\Delta(\log L) - \Delta(\log A)]. \tag{10.27}$$

Thus, we would expect the relative earnings of more educated labor to decrease if their relative supply increases and to increase if there is a technical change favoring them.

It was shown above that the rate of return to schooling unadjusted for resource costs, RR', satisfies the equation $P=(1 + RR')^4$. Thus, since $\log P \simeq 4RR'$, the change in the estimated rate of return is approximately a fourth of the value of equation (10.27), or

$$\Delta(RR') = -\frac{1}{4\sigma} [\Delta(\log L) - \Delta(\log A)] . \qquad (10.28)$$

If the relative demand function had remained stable between 1952 and 1979, the reduction in rate of return would have been $\Delta(\log L) = 1.01$ times $\frac{1}{4}\sigma$. The range of cross-sectional estimates of σ (1.4 to 3.3) imply a large fall in RR'—of 8 to 18 percentage points. This, of course, did not happen, which suggests either that (1) there was a significant technological change that favored educated labor or (2) the "true" elasticity of substitution is much greater than even the largest of the received estimates. Which of these explanations is the more correct is a question of considerable importance but at present is not answerable.

The Effect of Education on Unemployment

One of the more intriguing stylized facts in labor market analysis is the negative relation between individual unemployment rates and educational attainment. A simple graph of the relation between average unemployment and age and education shows that for all workers above age 30—when they "settle down"—attendance at high school is worth a reduction of 1.5 to two percentage points in unemployment, attendance at college is worth about one percentage point. Ashenfelter and Ham (1979) estimate that on average for the 1967–74 period an additional year of schooling increases the logarithm of annual earnings by 0.006 more than it increases the logarithm of wages. This result is consistent with a Tobit analysis of unemployment experience, and further tests by Ashenfelter and Ham suggest that this unemployment is involuntary (rather than simply a supply of labor phenomenon).

The interesting question about the negative association between unemployment and schooling levels concerns *why* it exists. One strong possibility is that firms tend to provide more specific training to employees with higher schooling levels and thus do not reduce their employment in the face of a business downturn as rapidly as they do the employment of less skilled workers. Persons with higher educational levels, therefore, would be more likely to have "lifetime jobs" than persons with lower educational levels. Consistent with this, Ashenfelter and Ham find that education decreases only the incidence of unemployment, not its duration.

Would a general increase in educational attainment lower the overall natural rate of unemployment by an amount consistent with the cross-sectional estimates? Weighing against an affirmative answer to this question is the fact that the estimated natural rate increased from 4.5 to 7.5 percent between 1950 and 1983 (Barro 1977: Johnson and Layard 1984) concurrently with the upward shift in the distribution of educational attainment. If, for example, the proportion of jobs that have a high specific training component (and low unemployment incidence) were fixed and these tended to be filled on the margin by those in the upper part of the educational distribution, we would observe a shift in unemployment by education relations for younger persons (ages 20–35) between 1970 and 1980. Specifically, in the latter period the large reduction in unemployment due to schooling would occur at a higher level of S than was true in the earlier period. On the other hand, if the effect of S on U remained stable between 1970 and 1980, one might conclude that the cross-sectional pattern can in fact be blown up to the aggregate.

Estimated Returns to Schooling Intensity

As pointed out earlier, the rate of return to investment in education can be decomposed into the return to length of schooling and the return to resources per year of schooling. Most studies of this question (Johnson and Stafford 1973; Link and Ratledge 1975; Akin and Garfinkle 1977; Rizzuto and Wachtel 1983) have found that the intensive rate of return exceeds the extensive return. The estimation procedure is as follows: For a data set that obtains detailed information on the area in which the respondent grew up, real per pupil expenditure on schooling can be entered as a separate explanatory variable in the earnings function; this permits estimation of $\partial(\log W)/\partial(\log C)$ as well as $\partial(\log W)/\partial S$. There are, of course, several problems with this. Two of the major ones are (1) the allocation of educational resources may not be fully efficient and (2) the cost variable applied to individuals is measured with error.

Despite these measurement problems that bias estimates of the effect of school quality downward, quality appears to have a large impact on future earnings. All of the above-mentioned studies find that there is a larger estimated return to schooling expenditure than to schooling years. The results of Rizzuto and Wachtel (1980), which are based on data on the earnings of males from the 1960 and 1970 Censuses of Population, are typical (see Table 10–9). The studies by Link and Ratledge (1975) and Akin and Garfinkle (1977) also show that as of the late 1960s the rate of return to school quality was greater for blacks than for whites. This is due to (1) the result that there are diminishing returns to intensive investment in schooling and (2) the fact that average per pupil expenditure on whites has been historically larger than that for blacks. (The latter of these facts, Welch (1970) has argued, accounts for a large share of the black/white wage differential.)

Another reason why expenditure per pupil is importatn for a policy analysis of social investment in education is that C is a variable that can be controlled in budgets while S can be influenced only indirectly. All of the studies cited above show that the value of S by

Table 10–9. Estimates of Intensive and Extensive Rates of Return to Education.

	1959		*1969*	
At Educational Level:	*Whites*	*Blacks*	*Whites*	*Blacks*
Returns to years of schooling				
High school (8–12)	6.5	5.2	7.3	5.7
College (12–16)	6.5	4.2	7.3	5.3
Return to expenditure per year (at mean value of C).				
8	17.0	15.6	11.3	14.5
12	13.2	12.4	9.2	11.2
16	12.0	11.1	9.1	10.5

Source: Rizzuto and Wachtel (1983).

someone currently in the labor force is positively associated (other things, like father's educational level, held constant) with the amount spent on their schooling. Interpreting the causation as an exogenous C influencing an exogenous S, the impact of an increase in expenditure per pupil of future earnings is given by:

$$\frac{dW}{dC} = W \frac{\partial(\log W)}{\partial S} \frac{\partial S}{\partial C} + \frac{\partial(\log W)}{\partial C} . \tag{10.29}$$

Thus, the relevant policy analysis of the rate of return to resources allocated to education would reflect both direct effects (the second term in equation (10.29), and the indirect effects (the first term).

There is, of course, another interpretation of the positive association between S and C—that the causation goes (at least in part) the other way: Parents of bright, motivated children, who are going to spend a long time in school, tend to congregate in communities that allocate substantial resources to their educational system. This possibility clouds the interpretation of both $\partial S/\partial C$ and $\partial(\log W)/\partial C$.

CONCLUSIONS AND IMPLICATIONS

This chapter has surveyed the evidence concerning several of the more important questions pertaining to the economic effects of education. The major conclusion is that there appears to be a rather robust relationship between the earnings of workers and both their quantity and quality of schooling. While this relationship may have weakened a little during the past decade as the distribution of educational attainment shifted up, schooling appears to remain a good investment from both a private and a social point of view.

Does this imply that the United States ought to increase the fraction of GNP that is allocated to educational investment? The answer depends on two factors. If one specifies a model in which there is investment in human capital, social infrastructure, plant and equipment, and housing, long-run social welfare is maximized when the (after-tax) rate of return to each of these forms of capital is equal to the equilibrium rate of economic growth (3 to 4 percent). Many economists (Feldstein and Summers 1978; Hendershott and Hu 1980) have argued that the rate of return to plant and equipment is in excess of 11 percent—although this is by no means a unanimous view

(Gordon 1984). There is also a perception–albeit not as yet well-documented–that there is also a very high rate of return to social infrastructure (roads, water systems, and so forth).

If more resources were allocated to investment in schooling, it would matter a great deal where these resources were obtained. If they were from consumption or investment in private housing, long-run consumption per capita would increase. On the other hand, if the expansion of the rate of investment in schooling were undertaken at the expense of investment in plant and equipment and social infrastructure (as might be the case if the additional schooling expense were financed by increasing government debt), long-run social welfare could fall.

REFERENCES

Akin, John S., and Irwin Garfinkle. 1977. "School Expenditure and Economic Returns to Schooling." *Journal of Human Resources* 12 (Fall):460–81.

Ashenfelter, Orley, and John Ham. 1979. "Education, Unemployment, and Earnings." *Journal of Political Economy* 87, pt. 2 (October):S99–S116.

Barro, Robert S. 1977. "Unanticipated Money Growth and Unemployment in the United States." *American Economic Review* 67 (March):101–15.

Becker, Gary S. 1964. *Human Capital.* New York: Columbia University Press.

———.1967. *Human Capital and the Personal Distribution of Income.* Ann Arbor: University of Michigan, Institute of Public Administration.

Becketti, Sean; William Gould; Lee Lillard; and Finis Welch. 1983. *Attrition from the PSID.* Santa Monica: Unicorn Research Corporation.

Chiswick, Barry R. 1983. "The Earnings and Human Capital of American Jews." *Journal of Human Resources* 18 (Summer):313–36.

Corcoran, Mary, and Greg J. Duncan. 1979. "Work History, Labor Force Attachment, and Earnings Differences Between Races and Sexes." *Journal of Human Resources* 14 (Winter):3–20.

Duncan, Greg. 1976. "Earnings Functions and Nonpecuniary Advantages." *Journal of Human Resources* 11 (Fall):462–83.

Dougherty, C.R.S. 1972. "Estimates of Labor Aggregation Functions." *Journal of Political Economy* 80 (November):1101–19.

Economic Report of the President. 1983. Washington, D.C.: U.S. Government Printing Office.

Filer, Randall. 1981. "The Influence of Effective Human Capital in the Wage Equation." *Research in Labor Economics* 4:367–416.

Feldstein, Martin S., and Larry Summers. 1978. "Inflation, Tax Rules, and the Long-Term Interest Rate." *Brookings Papers on Economic Activity* 1:221–77.

Freeman, Richard B. 1975. "Overinvestment in College Training?" *Journal of Human Resources* 10 (Summer):287–311.

———. 1977. "The Decline in the Economic Rewards to College Training," *Review of Economics and Statistics* 59 (February).

———. 1980. "The Facts about the Declining Economic Value of College." *Journal of Human Resources* 15 (Winter):124–42.

Gintis, Herbert. 1971. "Education, Technology, and the Characteristics of Worker Productivity." *American Economic Review* 61 (May):266–79.

Gordon, Roger H. 1984. "Taxation of Corporate Capital Income: Tax Revenue versus Tax Distortion." *Quarterly Journal of Economics.*

Gramlich, Edward M. 1981. *Benefit-Cost Analysis of Government Programs.* New York: Prentice-Hall.

Grilliches, Zvi. 1969. "Capital-Skill Complimentarity." *Review of Economics and Statistics* 51 (November):465–68.

Grilliches, Zvi, and Edward M. Mason. 1972. "Education, Income, and Ability." *Journal of Political Economy* 80 (May/June):S74–S103.

Gustman, Alan L., and Frank P. Stafford. 1972. "Income Expectations and the Consumption of Graduate Students." *Journal of Political Economy* 80 (November/December):1246–58.

Hamermesh, Daniel S., and James Grant. 1979. "Econometric Studies of Labor Substitution and Their Implications for Policy." *Journal of Human Resources* 14 (Fall):518–42.

Hansen, W. Lee. 1963. "Total and Private Rates of Return to Investment in Schooling." *Journal of Political Economy* 71 (April):128–40.

Hendershott, Patric H., and Sheng-Cheng Hu. 1980. "Government-Induced Biases in the Allocation of the Stock of Fixed Capital in the United States." In *Capital, Efficiency and Growth,* edited by George M. von Furstenberg, pp. 323–61. Cambridge, Mass.: Ballinger Publishing Company.

Hoffman, Saul. 1983. "Black-White Differences in Returns to Higher Education: Evidence from the 1970s." *Economics of Education Review* 3 (Spring):311–18.

Johnson, George E. 1984. "Subsidies for Higher Education." *Journal of Labor Economics* (July).

———. 1970. "The Demand for Labor by Educational Category." *Southern Economic Journal* 37 (October):190–204.

Johnson, George E., and P.R.G. Layard. 1984. "Long Run Unemployment and Labor Market Policy." In *Handbook of Labor Economics.* Amsterdam: North-Holland Publishing Co.

Johnson, George E., and Frank P. Stafford. 1973. "Social Returns to Quantity and Quality of School." *Journal of Human Resources* 8 (Winter): 139–55.

Johnson, George E., and Kenwood C. Youmans. 1971. "Union Relative Wage Effects by Age and Education." *Industrial and Labor Relations Review* 24 (January):171–79.

Link, Charles R., and Edward C. Ratledge. 1975. "Social Returns to Quantity and Quality of Education: A Further Statement." *Journal of Human Resources* 10 (Winter):78–89.

Office of Education. 1982. *Digest of Educational Statistics.*

Podgursky, Michael. 1983. "Unions and Family Income Inequality." *Journal of Human Resources* 18 (Fall):574–91.

Rizzuto, Ronald, and Paul Wachtel. 1983. "Further Evidence on the Returns to School Quality." *Journal of Human Resources* 15 (Spring):240–54.

Schultz, Theodore W. 1961. "Investment in Human Capital." *American Economic Review* 51 (March):1–17.

Smith, Sharon O. 1976. "Government Wage Differentials by Sex." *Journal of Human Resources* 11 (Spring):185–99.

Taubman, Paul. 1976. "The Determinants of Earnings: A Study of White Male Twins." *American Economic Review* 66 (December):858–70.

Welch, Finis. 1970. "Education in Production." *Journal of Political Economy* 78 (January):35–59.

Willis, Robert J., and Sherwin Rosen. 1979. "Education and Self-Selection." *Journal of Political Economy* 87 pt. 2 (October):S7–S36.

INDEX

After-tax income, 5, 8, 15, 232
Aggregate consumption, 18–19
Aid to Families with Dependent Children (AFDC), 10, 190–96, 199–200, 202
Akin, John S., 290–91
Akison, Patricia, 101
American Council of Life Insurance, 246
Ando, Albert, 106
Annuities, 159, 238
Arena, John, 59
Ashenfelter, Orley, 286, 289–90
Auerbach, Alan J., 4–5, 34–35, 37, 63
Autos and parts (of consumer durables), 11, 206, 209–10, 213–18, 222, 225, 227–31, 233

Bach, G.L., 162
Bailey, Martin J., 97
Baily, Martin N., 30
Balance Sheet Accounts, 79–80
Balance Sheets for the U.S. Economy 1945–82, 47, 58
Barro, Robert J., 26, 32–33, 35, 110, 290
Battese, George E., 176
Becker, Gary S., 271, 274–75, 281
Becketti, Sean, 286
Bequests, 4, 32, 72, 89, 106, 154, 163–66, 174, 176
Bhatia, Jul B., 59, 152
Black, D., 235
Blades, Derek W., 24, 63
Blinder, Alan S., 36, 173, 236, 264
Bonds, 22, 30, 43–44, 46–47, 49, 52–53, 57–59, 67, 76–77, 82–83, 85–89, 103–5, 108, 112, 116–17, 151, 159, 161–63, 237; government, 25, 28–29, 32, 109; long-term, 19
Boskin, Michael J., 3, 63, 258
Bracket drift, 110
Brown, E. Cary, 37
Brumberg, R., 106, 154
Buckley, Robert M., 183, 202
Budd, Edward C., 162
Bulow, Jeremy I., 45, 264
Bureau of Economic Analysis, 206
Burke, Vee, 202
Burke, Vincent J., 202
Business capital, 27
Business saving, 31, 34–35

Cagan, Phillip, 168

Capital assets, 24–25, 45, 164, 169
Capital consumption, 19
Capital formation, 3
Capital gains, 5–9, 19, 30, 34, 41–59, 66, 72, 74–81, 86–89, 91, 101, 110–11, 114, 129, 144, 146–47, 151–57, 160, 162–66, 168–73, 175–78, 241–42, 248, 254
Capital income taxation, 29, 32, 110, 250
Capital losses, 5, 30, 41, 51
Capital stock, 3, 30
Carliner, Goeffrey, 190
Carliner, Michael, 106
Carmichael, Jeffrey, 98
Center for Human Resource Research (OSU), 178
Certificates of deposit (CD) accounts, 112
Chan-Lee, James H., 160
Chen, A., 237
Chi-square tests, 146
Chiswick, Barry R., 282–83
Chow, G.C., 233
Cobb-Douglas form, 242, 262
Cochrane-Orcutt iterative method, 253
Collective bargaining, 284
Consumer confidence, 222, 224–25, 227–28, 230–31, 233
Consumer credit survey (1977), 102–3
Consumer durables, 5–11, 23–24, 26, 29–30, 36, 46–52, 54–57, 63–65, 68, 76–77, 79, 82–83, 85–87, 91, 94, 159, 205–14, 216, 221–24, 227–33. *See also* Autos and parts, Household and furniture
Consumer Price Index (CPI), 20, 112, 160–61, 187–88, 202, 249, 251
Consumption: first-period, 18; second-period, 18
Consumption behavior, 33, 64–66
Consumption tax, 274
Corcoran, Mary, 282–83
Corporate assets, 22–23
Corporate equity, 7, 9, 29, 41–44, 47–58, 76, 81–83, 85–88, 104–5, 151
Corporate income tax, 28, 33–34, 53
Corporate saving, 4, 32, 34, 36–37
Corporate securities, 19, 23
Credit unions, 159, 161–63
Cuban missile crisis, 93
Current population survey (CPS), 200–1, 287

David, Paul, 32, 34
DeLeeuw, Frank, 110
Denison, Edward, 17, 34
Deposit rate ceilings, 110–11
Depreciation, 10, 15–16, 19, 24, 28, 147, 212, 229, 231
Diamond, Douglas, 101
Dicks-Mireau, Louis, 147
Displacement effect, 172
Disposable income, personal, 15, 22–23, 98, 187, 189, 206–7, 211, 215, 221, 228, 231, 245
Dividends, 53, 55–56
Dividend taxes, 34
Divorce rate, 189–92, 194–95, 200
Dolde, Walter C., 4, 98
Dougherty, C.R.S., 279
Duncan, Greg J., 282–84
Durbin *h* statistics, 55–56
Durbin-Watson statistic, 215, 219, 221
Durkin, Thomas A., 104

Education: effect on earnings: 281–88, 292; effect on unemployment, 289–90. *See also* Human capital
Economic Report of the President: (1982), 36–37; (1983), 36, 75
Eisner, Robert, 4, 36, 47, 58–59
Elliehausen, Gregory E., 104
Employee Retirement Income Security Act (ERISA), 11–12, 60, 236–38, 254–56, 259–60, 264
Empty-nest housing, 122, 134
Engels coefficients, 125
Engels curves, 114, 124, 126
Equity values, 4, 8, 22, 31–32
Estrella, Arturo, 110, 250
Excise tax, 11, 228, 231–32

Federal Civilian Employees plan, 246
Federal Reserve Bank of Philadelphia, 96
Federal Reserve Survey (1963), 147
Federal Reserve System, Board of Governors, 20, 47, 79, 96, 103, 212
Feldstein, Martin S., 3, 26, 37, 63, 90, 98, 156, 236, 251, 253, 255, 259, 261, 263–64, 292
Ferber, Robert, 103, 146
FICA, 274
Filer, Randall, 284–85
Financial assets, 8, 42, 47–52, 56–57, 60, 66, 76, 81, 86, 88–89, 91, 101,

103, 114, 116–19, 134, 138, 142, 146, 151, 166
Fixed-income wealth, 5, 94, 96
Flow-of-Funds (FOF) data, 20, 22–23, 25–26, 29–30, 36–37, 47, 96, 103–4, 206, 246–49
Follain, James, 183, 188
Freeman, Richard B., 286
Friedman, Benjamin, 124
Friedman, Milton, 154
Friend, Irwin, 146, 152
Fuhrer, Jeffrey C., 110, 250
Fuller, Wayne A., 176
Future consumption, 5, 18–19, 23, 30

Garfinkel, Irwin, 290–91
General Price Index, 48
Gersovitz, M., 237, 255
Gintis, Herbert, 284
Golden rule, 272, 278
Goldsmith, Raymond, 103–4
Gordon, Roger, 173, 236, 293
Government assets, 25–26
Government capital, 27
Government deficits, 4, 15, 25, 37, 293
Government saving, 4, 28, 32, 35–36
Government securities, 264
Government subsidization of education, 272–74; in U.K., 274
Government unemployment insurance benefits, 91, 95, 97
Gramlich, Edward M., 270
Grant, James, 279
Grilliches, Zvi, 284
Gross National Product (GNP), 12, 53–56, 74, 79, 83, 86, 91–93, 97, 158, 205, 227, 267–68, 276, 282, 292
Gustman, Alan L., 275

Haig, Robert Murray, 44–47
Hall, Robert E., 33
Ham, John, 286, 289–90
Hamburger, M.J., 233
Hamermesh, Daniel S., 279
Hansen, W. Lee, 281
Hanushek, Eric A., 10
Hendershott, Patric H., 5–6, 8, 10, 41, 96, 101, 110–11, 151–52, 183, 187–88, 201, 233, 235, 292
Hicks, John R., 45–46, 48, 76, 96
Hoffman, Saul, 287
Household and furniture (of consumer durables), 11, 206, 219–10, 214, 217, 219–20, 222, 225, 227–31
Household appliances, 11
Household capital, 3
Housing, 8, 41–42, 46–50, 52, 56–57, 76–77, 82–83, 85–88, 91, 93–96, 122–23, 129, 166–67, 183–84, 187–89, 191, 242, 292–93
Hu, Sheng Cheng, 11, 110–11, 201, 233, 235, 292
Huang, Roger, 96
Human capital, 3–4, 6, 9, 12, 24–25, 72, 124, 134, 151, 159, 267–95. *See also* Education
Hurd, Michael, 162
Hymans, S., 233

Implicit claims, 25–27, 31–32
Income distribution, 24–25
Income tax rebate (1975), 97
Index of Consumer Sentiment, 212
Index of personal finances, 224, 226
Individual Retirement Accounts (IRAs), 264
Industrial capital, 3
Inflation, 5, 19, 22, 30, 35, 42, 48–49, 53, 55–56, 59–60, 63, 66–72, 79, 82, 84, 94, 96–97, 109–13, 122, 144, 146, 151–53, 157–58, 160, 162–63, 172, 177–78, 188, 205, 212, 225, 227–28, 238, 240–42, 249, 251–52, 258–60
Interest income, 5
Intriligator, Michael D., 168

Jaffee, Dwight M., 189
Jianakoplos, Nancy A., 4, 6–8, 12, 113, 151
Johnson, George, 197
Johnson, George E., 267, 274, 279, 283–84, 290
Johnston, J., 174
Jorgenson, D.W., 211
Jump, Gregory V., 66–67
Juster, F. Thomas, 86, 233

Kane, Edward J., 4, 7–8, 12, 98, 101, 111, 125, 127, 151, 166
Katona, George, 104
Kearl, James R., 188
Kendrick, John W., 59
King, Mervyn A., 147
Kotlikoff, Laurence J., 37

Kurz, M., 236

Lagrange function, 261
Land, 8, 41–42, 45, 48–52, 52, 56–58, 76–77, 82–83, 85–88, 91, 93–95, 183
Layard, P.R.G., 290
Lehvari D., 155
Lessard, Donald, 201
Lieberman, Charles, 116, 146, 152
Life cycle hypothesis, 64
Link, Charles R., 290–1
Lipsey, Robert E., 168
Liquidity constraint, 4
Livingston survey, 53, 79, 88, 96, 160–61, 248–49, 251
Lorenz curves, 114, 117
Lorenz distributions, 130
Lowry, Ira S., 187

Maddala, G.S., 168, 174
Mankiw, N.G., 233
Market interest rate, 18
Marketable government debt, 26
Mason, Edward M., 284
Mayers, David, 124
McCulloch, J. Huston, 63, 151
McElroy, Michael B., 46–47, 59
Medicaid, 190
Miller, Merton, 31–33, 35
Minutes-to-midnight, 83, 85, 89–93, 95
Mirman, L.J., 155
Mishkin, Frederic S., 33, 233
Modigliani, Franco, 31–33, 35, 80, 106, 154
Modigliani/Miller theorem, 35
Monetary policy, 232
Money market mutual funds, 112
Money supply, 53, 55, 98
Moody's Aaa bond rate, 250
Moody's corporate bond yield, 53–55
Mortgage debt, 7, 9, 49, 56, 103–4, 111, 116–17, 123, 134–35, 145, 147, 188–89, 191–92, 195–96
Mundell effect, 245
Munnell, Alicia, 112, 178, 235, 255, 263–64
Musgrave, J.C., 206
Mutual funds, 159, 161–63, 166–67

National income accounts (NIA), 16, 20, 22–23, 25–26, 28–31, 35, 90, 98
National income and product accounts (NIPA), 41, 48, 59, 64–68, 72, 79–80, 94, 96, 206, 224, 229–32, 248, 253
National Longitudinal Survey (NLS), 157–60, 166, 178, 235, 263
National saving, 15–16, 20–23, 25, 31, 35–36
Negative unfunded pensions effect, 90
Nerlove, M., 233
Net national product, 15, 22
Net worth, 4, 158–59; household, 6
Nichols, Donald A., 97
Nominal assets, 19
Nominal wealth, 116–17, 128–29, 138, 142
Noncorporate equity, 7–8, 41–43, 48–52, 54–58, 76, 82–83, 85–88, 91, 93–95
Nuclear-fear variable. *See* Minutes-to-midnight

Official saving measure, 5
Ohio State University: Economics Dept., 183; Instruction and Research Computer Center, 168
OLS coefficient estimates, 168–71, 173–75, 177
Omnibus Budget Reconciliation Act of 1981 (P.L. 97–35), 202
Output, 15, 18
Owner-occupied housing, 6–7, 9–10, 19, 23, 27, 36, 49–50, 76, 104–5, 110, 113–14, 117, 138, 140, 187, 189, 191, 199–200
Ozanne, Larry, 110

Packard, M., 263
Panel Study on Income Dynamics (PSID), 286–87
Parsons, Donald O., 151
Partial Test Ban Treaty, 93
Peek, Joe, 5–6, 8, 41, 59, 65, 80, 96, 146, 152, 172
Pension assets, 9, 30, 238, 248–49, 263–64
Pension Benefit Guaranty Corp., 60, 236–37
Pension fund reserves, 48, 58, 63, 65
Pension savings, 4, 235–66
Pensions: funded, 29; private, 66, 68, 235–37, 263–64; unfunded, 6, 90, 93, 95, 98

Pension wealth, 11–12, 59–60, 79, 147, 240, 245–48, 254, 256–60, 263
Permanent income hypothesis, 64
Personal consumption expenditure (PCE), 24, 64–66, 117, 158, 215
Personal income, 20, 22, 33
Personal interest income, 19
Personal loans, 159, 161–163
Personal saving, 16, 18–23, 26, 28–31, 34–35, 44, 57, 63–73, 75–76, 78, 81–82, 84–85, 89–90, 93, 96, 205, 246
Physical assets, 19, 57–58
Physical capital, 42–44, 46, 268–69, 272, 278
Pieper, Paul J., 4, 36, 58
Pigou, A.C., 45
Plosser, Charles I., 98
Podgursky, Michael, 282–83
Poole, William, 96
Portfolio allocation, 6–9
President's Commission on Housing, The, 201
President's Commission on Pension Policy, The, 236, 260, 263
Private saving, 15–16, 20–23, 28, 31, 34–36, 258
Productivity, 19
Property income, 80
Purchasing power, 48, 59

Quigley, John M., 10

Railroad Retirement plan, 246
Ratledge, Edward C., 290–91
Reagan, Ronald: administration, 205
Real after-tax mortgage rate, 10
Real estate wealth, 101–3, 105, 108, 114, 116–21, 124–27, 129–34, 138–40, 142, 146, 151, 159, 161–63
Real household wealth, 42–44, 51, 124
Real house prices, 7, 10
Real (per capita) income, 10, 217
Real interest rate, 11, 222, 224–25, 227–28, 231–33
Real wealth, 4–6, 116–17, 128, 138, 142
Retail financial assets, 7, 116–21, 124–27, 130–33, 139, 142
Retained earnings, 4, 31, 34
Retirement History Survey, 236, 263
Ricardian equivalence theorem, 32
Rizzuto, Ronald, 283, 290–91
Rosen, H.S., 217
Rosen, Kenneth T., 183, 189
Rosen, Sherwin, 284

Sahasakul, Chaipat, 110
Sales tax, 228, 232
SAS computer programs, 168
Saving rate, 6, 15, 17, 20–23, 25, 34–35, 44, 64, 72, 92, 95, 137
Scadding, John L., 32, 34
Schooling costs, 267–69, 272–73
School taxes, 134
Schultz, Theodore, 267
Schwab, Robert M., 188
Schwert, G. William, 98
Seiders, David F., 162
Seltzer, Lawrence H., 44
Shilling, James D., 187, 201
Shoven, John B., 45, 162
Shumay, Alexander, 101, 103
Simons, Henry C., 44–47
Simonson, John C., 202
Slemrod, Joel, 89, 98, 188
Smith, Mark, 10, 183
Smith, Sharon O., 282–83
Social security, 6–7, 11–12, 28, 37, 80, 90, 95, 97–98, 112, 160, 165–66, 173–74, 176, 199, 235–36, 238–39, 243, 246, 251–53, 255–56, 258, 261–64
Social Security Amendment (1972), 11, 259–60
Social security indexing, 116, 129
Social security taxes, 25
Social security trust fund, 25
Social security wealth, 25–26, 37, 59–60, 89–90, 240, 244, 251, 253–54, 256, 259, 261, 263
Stafford, Frank P., 275, 283, 290
Standard and Poor's Industrial Stock Price index, 88
Standard and Poor Index of 500 stocks, 248
State and Local Employees plan, 246
Statistics of Income, Individual Income Tax Returns (SOI), U.S. Internal Revenue Service, 65, 80, 247
Steindel, Charles, 80
Stephenson, James B., 162
Sturm, Peter H., 24, 63
Summers, Lawrence H., 110, 292
Survey of Consumer Finances: (1962), 102; (1970), 102

Taubman, P., 264, 284
Tax adjustments, 64–66, 82, 84, 86
Taxes: personal income, 33, 53–56, 66, 110, 159, 212, 214–17, 222, 231, 238–39, 250, 253, 258, 262, 273–74; state and local, 68
Taylor, Lester D., 86
Temporary personal income tax surcharge (1968–70), 97
Tepper, I., 237
Tobin, James, 98
Tobit limited-dependent-variable estimation procedure, 124, 126
Transactable wealth: mean, 115–16, 119, 128, 131, 137, 141; net, 7, 102, 104–5, 117–18, 120–24, 129–30, 132–33, 139–40, 146
Transactable savings, 112–13
Treasury bills, 53–55, 79, 108–9, 112, 127, 160
Turner, J., 255

Unemployment, 95, 216–17, 222, 224–25, 256, 270–71, 282, 286–87, 289–90
U.S. Bureau of the Census, 163, 200–1, 281
U.S. Council of Economic Advisors, 79
U.S. Department of Housing and Urban Development, 183
U.S. Department of Labor, 157, 236
University of Michigan, Survey Research Center, 102–4, 129, 144, 146, 212

Value-added tax, 11

Wachtel, Paul, 101, 116, 172, 233, 283, 290–91
Wealth accumulation: planned, 72, 73–76, 78; unplanned, 86
Welch, Finis, 279, 291
White, Betsey B., 173
Wholesale financial assets, 7, 116–21, 124–27, 130–34, 139, 142, 144
Willis, Robert J., 284
Wise, Donald E., 173, 236
WLS coefficient estimates, 168–71, 173–74, 177
Wright, Colin, 96

Yaari, M., 239, 261
Youmans, Kenwood C., 284

ABOUT THE CONTRIBUTORS

Alan J. Auerbach is Associate Professor of Economics at the University of Pennsylvania and a Research Associate of the National Bureau of Economic Research. He is Associate Editor of the *Journal of Public Economics* and has served as a consultant to the U.S. Treasury on tax policy. He received his doctorate from Harvard University in 1978.

Sheng Cheng Hu is Professor of Economics at Purdue University. He has consulted for the Social Security Administration and received his doctorate from Rochester University in 1970.

Nancy Ammon Jianakoplos is an Assistant Professor of Economics at Michigan State University. She received her doctorate from The Ohio State University in 1983.

George Johnson is Professor of Economics at the University of Michigan. He has consulted for the U.S. Department of Labor and was Senior Staff Economist of the President's Council of Economic Advisers. He received his doctorate from the University of California at Berkeley in 1966.

Edward J. Kane occupies the Everett D. Reese Chair of Banking and

Monetary Economics at The Ohio State University and is a Research Associate of the National Bureau of Research. He has consulted for the Federal Deposit Insurance Corporation, the Federal Home Loan Bank Board, the Department of Housing and Urban Development, various components of the Federal Reserve System, and the Joint Economic Committee and Office of Technology Assessment of the U.S. Congress. Professor Kane is a past president of the American Finance Association, a former Guggenheim fellow, and serves currently on six editorial boards. He received his Ph.D. from Massachusetts Institute of Technology in 1960.

Richard C. Lemmon is the Manager of Economics and Surveys for General Motors. He received his doctorate in economics from Purdue University in 1973.

Joe Peek is an Associate Professor of Economics at Boston College. He received his Ph.D. from Northwestern University in 1979.

Marc Smith is an Assistant Professor of Real Estate at Temple University. He received his doctorate from The Ohio State University in 1984.

ABOUT THE EDITOR

Patric H. Hendershott is holder of the John W. Galbreath Chair in Real Estate in the Faculty of Finance at The Ohio State University. He is also a Research Associate of the National Bureau of Economic Research, participating in their programs in Financial Markets and Taxation. He has been a research economist at the Federal Reserve Board and has taught at the University of Florida, Northwestern, New York, Stanford and, most recently, Purdue University where he received his doctorate in economics in 1965.

Hendershott is currently an Associate Editor of the *Journal of the American Real Estate and Urban Economics Association,* the *Housing Finance Review,* and the *Journal of Money Credit and Banking,* a member of the Board of Directors of the National Tax Association and President of the American Real Estate and Urban Economic Association. He has been an Associate Editor of the *Journal of Finance Association* and has served on the Board of Directors of the American Finance Association.

Hendershott is also currently a consultant for the U.S. Government

Accounting Office (on housing issues) and the Federal Home Loan Bank of Cincinnati and has consulted for the U.S. Departments of Housing and Urban Development and the Treasury. He is the author of over 75 articles, books, and monographs.